Examining
GCSE Chemistry

Bob McDuell BSc
Deputy Headmaster, Berry Hill High School, Stoke-on-Trent
Chief Examiner and Chief Coursework Moderator in Chemistry

Hutchinson

London · Melbourne · Auckland · Johannesburg

Hutchinson Education

An imprint of Century Hutchinson Ltd
62-65 Chandos Place, London WC2N 4NW

Century Hutchinson Australia Pty Ltd
PO Box 496, 16-22 Church Street, Hawthorn,
Victoria 3122, Australia

Century Hutchinson New Zealand Ltd
PO Box 40-086, Glenfield, Auckland 10, New Zealand

Century Hutchinson South Africa (Pty) Ltd
PO Box 337, Bergvlei 2012, South Africa

First published 1989 by Century Hutchinson Ltd

© Bob McDuell 1989

Illustrations © Century Hutchinson Ltd 1989

Edited by Sarah Ware, Editorial Plus
Designed, illustrated and typeset in Plantin by 𝕋 Tek-Art Ltd., Croydon, Surrey.

Printed in Singapore by Singapore National Printers Ltd

British Library Cataloguing in Publication Data
McDuell, G.R. (Godfrey Robert), 1944-
　Examining GCSE Chemistry.
　1. Chemistry
　I. Title
　540
ISBN 0-09-164631-6

Contents

Preface

Examining GCSE Chemistry is a textbook designed to give students an insight into the requirements of GCSE examinations in Chemistry. It also covers the Chemistry content of Balanced Science schemes. It conforms to National Criteria in Chemistry and new National Criteria in Science.

The book is intended for students of all abilities. It is written in a simple style. Only word equations are given in the text so that students are not put off by symbol equations. The symbol equations are given in the appendix so that students can look them up and incorporate them into notes. Chemical calculations are also given, which enable more able students to attempt the calculations required on higher level papers.

In line with National Criteria, there is a great emphasis on social, economic, environmental and technological aspects of Chemistry throughout the book. In particular, the ten double-page Case Studies are intended to give teacher and student opportunities for discussion and project work on relevant themes such as pollution, siting of factories, field-work studies, etc. I hope these Case Studies will stimulate teachers and students to develop similar exercises.

Chemistry, like other sciences, has been divided into three domains:
 I Knowledge and understanding
 II Handling information and solving problems
 III Experimental skills and investigations

In the interest of keeping this book to a reasonable size, no attempt has been made to incorporate practical work or attempt to test Domain III. There are questions throughout this book to test 'knowledge and understanding' and 'handling information and solving problems'. In a separate section at the end of the Units, there is a selection of past GCSE examination questions.

Author's acknowledgements

My thanks to Pat Rowlinson and staff at Hutchinson Education for their patience while I waited until I was confident about what is required for GCSE Chemistry. Also to Sarah Ware for her help in the editing of the manuscript and picture research, and to Mike Hauser for his work on the design.

To Dr Phil Sanderson in Durham for writing Case Studies 1 and 6.

To the publishers listed over the page for permission to reproduce extracts from their various publications.

To the following for permission to reproduce examination questions: Midland Examining Group, London and East Anglian Group, Southern Examining Group, and the Northern Examining Association.

To the many organisations and individuals for permission to reproduce photographs.

And finally, but not least, to my wife Judy and sons Robin and Timothy for their help, encouragement and patience through this long project.

Bob McDuell 1989

Acknowledgements

The author and publishers would like to thank the following for kind permission to reproduce extracts and other material from previous publications:

Page 9: The Whitefriars Press Ltd (Fig. 2.3); **74–5:** The Warmer Campaign (illustrations); **98:** The Daily Telegraph plc (article); **178:** Times Newspapers Ltd (article); **269–76** Charles Letts & Co Ltd (glossary).

and to the following for kind permission to reproduce photographs:

Page 3: (left) Claire Starkey; (centre) D. Parker/SPL; (right top & bottom) Sally & Richard Greenhill. **6:** University of Kent & BBC/Hawkins (4). **7:** (top) French Government Tourist Office; (bottom) J. Burgess/SPL. **10:** (top left) Greenpeace; (top right) Chubb Fire Security Limited; (bottom left) ICI Chemicals & Polymers; (bottom right) West Midlands Fire Service. **14:** (top) Maria Saile/ACE; (bottom) A. McClenaghan/SPL. **16:** The Royal Society. **22:** Ann Ronan Picture Library. **23:** Long John International. **26:** (top left & right) S. Stammers/SPL; (bottom) R. McDuell. **30:** (left) A. Bartel/SPL; (right) Claire Starkey. **31:** (left) Claire Starkey; (right) Danish Tourist Board. **34:** (left) British Museum (Natural History); (right) Clay Perry/ACE. **35:** J. Walsh/SPL. **38:** British Railways Board (Research Division) (3). **42:** Manchester City Council. **43, 46:** J. Burgess/SPL. **47:** Dr A. Lesk/SPL. **52:** Ann Ronan Picture Library. **53:** Trustees of the Science Museum. **59:** P. Sanderson (2). **62:** (left) British Steel Corporation; (top) Steve Benbow/Telegraph; (bottom) J. Stevenson/SPL. **63:** British Alcan Aluminium plc (3). **67:** (top) Sofianopoulos/ACE; (bottom) A–Z Collection. **69:** Royal Mint. **70:** (top left) Geoff Childs; (top right) St Regis Paper Company (Taplow) Ltd; (bottom left & right) North London Waste Authority. **71:** (top) Claire Starkey; (bottom) A. McClenaghan/SPL. **74:** Derby Evening Telegraph (2). **78:** (top left & right) Geoff Childs; (bottom) C. Raymond/SPL. **83:** (left & bottom right) BOC Limited; (top right) D. Kasterine/Telegraph. **86:** (left) V. Fleming/SPL; (top) J. Sanford/SPL; (bottom) J. Heseltine/SPL. **89:** The Keystone Collection. **90:** S. Stammers/SPL. **94:** (left) A. Hart/SPL; (top right) Westair/Telegraph; (bottom right) D. Kasterine/Telegraph. **95 & 97:** Ann Ronan Picture Library. **99:** (top) Netherlands Board of Tourism; (bottom) Food & Wine from France. **102:** (top) Shell; (middle) Brighton West Pier Trust; (bottom) Ford Motor Company Ltd; (right) C. Ware. **106:** (top) R. McDuell; (bottom) J. Mason/SPL. **110:** (top) Thames Water; (left) Geoff Smyth/ACE; (right) J. Burgess/SPL. **111:** (left) Claire Starkey; (right) UK Paper (Southern) Ltd. **117:**

Media/Telegraph (2). **122:** Hydro Fertilizers Ltd. **123:** (top & middle) Shell; (bottom) Croda Chemicals International Ltd. **127:** P. Sanderson (3). **128:** Ian Berry/Christian Aid. **129:** (left) BASF UK Ltd; (top right) ICI Agrochemicals; (bottom right) J. Perkins/Telegraph. **131:** (top & middle left) ICI Agrochemicals; (bottom left) Claire Starkey; (top & bottom right) Hydro Fertilizers Ltd. **135:** A. Bartel/SPL. **138:** BASF UK Ltd. **140:** ICI Paints. **142:** Geoff Childs. **143:** (left & top right) Claire Starkey; (bottom) Ford Motor Company Ltd. **146:** E. Jobbins. **147:** (left) Mike Hardy/Telegraph; (right) M. Dunn. **148:** The Keystone Collection. **151:** CEGB. **154:** (top left) M. Bond/SPL; (bottom left & right) Shell; (top right) British Alcan Aluminium plc. **158:** L. Georgia/SPL. **159:** (top) CEGB; (bottom) Marchwood Engineering Laboratories (CEGB). **162:** (left) Geoff Childs; (right) J. Burgess/SPL. **163:** (top left) BASF UK Ltd; (top right) P. Biddle & T. Mason/SPL; (bottom left & right) West Midlands Fire Service. **165:** Ford Motor Company Ltd. **167:** (top left) Food & Wine from France; (top right) Croda Chemicals International Ltd; (bottom left & right) Metropolitan Police. **171:** (left) RSPB/M. W. Richards; (right & bottom) Watney Truman Ltd. **174:** S. Stammers/SPL. **175:** (top) Dover District Council; (left) James Longley & Co Ltd; (right) R. Howard/ACE. **178–9:** Peak Park Joint Planning Board (2). **181:** Cheshire County Council. **182–3:** ICI Chemicals & Polymers (3). **186:** The Director of The Royal Institution. **187:** Claire Starkey (2). **190:** Geoff Childs. **191:** (left) ICI Chemicals & Polymers; (right) Biwater Filtration Ltd. **194:** (left) The Sulphur Institute, Washington D.C.; (right) S. Fraser/SPL. **195:** Claire Starkey. **198:** (left) Goodyear GB Ltd; (right) ICI Chemicals & Polymers. **203:** Claire Starkey. **206:** (top) A. McClenaghan/SPL (4); (bottom) Ann Ronan Picture Library. **208:** (top) BASF UK Ltd; (middle right) Albright & Wilson Ltd; (middle left) GEOC UK/SPL. **211:** Andy Huntley. **215 & 218:** Claire Starkey. **276:** Croda Chemicals International Ltd.

UNIT 1 Laboratory apparatus and safety

1.1 Laboratory apparatus

In lessons in Science you will use a number of pieces of apparatus. Each item has a special name and use.

Fig. 1.1 shows some pieces of apparatus you will use.

These pieces of apparatus may be made of different materials.

Fig. 1.1 Common pieces of apparatus

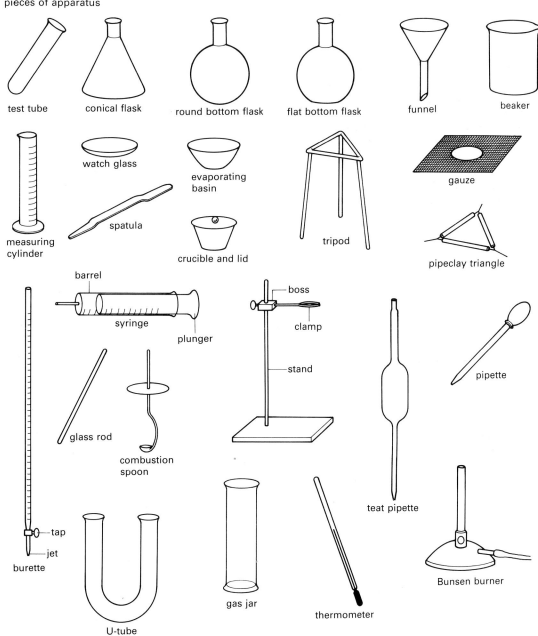

test tube

conical flask

round bottom flask

flat bottom flask

funnel

beaker

measuring cylinder

watch glass

evaporating basin

spatula

crucible and lid

tripod

gauze

pipeclay triangle

barrel

syringe

plunger

boss

clamp

stand

pipette

glass rod

combustion spoon

teat pipette

tap

jet

burette

U-tube

gas jar

thermometer

Bunsen burner

1.2 Drawing diagrams

In Fig. 1.1 the diagrams are in three dimensions, i.e. they are drawn to look like the pieces of apparatus as we see them. In Chemistry we do not usually try to draw them like this. We draw **section diagrams,** i.e. what the pieces of apparatus would look like if they were cut in half (e.g. Fig. 1.2 below).

You will draw many diagrams in Chemistry and you should remember the following points when doing so:

> - Draw your diagrams in pencil and label in ink.
> - Do not draw your diagrams too small.
> - Do not draw all the stands, bosses and clamps necessary to support the apparatus. They will only make the diagram confusing.
> - Make sure all of the corks and connecting tubes needed are drawn.
> - Do not draw a Bunsen burner each time. An arrow labelled 'HEAT' is enough.
> - Label every piece of apparatus in the diagram.

1.3 Apparatus used for heating

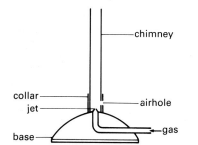

Fig. 1.2 Section diagram of a Bunsen burner

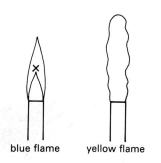

Fig. 1.3 Types of flame

Until 1855, heating for experiments was done with a large coke furnace or a large magnifying glass which directed the sun's rays onto the object being heated.

The invention of the **Bunsen burner** by Robert Wilhelm Bunsen in 1855 changed everything (see page 206). The Bunsen burner burns a mixture of natural gas, coal gas or Calor gas with air.

Fig. 1.2 shows a section diagram of a Bunsen burner. The gas enters the burner through the tube in the base. Air can enter the burner through the airhole but the amount of air entering can be altered by turning the collar. At the top of the chimney the mixture of gas and air burns.

Fig. 1.3 shows two possible flames which can be produced. The blue (or non-luminous) flame is a very hot flame with a regular cone shape. It is produced when the airhole is open and plenty of air mixes with the gas. The temperature at the hottest point of the flame (labelled X in Fig. 1.3) can be as high as 1000°C.

The yellow (or luminous) flame is a very cool flame. Little air is available to burn the gas. Soot is formed when this flame is used.

In many experiments in the laboratory the best flame to use is the one obtained when the airhole is half open.

1.4 Apparatus used for measuring

Weighing   Measuring weight is carried out using a **balance.** The word balance comes from the kind of scales that were once used. Now balances are usually electronic and give a direct weighing either as a digital reading (like a calculator) or a scale reading.

The units used for weighing are **grams** (g).

$$1000 \text{ g} = 1 \text{ kilogram (kg)}$$
$$1000 \text{ kg} = 1 \text{ tonne}$$

Mass changes in Chemistry are often very small and a balance usually weighs to two decimal places.

Measuring volume   The metric system is widely used in Chemistry when making measurements.

$$1 \text{ metre (1 m)} = 10 \text{ decimetres (10 dm)}$$
$$= 100 \text{ centimetres (100 cm)}$$
$$= 1000 \text{ millimetres (1000 mm)}$$

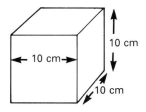

Fig. 1.4

Volume is the amount of space that an object occupies. Fig. 1.4 shows a cube with each side 10 cm or 1 dm long. The volume of this cube is obtained by multiplying the length, breadth and height of the cube.

$$\text{Volume} = 10 \times 10 \times 10 = 1000 \text{ cubic centimetres} = 1000 \text{ cm}^3$$

Alternatively, the volume is 1 cubic decimetre (1 dm^3).

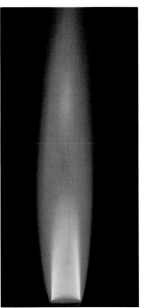

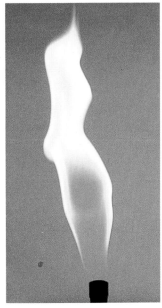

ABOVE   The flames produced by a Bunsen burner. The blue flame is produced when the airhole is open and the yellow flame is produced when the airhole is closed.

RIGHT   Students working in a school laboratory. Are all these students working safely? If not, what would you advise to ensure their safety?

We now use the litre widely as a unit. A litre (l) is the same as a cubic decimetre. A thousandth part of a litre is equal to a cubic centimetre, and may be called a millilitre (ml).

A **measuring cylinder** is a good general-purpose piece of apparatus for measuring out approximate volumes of a liquid. Alternatively, a **syringe** may be used.

A **burette** is better for measuring out volumes of liquid accurately. If, however, a number of equal volumes of the same liquid have to be measured out accurately a **pipette** may be used.

Measuring temperature

A **thermometer** is used to measure temperature. The usual 'mercury-in-glass' thermometer is a useful laboratory instrument.

More accurate temperature measurements can be made with an electronic thermometer.

Temperature is usually measured using the Celsius (or Centigrade) scale. Fig. 1.5 shows some common temperatures.

1.5 Safety in the laboratory

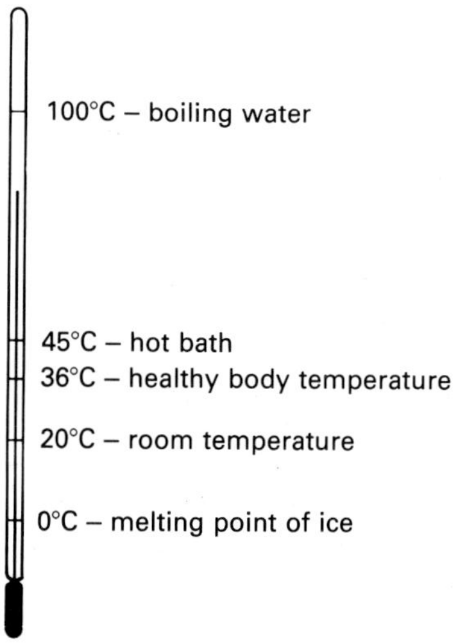

A laboratory can be a dangerous place. Accidents are always possible but many of them can be avoided by developing safe working habits. In industry accidents occur, and a great deal of time is spent investigating them and making sure they do not occur again.

Some of the rules you should follow to ensure your safety are listed below:

100°C – boiling water

45°C – hot bath
36°C – healthy body temperature

20°C – room temperature

0°C – melting point of ice

Fig. 1.5 Some common temperatures

- Never run around in the laboratory.
- Never eat or drink in the laboratory.
- Wear safety goggles or safety spectacles in all experiments.
- Never block exits with coats, bags or boxes.
- Do not leave apparatus close to the edge of the bench.
- Leave any lit Bunsen burner on the yellow flame so that it can be seen clearly.
- Make sure you know where all fire extinguishers are and how to use them.
- Wipe up spills of chemicals on the bench or floor as soon as possible.
- Be careful when picking up pieces of apparatus that could be hot.

QUESTIONS ON UNIT 1

Domain I: Knowledge and understanding

1. Name pieces of apparatus suitable for each of the following tasks:
   (a) Measuring out approximately 30 cm^3 of water.
   (b) Measuring the temperature of a liquid.
   (c) Measuring out exactly 16.6 cm^3 of dilute acid.
   (d) Heating a small amount of a solid in a Bunsen burner flame.
   (e) Grinding some lumps of solid into a fine powder.
   (f) Lifting the lid on a crucible during a heating experiment.

2. Below are some section diagrams of pieces of apparatus. Draw these section diagrams and label each piece of apparatus.

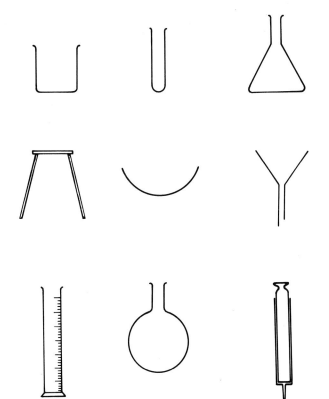

Domain II: Handling information and solving problems

3. Test tubes vary greatly in price depending upon the type of glass used. The table below shows information about three types of test tube from a chemical catalogue:

Type	Size	Type of glass	Price per 100
A	125 × 16 mm	Soft glass	£ 3.75
B	125 × 16 mm	Hard glass	£ 6.70
C	125 × 16 mm	Borosilicate glass	£19.77

Soft glass softens at a low temperature and easily loses its shape. Hard glass does not easily soften when heated. Borosilicate glass is a toughened glass which does not crack when rapidly cooled, for example with cold water.

(a) Why is the comparison about cost of test tubes in the table above a fair comparison?
(b) Work out the cost of one test tube of each type.
(c) Which type of glass is used in the kitchen to make 'oven-proof' kitchen-ware, e.g. casserole dishes?
(d) Which type of test tube would you recommend for each of the following:
   (i) a test tube which is going to be used just to heat a solid to a high temperature?
   (ii) a test tube which is going to be heated and bent to a different shape?

4. Many pieces of apparatus are now made of plastic instead of glass. For each of the following pieces of apparatus, state whether it could be made of plastic or not. If not, give a reason why plastic is not suitable.

   (a) Tripod   (d) Evaporating basin
   (b) Beaker   (e) Spatula
   (c) Measuring cylinder

5. You are given a measuring cylinder, some water and a pebble. How could you find the accurate volume of the pebble?
   Why is it not possible to find the volume of the pebble by measuring with a ruler?
   Why is it not possible to find the volume of a salt crystal by the method you suggested?
   Can you suggest a way of changing this simple experiment to find the volume of a salt crystal?

6. Jenny weighed an empty measuring cylinder and then she weighed it again containing 40 cm^3 of water. Finally, she weighed it containing 40 cm^3 of an oil which was less dense than water.

   Unfortunately, although she wrote down the three masses, she got the three masses mixed up.

   The three masses were:

   139.75 g   150.47 g   110.53 g

   Decide which mass applies to each of the three test tubes.

7. Shiraz wanted to find the mass of a filter paper but only had a balance which weighed to the nearest gram.

   How could he find the accurate mass of a filter paper?

   What does he assume about filter papers when doing this?

A practical Chemistry session for first year undergraduates. Can you identify the various pieces of apparatus which they are using?

UNIT 2 Chemicals in use

2.1 Sources of chemicals

The chemicals we use, and often take for granted, come from different places. We often forget that a great deal of time, effort and money is required to produce them.

Chemicals from the Earth

Evaporation of sea-water to produce salt. What is the source of energy for this evaporation? Why are large shallow pools better than small deep ones?

Foxglove, which is used as a source of the drug digitalis. This is extracted from the leaves and used in cases of heart failure.

The Earth is a 'store-house' of chemicals. Most of the rocks of the Earth are composed largely of oxygen, silicon and aluminium. Metals such as gold and copper can be found in the Earth as small flakes or nuggets (see page 34). Other metals exist only hidden in the form of **ores**. Chemical treatment of ores will produce pure metals (Unit 9).

Minerals such as salt (sodium chloride), sulphur and limestone are mined in large quantities to provide raw materials for the chemical industry.

The Earth also provides **fossil fuels** (Unit 21) including coal, petroleum and natural gas. Chemical industry depends greatly upon fossil fuels both as sources of energy and of chemicals. There are only limited amounts of these fossil fuels in the Earth and they cannot be replaced.

Table 2.1 summarises some of the useful minerals obtained from the Earth.

Table 2.1 Important minerals of the Earth

Mineral	Chemical composition	Origin	Uses
Salt	Sodium chloride	Evaporation of inland salty lakes	Making chlorine, bleaches, pottery glazes, sodium carbonate (washing soda) Flavouring and preserving food
Marble Limestone Chalk	Calcium carbonate	Shells of dead sea animals	Making lime (calcium hydroxide), cement (roasting limestone with sand and aluminium oxide), glass (heating limestone with sand and sodium carbonate)
Coal	Largely carbon	Effect of pressure and temperature on trees and plants over millions of years	Fuel and source of of carbon chemicals
Oil and natural gas	Largely a mixture of hydrocarbons	Effect of pressure and temperature on animals and vegetable material over millions of years	Fuel and source of carbon chemicals
Sulphur	Sulphur	Decomposition of calcium sulphate – volcanic gases	Making sulphuric acid Vulcanising (hardening) rubber

Chemicals from the sea

Three quarters of the Earth's surface is covered with sea. Sea-water can provide a number of important chemicals.

Sodium chloride (salt) is the most important chemical obtained from the sea. Evaporation of sea-water produces sodium chloride.

Magnesium and bromine are also produced commercially from sea-water. In theory, other substances could be obtained from sea-water, but at present it is not economical. It has been estimated that one cubic mile of sea-water contains £100 000 000 worth of gold. However, this gold is dissolved in the sea-water along with 150 000 000 tonnes of other substances.

The sea-bed could provide a wide range of chemicals in the future. Lumps of metal called nodules are on the sea-bed. Recovering them could provide new stocks of nickel, chromium and other metals, but this would be very expensive. It could become economical in the future.

Chemicals from the air

The air is a mixture of gases. Chemical industry separates this complex mixture to produce oxygen, nitrogen, carbon dioxide and noble gases (see Unit 12).

Chemicals from plants

Plants have always been used by man as a source of chemicals. Plants take in energy from the Sun as they grow. They store up this energy.

Many important drugs, dyes and other chemicals were first found in plants. Now it is often cheaper to make these substances in the laboratory from other chemicals. They are said to be made **synthetically.**

2.2 Grades of chemicals

The chemicals that we use can be bought in different grades of purity. For some purposes pure chemicals are necessary. For example, accurate **analysis** or chemistry in the food industry requires purest chemicals. For other purposes the purity is not important. Purification of chemicals (Unit 4) is an expensive process.

Common grades of chemicals are:

1. Analar (or AR)   This is the highest grade of purity. It is as near to 100% purity as possible. The maximum levels of possible impurities are stated on the label.

2. Laboratory grade   These are less pure than AR grade and are cheaper to buy. They are suitable for normal laboratory use.

3. Technical grade   These are less pure, often containing large amounts of impurities. They are used when chemicals are required in bulk and purity is not important.

2.3 Safety symbols

In any chemical catalogue or on any bottle of chemical you should be warned of the potential dangers of a chemical. This information is usually given by using safety symbols that are understood throughout the world. The safety symbols and their meanings are shown in Fig. 2.1.

toxic

 corrosive

 harmful or irritant

 oxidising

 explosive

 highly flammable or flammable flash point below 32°C

 radioactive

Fig. 2.1 Safety symbols

2.4 Using chemicals safely in the laboratory

The following rules should be remembered when using chemicals in the laboratory:

- Never taste any chemical in the laboratory.
- Read the label and note every warning given by the manufacturer.
- Never handle chemicals with your fingers. Use a clean, dry spatula to transfer chemicals.
- Never take more chemical than you need.
- Never return chemicals to the bottle. You run the risk of adding impurities when you return chemicals to the bottle.
- Dispose of chemicals with care at the end of the experiment. If you have any doubts about how the chemicals should be disposed of, get advice from your teacher.
- Always put the top back on every bottle of chemical as soon as you have used it.

2.5 Transport of chemicals

Chemicals are moved around the country in bulk. Every year about 40 million tonnes of chemicals are transported. Usually they are transported in special road tankers or railway wagons. It is important that emergency services should know what is in each container and how the chemical should be treated if it should escape, especially after an accident.

Tankers carry labels to identify the load being carried (Fig. 2.2). Inside the cab there should be a card (Fig. 2.3) giving important advice.

Because of the care that is taken and the training of all people concerned, there are few serious incidents involving transport and storage of chemicals.

Fig. 2.2 BELOW A chemical warning sign on road tankers. Most of this panel, on the back and sides of every tanker, provides coded information which the emergency services can quickly check and understand. It tells them what the chemical is, and how to deal with a spillage, leak or fire.

Fig. 2.3 RIGHT Example of a safety card carried in the cab of a road tanker.

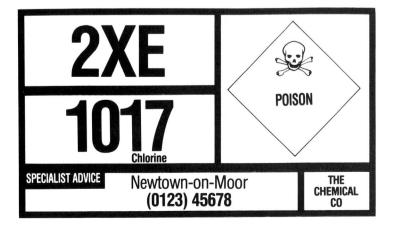

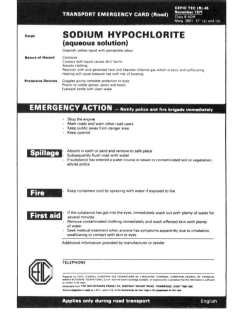

2.6 Disposal of chemicals

NEWS BRIEF NEWS BRIEF

Widespread death of seals in the North Sea has provoked concern amongst environmentalists and scientists, many of whom think that the deaths may be due to toxic chemicals reducing the immunity of seals to natural viruses.

Great care has to be taken in the disposal of chemicals. Strict laws control the tipping of chemical waste, the emission of waste gases into the air and the pumping of liquid waste into rivers.

In the ideal world no chemicals would be disposed of in the environment. In reality other ways of disposal are not always practical. There is considerable evidence that disposal of chemicals in the North Sea, for example, is causing serious pollution problems.

Chemical manufacturers and users spend a great deal of money finding safe ways for disposing of chemicals. As a result there have been considerable improvements in the environment. However, the dumping of chemical waste is a highly controversial issue and one of the inevitable consequences of an industrial society.

ABOVE Toxic chemicals being burnt at sea on an incinerator ship. Harmful fumes may be produced but 'out of sight, out of mind'. What alternatives are there for dumping waste chemicals?

TOP RIGHT Fighting a fire after a road accident. What precautions are the fire-officers taking?

ABOVE Dealing with an overturned lorry which was carrying barrels of chemicals. What are the gas cylinders being used for and why?

ABOVE Transferring the contents of a crashed tanker to another tanker after an accident. What would you suggest should be done if some of the contents of the crashed tanker had spilled onto the road?

QUESTIONS ON UNIT 2

Domain I: Knowledge and understanding

1. Methane (natural gas), iron ore, sucrose (sugar), oxygen, aluminium.

   From the list above, choose:

   (a) a fossil fuel
   (b) a chemical obtained from plants
   (c) a chemical obtained straight from the ground
   (d) a chemical obtained from the air
   (e) a renewable fuel
   (f) a metal extracted from an ore.

Domain II: Handling information and solving problems

2. Table 2.2 contains part of a chemical catalogue. Use this to answer the questions which follow:

   (a) Name the three forms of calcium carbonate sold. Which form is cheapest and which is most expensive?
   (b) Explain the meaning of the word 'assay'.
   (c) Name two impurities in LR calcium carbonate not present in AR calcium carbonate.
   (d) How would you suggest that calcium is stored?
   (e) Why is it unlikely that calcium chloride crystals are made from calcium?

Table 2.2 A sample page from a chemical catalogue

Calcium metal, granules				Calcium carbonate, Iceland spar		
	25 g		£2.75		25 g	£2.85
	100 g		£4.75			
	250 g		£7.50	Calcium carbonate (Marble chippings) approx. 13mm (irregular) (Calcium carbonate ore)		
Ca						
Contact with water liberates					1 kg	£2.06
highly inflammable gas					3 kg	£3.70
Calcium carbonate, LR (powder)				**Calcium chloride LR, hexahydrate** (crystals)		
	1 kg		£2.16		500 g	£3.61
	3 kg		£4.40			
CaCO₃				CaCl₂.6H₂O		
Assay, min. 98.5% (on dried)				Assay, min. 98%		
Maximum limits of impurities				Maximum limits of impurities		
Acid insoluble		0.05%		Aluminium, iron and acid insoluble	0.2%	
Arsenic (As)		0.0004%		Arsenic (As)	0.0002%	
Chloride (Cl)		0.05%		Free acid (HCl)	0.01%	
Iron (Fe)		0.02%		Free alkali (Ca(OH)₂)	0.01%	
Lead (Pb)		0.002%		Lead (Pb)	0.025%	
Loss on drying (105°C)		1%		Sulphate (SO₄)	0.025%	
Sulphate (SO₄)		0.25%		*Low melting point substance*		
Calcium carbonate, AR (powder)				**Calcium hydroxide, LR** (powder)		
	250 g		£9.50		1 kg	£3.33
	500 g		£18.80			
CaCO₃				Ca(OH)₂		
Assay, min.99.5%				Assay, min. 90%		
Ammonia (NH₃)		<0.1%		Maximum limits of impurities		
Barium and strontium (Ba)		<0.04%		Aluminium, iron and acid insoluble	1%	
Chloride (Cl)		<0.001%		Arsenic (As)	0.0005%	
Heavy metals (Pb)		<0.001%		Chloride (Cl)	0.05%	
Iron (Fe)		<0.001%		Lead (Pb)	0.005%	
Magnesium (Mg)		<0.01%		Sulphate (SO₄)	0.5%	
Nitrate (NO₃)		<0.01%				
Phosphate (PO₄)		<0.001%		**Calcium oxide, Technical,** lump (Quicklime)		
Potassium (K)		<0.01%			1 kg	£3.46
Silicate (SiO₂)		<0.01%			1 kg	£4.46
Sodium (Na)		<0.02%				
Soluble alkali	<0.25 milli	equivs %		*Cause burns*		
Sulphate (SO₄)		<0.005%				

NEWS BRIEF NEWS BRIEF NEWS BRIEF NEWS BRIEF NEWS BRIEF NEWS BRIEF NEWS BRIEF

One of the world's worst industrial accidents, the explosion on the Pipa Alpha oil rig in July 1988, has left its mark in the North Sea. Nearly five tonnes of polychlorinated biphenyls (PCBs) were released in the explosion. These toxic chemicals, contained in the rig's four electrical transformers, have been shown to have disastrous effects on sea life.

3. Questions (a) – (g) concern hazard symbols and their use.

The symbols on the right are part of a set which has been used in Canada to represent different hazards; their meaning is given underneath.

What are the meanings of the three new symbols below:

(a)   (b)   (c)

Use these answers to (a), (b) and (c) to answer questions (d) to (g).

(d) Which **one** of these symbols would you expect to be displayed in an emergency near to a leaking tank of ethanol?

(e) Which **two** of these symbols might you find on a bottle of concentrated sulphuric acid?

(f) Which **one** of these symbols would you find on a bottle of household bleach?

(g) Which **one** of these symbols would you see on a bottle of dry cleaning fluid?

NEWS BRIEF NEWS BRIEF NEWS BRIEF NEWS BRIEF NEWS BRIEF NEWS BRIEF NEWS BRIEF

The disposal of hazardous industrial waste has hit the headlines as the extent of Britain's so-called Dirty Business has been revealed.

Between 1981 and 1986 the amount of imported toxic waste has grown from 4000 tonnes to 53 000 tonnes. Another 130 000 tonnes of less hazardous waste is also brought into the country each year.

The waste is composed mainly of contaminated soil, gypsum, ash and other bulky industrial waste. It is imported for treatment, incineration or disposal with domestic waste in landfill sites.

Many countries such as Italy cannot handle all their waste, so they have resorted to shipping it round the world. In Nigeria, over 10 000 leaking drums of assorted poisons were discovered in a farmyard. Ships such as the Zanoobi and Karin B, laden with hazardous cargo, have been turned away from ports all over the world and eventually returned to Italy, where the chemicals will have to be incinerated at vast cost.

There have even been reports of waste being flown into Britain on passenger aircraft, although the authorities have given an assurance that safety precautions of the highest standard were taken.

UNIT 3 States of matter

3.1 States of matter

Chemistry is the study of all of the objects in the world around us and how they change. Everything about us we call **matter**. Matter can exist in three different forms or **states**.

Water is a very common substance. You will know that water can exist in three forms:

ICE   –   solid
WATER   –   liquid
STEAM   –   gas

(Sometimes we call water which is in a gas form 'water vapour'.)

When liquid water is heated it turns to steam at 100°C. The water is said to be **boiling** and this temperature is called the boiling point of water.

When steam is cooled down it turns back to water. You will have seen the water which forms on a cold window in a steamy kitchen. This change back from steam to liquid water is called **condensation**.

When water is cooled it turns to ice at 0°C. This is called **freezing** and 0°C is called the freezing point of water. At 0°C, **melting** of ice also takes place and ice turns to liquid water.

You will know that steam (or water vapour) can turn directly into a solid. This happens inside a freezer. Solid ice forms inside the freezer when the steam in the air rapidly cools. This change is called **sublimation**.

These changes of state can be summarised in Fig. 3.1.

Similar changes take place with other substances. All substances can exist in three states of matter under certain conditions. These states are **solid, liquid** and **gas**. The typical properties of solids, liquids and gases are compared in Table 3.1.

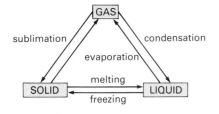

Fig. 3.1 Changes in the state of matter

Table 3.1 Properties of a solid, liquid and gas

	Solid	Liquid	Gas
Volume	Definite	Definite	Changes to fill the whole container
Shape	Definite	Takes up the shape of the bottom of the container	Takes up the shape of the whole container
Density	High	Medium	Low
Expansion on heating	Low	Medium	High
Ease of compression	Very low	Low	High
Movement of particles	Very slow	Medium	Fast moving particles

3.2 Predicting the state of a substance

Table 3.2 compares the melting and boiling points of some common substances:

A thermal geyser in New Zealand. Water can be seen in three states of matter. Can you identify them?

Table 3.2 Melting and boiling points of some common substances

Substance	Melting point in °C	Boiling point in °C
Hydrogen	− 259	− 253
Nitrogen	− 214	− 196
Oxygen	− 219	− 183
Ethanol	− 117	+ 78
Ammonia	− 78	− 33
Mercury	− 39	+ 357
Bromine	− 7	+ 58
Sodium	+ 78	+ 890
Iodine	+ 114	+ 183
Sulphur	+ 119	+ 445
Zinc	+ 419	+ 908
Potassium chloride	+ 776	+1427
Sodium chloride	+ 801	+1420
Copper	+1083	+2582
Iron	+1539	+2887

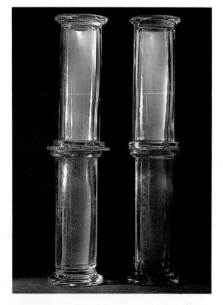

Diffusion of bromine. On the left, bromine and air are separated by a glass lid. Which gas is in the lower gas jar? On the right the gases have been allowed to mix. What can you conclude about the gases in each gas jar now?

We will assume for this exercise that room temperature is 20°C. A substance will be a solid at room temperature if both the melting and the boiling points of the substance are above 20°C. Looking through the list of substances in Table 3.2 the following are solid at room temperature:

sodium	potassium chloride
iodine	sodium chloride
sulphur	copper
zinc	iron

A substance will be a liquid at room temperature if the melting point is below 20°C and the boiling point is above 20°C. Liquids in Table 3.2 are:

ethanol
mercury
bromine

A substance is a gas at room temperature if both the melting and boiling points are below 20°C. Gases in Table 3.2 are:

hydrogen
nitrogen
oxygen
ammonia

You should now be able to work out whether any substance is a solid, liquid or a gas, providing you are given the necessary information.

Robert Boyle (1627–1691)

Robert Boyle was an Irishman, the seventh son of the first Earl of Cork, Richard Boyle. He is known for two things: he was the first to impose a systematic approach to his science, and secondly, in 1670 he published his famous Boyle's Law. For the first he was justly famous. For the second . . . Boyle's Law was actually worked out by Richard Towneley and Henry Power, and only later verified by Boyle's assistant, Robert Hooke!

Boyle was educated by a private tutor at his father's castle in Lismore, Ireland, before being sent to Eton in England when he was eight. He had an excellent memory and a talent for languages, which he used while completing his education in France, Switzerland and Italy.

In 1645, aged 18, he moved to Dorset and began performing systematic experiments. These were a great advance on the random tests and tricks used by the alchemists of the time. Boyle attacked alchemists' methods and put their findings into a sensible order. It was his disciplined work, in the face of an unformed science, which led to him becoming thought of as The Father of Chemistry.

In 1654 he moved to Oxford and became friends with the people who, in 1663, formed The Royal Society to study and advance science. However, in 1680 Boyle turned down their offer to become President of The Royal Society because he said he did not want to take an oath.

His early experiments were based on the use of the air pump, which was how he – or rather Towneley, Power and Hooke – came to show that water boils at a lower temperature under reduced pressure. This was sum-marised in **Boyle's Law,** which says the volume of a gas varies inversely with its pressure.

As well as Chemistry, he was deeply interested in diseases – possibly because he suffered from ill health for much of his life.

NEWS BRIEF NEWS BRIEF NEWS BRIEF NEWS BRIEF NEWS BRIEF NEWS BRIEF NEWS BRIEF

Britain's last incinerator for burning polychlorinated biphenyls (PCBs) may be spreading dioxin over local houses.
Public concern about the safety of the Pontypool incinerator has grown since the sister plant in Bonnybridge, Scotland was closed and following articles in a national newspaper. These articles linked the incinerators with illness in young children and farm animals living around the factory.

The environmental group, Greenpeace, has provided evidence that to destroy PCBs completely they must be burnt in an incinerator at more than 2000°C for at least 22 seconds. Incomplete combustion could lead to the formation of highly toxic materials such as chlorinated dioxin and dibenzofurans.

The factory at Pontypool, however, can achieve a temperature of only 1200°C for just four seconds. Tests on soil and biological material around the factory show that the concentrations of PCBs and dioxin are comparable with background levels in unpolluted areas.

3.3 Matter is made up of particles

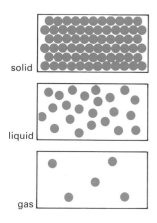

Fig. 3.2   Distribution of particles

If you leave a saucer of water in a warm room for a couple of days you will find that the saucer is empty. The water has not boiled but evaporation has taken place. Evaporation, like boiling, involves a change from liquid to gas but it is at any temperature, not necessarily boiling point. We can understand it if we imagine that the saucer of water is made up of millions of tiny water particles that escape into the room as evaporation occurs.

Fig. 3.2 shows a simple representation of particles in a solid, a liquid and a gas. These diagrams are only in two dimensions but they do show some important points to remember:

1. Particles are usually regularly arranged in solids but irregularly distributed in liquids and gases.
2. Generally, particles are more closely packed in solids than in liquids and more closely packed in liquids than in gases.

The diagrams, however, cannot show that the particles are moving. In a solid the particles are not moving very much. It is rather like being in a very crowded room and trying to get to the door! In gases the particles are moving rapidly and in all directions. The particles in a gas collide frequently with each other and with the walls of the container. There is no pattern to the movement of particles in solids, liquids and gases. It is said to be 'random movement'.

When a liquid boils the particles are given more energy so they break away from the liquid and move faster. They move apart and occupy more space than they did in the liquid:

one gram of water (i.e. 1 cm^3) produces over 1000 cm^3 of steam

If you trap some air in a bicycle pump, it is easy to push in the plunger and compress the gas. The particles are forced closer together (Fig. 3.3).

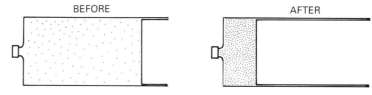

Fig. 3.3   Compressing a gas – the particles are forced closer together

Evidence for sizes of particles

There are different pieces of information which suggest to us that the particles which make up matter are very small:

Diffusion

If you open a bottle of perfume in a room, the smell of the perfume soon spreads throughout the room. We can understand it if the perfume is made up of millions of tiny particles and they can move around the room.

Diffusion is the movement of a gas to fill any space in which it is put.

We can demonstrate diffusion in the laboratory by putting a gas jar filled with air above a gas jar filled with heavier red-brown bromine vapour (see page 14).

After a few minutes the contents of the two gas jars mix and eventually they look the same. The bromine particles have spread out evenly into both gas jars. This movement of particles is called **diffusion.**

Diffusion also takes place in liquids, but more slowly. This is because the particles in a liquid are moving less than in a gas. If a purple crystal of potassium permanganate is dropped into a beaker of water, diffusion takes place. After some hours the whole solution is a pale pink colour. One small crystal of potassium permanganate must contain enough small particles to spread out and fill all of the water.

Brownian motion

In 1827, Robert Brown observed that fine pollen grains on the surface of water were not stationary but were constantly moving. The random movement of the pollen grains, he concluded, was caused by collisions between water particles (too small to be seen) and the pollen grains. He called this random motion **Brownian motion**. Three points are important:

1. The water particles must be moving very fast in order to move the larger pollen grains.
2. The direction of movement of the pollen grains is random because it depends upon how often the water particles collide and how they collide.
3. There is no pattern in the movement of pollen grains or water particles.

Surface films

A tiny drop of oil, when placed on the surface of water in a large beaker, will spread out to cover the whole surface. This is used in warm countries to reduce the evaporation of water from reservoirs. One drop of oil must contain a very large number of very small particles in order to spread out in this way.

Comparing the rate of diffusion of different gases

Ammonia and hydrogen chloride are two gases. They are both composed of tiny particles but the particles are, of course, not the same. The hydrogen chloride particles are larger and about twice as heavy as the ammonia particles. When these two gases mix they form a white solid called ammonium chloride.

The following experiment is frequently carried out to compare the rate of movement of ammonia and hydrogen chloride particles.

A long, dry glass tube is clamped horizontally. A piece of cotton wool soaked in ammonia solution is put at one end of the tube. At the same time a piece of cotton wool soaked in hydrogen chloride solution is placed at the other end (Fig. 3.5). The two gases move towards each other in the tube. When they meet they combine to form a white ring on the inside of the glass tube. If the particles of the two gases moved at the same speed, they would meet exactly in the middle and the white ring of ammonium chloride would form there. This does not happen. The ring forms much closer to the hydrogen chloride end. The ammonia particles travel about twice as far as the hydrogen chloride particles. Smaller, lighter particles travel faster than larger, heavier ones.

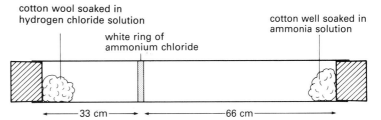

Fig. 3.5 Comparing the rates of diffusion of ammonia and hydrogen chloride

Despite the fact that the particles are moving quickly, the ring does not form for about five minutes. This is because:

(a) the particles are not just moving in one direction, and
(b) the tube is filled with air, which obstructs the movement of the particles.

QUESTIONS ON UNIT 3

Domain I: Knowledge and understanding

1. bromine, iron, oxygen, copper, mercury, sulphur

   Using only the elements in the list above, name:

   (a) two elements that are liquid at room temperature and atmospheric pressure;
   (b) the element with the lowest melting point;
   (c) two elements that are solid at room temperature;
   (d) one element that is a gas at room temperature and atmospheric pressure.

2. solid, liquid, gas, evaporates, melts, boils, sublimes, condenses, freezes

   Use the words above to complete the passage below:

   Water is a . . . . at room temperature and atmospheric pressure. If it is cooled in an ice-maker, it . . . . and turns to ice which is a . . . .

   If water is left in a saucer on a window sill, the water . . . . When water is heated to 100°C, it . . . . and a . . . . called steam is produced. When steam hits a cold surface such as a window, the steam . . . . and this can cause condensation problems.

Domain II: Handling information and solving problems

3. Look up the melting and boiling points of the following elements in the Data Section on page 248:

   potassium, phosphorus, mercury, bromine, oxygen, chlorine, lead, caesium, helium, calcium, sulphur, nitrogen

   Draw the diagram which is at the top of the next column on graph paper and complete the diagram using the data for each element. The horizontal dotted line shows normal room temperature.

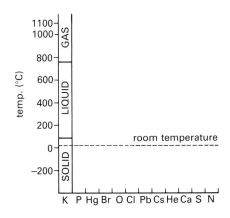

Use this diagram to help you answer the following questions:

(a) Which of the elements in the diagram are solid at room temperature?
(b) Which of the elements are liquid at room temperature?
(c) Which of the elements are gases at room temperature?
(d) Which element has the lowest melting point?
(e) Which element has the highest boiling point?
(f) Which element is liquid over the greatest range of temperature?
(g) Why is mercury not suitable for thermometers used to read temperatures over 400°C?
(h) Which elements would not melt in a Bunsen burner flame at 600°C?
(i) Divide the elements into solids, liquids and gases at a temperature of −50°C. (Hint: Draw another horizontal dotted line at −50°C.
(j) Divide the elements into solids, liquids and gases at a temperature of 125°C.
(k) Below is a pie chart of the elements in your diagram at room temperature. Draw a similar pie chart showing the states of the same elements at 300°C.

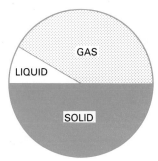

4. Some solid crystals were heated in a test tube until they melted. A thermometer was put into the liquid and the test tube removed from the heat. When the heat was removed the contents of the test tube started to cool. The temperature was recorded every half minute and the results are shown in the graph below:

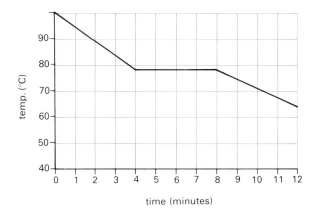

time (minutes)

(a) What was the temperature after two minutes?
(b) At what temperature did the crystals turn to a solid?

5. Explain each of the following:

(a) A person wearing spectacles finds it difficult to see when entering a hot, steamy kitchen.
(b) Ice forms on the inside of a freezer.
(c) The back of a refrigerator gets hot.
(d) Puddles in the road disappear faster on a warm day than a cold day.
(e) Droplets of water may be seen dripping from a car exhaust when a car starts in the morning but not when the engine has been running for some time.

6. A 90 cm long glass tube was clamped horizontally. A pad of cotton wool soaked in hydrogen sulphide solution (giving off hydrogen sulphide gas) and a pad soaked in sulphur dioxide solution (giving off sulphur dioxide gas) were placed at the same time in opposite ends of the glass tube:

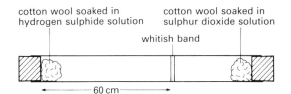

After about five minutes a band of whitish solid formed inside the tube.

hydrogen sulphide + sulphur dioxide → sulphur + water

(a) Name the whitish solid formed in the tube.
(b) What is this movement of particles called?
(c) What does the experiment tell you about the spread of movement of sulphur dioxide and hydrogen sulphide particles?
(d) Why does it take so long for the band of whitish solid to form?

UNIT 4 Purifying chemicals

4.1 What is a pure chemical?

A pure chemical is a chemical which does not contain **impurities**. A pure chemical has a definite melting point. The presence of impurities lowers the melting point and causes the substance to melt over a range of temperatures.

4.2 Methods of purification

There are a number of methods which can be used to produce pure chemicals. The method used has to be chosen carefully for each purification. Sections 4.3 to 4.7 describe these methods.

4.3 Filtration and evaporation

When salt is added to water and the mixture is stirred, the salt **dissolves**. The salt disappears and cannot be seen but it is, of course, still there. The water would taste salty!

The salt which dissolves in water is called the **solute**. The water which dissolves the salt is called the **solvent**. The resulting mixture of salt and water is called a salt **solution**.

Example   An impure form of salt found underground in Cheshire is called **rock salt**. This consists of salt mixed with impurities such as sand which do not dissolve in water. These are called **insoluble** impurities. The fact that the impurities do not dissolve in water is the basis of a method used to purify rock salt.

The rock salt is crushed using a pestle and mortar. The crushed rock is added to water and the mixture is stirred. The salt dissolves but the impurities sink to the bottom and form a **sediment** or **residue**. The salt solution can be removed by **decanting** (Fig. 4.1).

Alternatively, the salt solution can be removed by **filtering**. In the kitchen, flour may be sieved to remove any lumps. The flour passes through the small holes in the sieve but the lumps do not. Filtering is a very similar process. A filter paper has many very small holes in it. The solution passes through the holes but the solid impurities such as sand cannot, and therefore remain on the filter paper.

A filter paper is folded into a cone shape (Fig. 4.2) and placed in a funnel to support it. The mixture of salt solution and solid impurities is poured into the funnel (Fig. 4.3). The solid impurities remain on the filter paper and the solution passes through and is collected in a beaker. The solution collected in the beaker is called the **filtrate**.

Solid salt can be recovered from the salt solution by **evaporation**. The solution is heated in the apparatus shown in Fig. 4.4 until all of the water

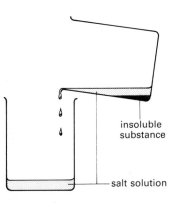

insoluble substance

salt solution

Fig. 4.1   Decanting to remove salt solution

has boiled away. Evaporating all of the water away is called **evaporating to dryness.** However, this often causes the crystals to decompose. To get good crystals the solution should be evaporated until a small volume of solution remains. The solution should then be left to cool, when crystals will form.

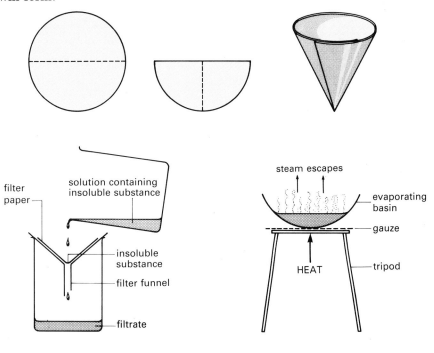

Fig. 4.2 Folding a filter paper

Fig. 4.3 Filtering

Fig. 4.4 Evaporation

4.4 Obtaining a solvent from a solution

Evaporation is used to obtain a solute, such as salt, from a solution. In some cases it is important to recover the solvent from a solution. This can be done by a process called **distillation.** This is evaporation followed by condensation.

Example   Fig. 4.5 (over the page) shows apparatus set up to recover some water from some ink. The ink is boiled and the steam is condensed. The liquid produced is called the **distillate.** If this experiment is carried out carefully, pure water can be produced, but it is difficult to stop the ink boiling over and to condense all of the steam.

Fig. 4.6 (over the page) shows an improved apparatus which uses a **condenser** (sometimes called a Liebig condenser). This piece of apparatus efficiently condenses the steam. Cold water passes through the condenser from a tap to cool down the steam.

The following points should be remembered:

1. Only steam leaves the flask. The other substances in the ink remain in the flask.
2. The thermometer measures the temperature of the steam. The bulb of the thermometer is alongside the side-arm of the flask and not dipping in the ink. The maximum temperature recorded on the thermometer when ink is distilled should be 100°C.

3. The condenser consists of two tubes – one inside the other. Steam passes through the inner tube and cooling water passes through the outer tube. The cooling water enters at the bottom of the condenser and leaves at the top, as shown in Fig. 4.5.
4. The condenser must slope downwards so that the water which condenses runs into the receiver.
5. The receiver should be open at the top, i.e. there should be no cork in it.

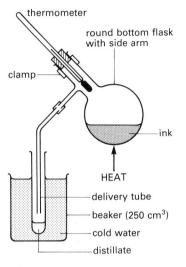

Fig. 4.5 Getting water from ink. The end of the delivery tube should **not** be in contact with the test tube.

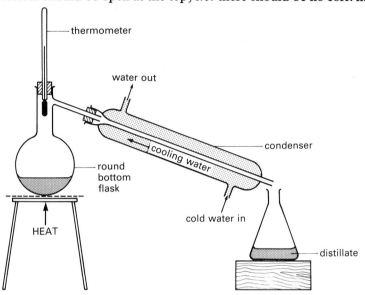

Fig. 4.6 Distillation

Baron Justus von Liebig (1803–1873)

Just as Bunsen invented the Bunsen burner, you might expect that Liebig invented the **Liebig condenser.** He did not. Nobody knows who *did* invent it! Liebig developed and popularised the condenser, which is the water-cooled glass tube still used today in most laboratories to help vapours condense into liquids. But it was as an organic chemist that the German made his greatest contribution to science.

Liebig was born in Darmstadt, Germany, and went to University in Bonn to study with Kastner, the most famous chemist of the day. Liebig went on to become Doctor of Chemistry in 1822, and Professor of Chemistry at Giessen in 1826. His expertise and reputation for hard work drew famous chemists from all over the world to study with him.

Liebig's main research was into organic chemistry. This research led him to isolate several organic chemicals for the first time, including trichloromethane (chloroform) and ethanol.

Above all, he is regarded as the founder of 'agricultural chemistry'. He showed that certain minerals are essential for plant growth. He also proved that the soil becomes barren unless these substances are added, either by manure or natural decay.

In 1845 he was made a baron and in 1852 became Professor of Chemistry at Munich University . . . but for all that, he never invented the Liebig condenser!

4.5 Separating mixtures of liquids

Fig. 4.7 Separating two immiscible liquids

liquid with lower density

liquid with higher density

tap

Some liquids mix together well. For example, ethanol and water mix together completely to form a single solution. Liquids which mix together completely to form one solution are said to be **miscible.**

Hexane and water do not mix well. They form two separate layers. The top liquid is almost completely hexane while the lower liquid is almost completely water. They are said to be **immiscible.** The liquid in the lower layer has a greater density than the liquid in the upper layer.

Immiscible liquids can be separated using a tap funnel (Fig. 4.7). A mixture of hexane and water is placed in a tap funnel. After standing, the tap is opened. The water layer runs out through the tap. The hexane layer remains in the tap funnel and can be run out into another beaker.

Miscible liquids are much more difficult to separate but their separation is important in industry. Mixtures of miscible liquids can be separated by **fractional distillation** providing the boiling points of the liquids are not too close together.

Example A mixture of ethanol (boiling point 78°C) and water (boiling point 100°C) can be separated by fractional distillation. However, the complete separation into pure ethanol and pure water is not possible even with this method. Fig. 4.8 (over the page) shows apparatus suitable for the fractional distillation of a mixture of ethanol and water in the laboratory.

The mixture to be separated is placed in the flask and small pieces of broken china are put into the flask to ensure that the liquid does not boil over.

The flask is heated slowly with receiver number 1 in place. The ethanol starts to boil first because it has a lower boiling point. The vapour passes up the fractional distillation column. Any water vapour which gets into the column at this stage condenses and drops back into the flask. The temperature reading on the thermometer remains below 80°C and only ethanol distils over. The liquid collected in the first receiver is called the first **fraction** and consists almost entirely of ethanol.

A traditional whisky still. The mixture of ethanol and water produced by fermentation is distilled. The first liquid distilled over is richer in ethanol than the original mixture. Can you suggest why this is so?

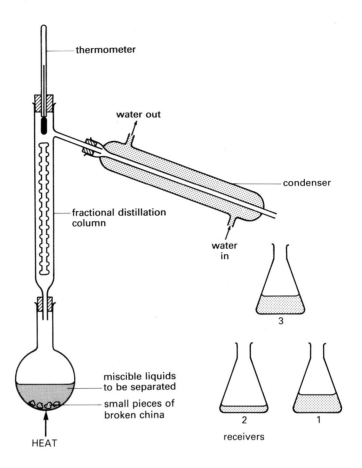

Fig. 4.8 Separation of a mixture of ethanol and water by fractional distillation

When the temperature reaches 80°C, receiver 2 is put in place and the temperature rises quickly to 95°C. A second fraction is collected.

When the temperature reaches 95°C receiver 3 is put in place and soon a large volume of liquid collects in the receiver. The results of this experiment are shown in Table 4.1:

Table 4.1 Fractional distillation of ethanol and water

Fraction collected in receiver	Boiling point in °C	Volume collected
1	Below 80	Large volume
2	80–95	Very little
3	Above 95	Large volume

Fraction 1 consists very largely of ethanol and fraction 3 very largely of water. Fraction 2 consists of a mixture of ethanol and water. It is difficult to separate completely a mixture of miscible liquids by fractional distillation.

Fractional distillation is used in industry in order to:

1. separate oxygen and nitrogen from air by fractional distillation of liquid air (Unit 12);
2. refine petroleum to produce valuable products (Unit 22);
3. concentrate ethanol in whisky production (see previous page).

4.6 Chromatography

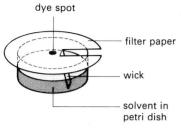

Fig. 4.9(a)

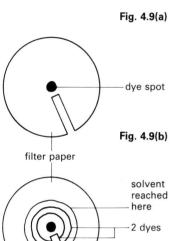

Fig. 4.9(b)

Fig. 4.9(c)

Chromatography is a relatively simple method used to separate mixtures of substances dissolved in a solvent. It can also be used to identify substances. The simplest form of chromatography is called **paper chromatography.**

Paper chromatography is often used to separate mixtures of inks or dyes. It relies upon the different rates at which the dyes spread across a piece of filter paper.

A flap is cut out of a piece of filter paper and folded down to form a 'wick'. A spot of dye mixture is dropped on the centre of the filter paper. The paper is then placed over a petri dish which contains a solvent, so that the wick dips into the solvent (Fig. 4.9a). When the solvent travels up a wick it reaches the spot. The spot spreads out on the piece of filter paper (Fig. 4.9c). Each dye spreads out at a different rate depending upon the relative liking of the dye for the solvent and the paper. Each dye in the original mixture produces a different ring. In the example in Fig. 4.9 the original mixture contains two dyes.

In practice, a square sheet of filter paper is often used. The sample spots are put on the base line and the paper is dried thoroughly. The paper is then coiled into a cylinder and put into a tank with a lid (Fig. 4.10). At the bottom of the tank is a small amount of solvent. The solvent travels up the filter paper and the spots are separated. When the solvent has nearly reached the top of the filter paper, the filter paper is removed and the position of the solvent marked. The paper is dried. Fig. 4.11 shows an example obtained in this form of chromatography which is sometimes called **ascending paper chromatography.**

Chromatography can be used to separate dyes in food. Each dye can be identified by the position it reaches after separation. Chemists can then check whether or not these are permitted dyes for use in food. In a similar way, chromatography can be used to diagnose medical problems. For example, some people are unable to use the amino acids that they eat to build up proteins. From a urine sample and chromatography they excess of amino acids leaving the body can be detected.

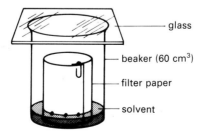

Fig. 4.10 Chromatography experiment

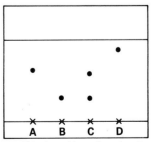

x original position of each substance

● final position of each substance

Fig. 4.11 Result of chromatography **A, B** and **D** have not separated. **C** is shown to be a mixture of **A** and **B**.

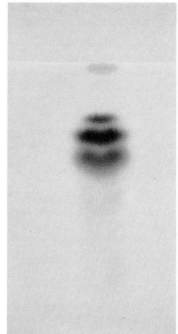

LEFT Scientists using chromatography to separate and purify proteins from plants. The method they are using is called fast protein liquid chromatography.

RIGHT A chromatogram produced on a glass plate coated with a thin layer of absorbent chemical. This shows the substances present in a plant extract called chlorophyll. How many compounds can you detect on the chromatogram?

4.7 Sublimation

Sublimation (Unit 3) can be used in the separation of mixtures of substances. For example, iodine can be separated from substances which do not sublime using the apparatus in Fig. 4.12. Ammonium chloride is another substance which can be separated by sublimation.

Fig. 4.12 Sublimation

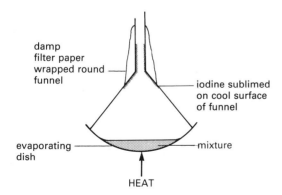

damp filter paper wrapped round funnel

iodine sublimed on cool surface of funnel

evaporating dish

mixture

HEAT

RIGHT Toilet deodorant blocks contain a chemical called paradichlorobenzene which vaporises slowly at room temperature. These blocks were put into a glass screwtop jar and left in a cupboard over a warm radiator for some months. Colourless crystals of paradichlorobenzene were produced by sublimation.

QUESTIONS ON UNIT 4

1. melts, dissolves, boils, solvent, solution, solute, soluble, insoluble, filter, residue

   Use the words in the above list to complete the following passage:

   When copper(II) sulphate is added to cold water, it . . . . and forms a blue . . . . Copper(II) sulphate is . . . . in water and forms an aqueous . . . . Copper(II) sulphate is called the . . . . while water is called the . . . .

   Copper(II) oxide, however, does not dissolve in water. It is . . . . in water. When it is added to water, it sinks to the bottom and forms a black . . . . The copper(II) oxide can be recovered by passing the mixture through a . . . .

2. The drawings below shows apparatus set up for various separation experiments.

   Which of the sets of apparatus A–D would be most suitable for each of the following tasks:

   (a) Obtaining salt from salt solution?

   (b) Obtaining a small amount of water from salt solution?

   (c) Obtaining sand from a mixture of sand and water?

   (d) Obtaining ammonium chloride from a mixture of ammonium chloride and salt?

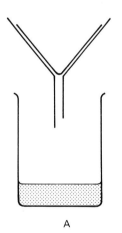

A

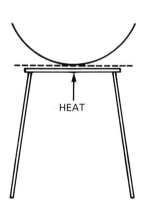

B

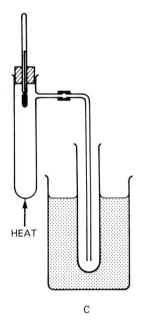

C

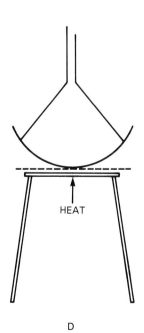

D

Domain II: Handling information and solving problems

3. Three solids X, Y and Z are mixed together. The table below contains information about some of the properties of the three solids:

Solid	Soluble in water?	Soluble in petrol?
X	No	Yes
Y	No	No
Z	Yes	No

Explain clearly how separate pure samples of X, Y and Z could be made from the mixture of all three.

4. Using the apparatus shown below plus corks, glass tubing and a Bunsen burner, draw a labelled diagram to show how the apparatus could be set up to separate a mixture of two liquids with boiling points of 80°C and 120°C.

5. A chemical fertiliser contains a mixture of three substances – urea, ammonium chloride and potassium chloride. Some of the properties of these three substances are given in the table below.

   (a) Which substances present in the fertiliser contain the element nitrogen?
   (b) Explain how pure samples of each substance could be obtained from a sample of the fertiliser.

6. A forensic scientist was asked to try to find out which one of four pens was used to write a 'poison-pen' letter.

   Ink on the letter was dissolved in ethanol and inks from the four 'suspect pens' A, B, C and D were also dissolved in separate samples of ethanol.

   The chromatogram shown below was obtained when these solutions were used in a chromatography experiment:

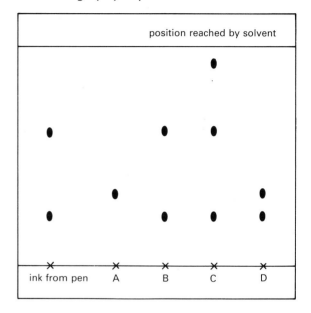

   (a) How many dyes were present in the ink from pen C?
   (b) Which pen was used to write the letter? Explain your answer.
   (c) Can the ink in pen C be made by mixing together the inks from the other pens? If so, which inks should be mixed?
   (d) Often a scientist works out the R_f value of a dye by measuring the distance moved by the dye (in mm) and dividing it by the distance moved by the solvent (in mm). R_f values must always be less than 1.

   Calculate the R_f values for each dye present in the ink from pen C.

Substance	Formula	State at room temperature	Solubility in water	Change on heating
Urea	$CO(NH_2)_2$	solid	does not dissolve	melts
Ammonium chloride	NH_4Cl	solid	dissolves well	sublimes
Potassium chloride	KCl	solid	dissolves well	melts

UNIT 5 Elements, mixtures and compounds

5.1 Elements

A pure substance has a definite melting and boiling point and contains no impurities.

Only a relatively small number of chemical elements make up pure substances. These elements are joined together in different ways to give us all of the substances around us, just as bricks can be put together to form all sorts of buildings (see page 31).

An **element** is a pure substance which cannot be split up by chemical reactions. Most elements occur in nature but a few are man-made.

Table 5.1 gives a list of common elements. On pages 248–9 there is a complete list of elements and some information about them. For each element there is a shorthand representation which we call a **symbol.**

Symbols   The symbol consists of one or two letters. If there is one letter, it is a capital letter. If there are two letters, only the first letter is a capital letter. If there is only a single letter, it is usually the first letter of the element's name, e.g. S for sulphur or O for oxygen. (There is one exception; tungsten is represented by the symbol W).

With only 26 letters in the alphabet and over a hundred elements, initial letters would not be enough! So often the first two letters of the name of the element are used, e.g. Ca for calcium and Br for bromine. Sometimes the first letter is used along with another letter in the name, e.g. Cl for chlorine and Mg for magnesium.

Some symbols seem to bear no relationship to the name of the element, e.g. Na for sodium, Fe for iron, etc. These symbols come from Latin names (Ferrum for iron and Natrium for sodium).

Table 5.1 The common elements and their symbols

Element	Symbol	Element	Symbol
Aluminium	Al	Bromine	Br
Calcium	Ca	Carbon	C
Copper	Cu	Chlorine	Cl
Iron	Fe	Fluorine	F
Lead	Pb	Helium	He
Lithium	Li	Hydrogen	H
Magnesium	Mg	Iodine	I
Potassium	K	Nitrogen	N
Silver	Ag	Oxygen	O
Sodium	Na	Phosphorus	P
Zinc	Zn	Sulphur	S

Most of the elements are solid and metallic. There are two liquid elements at room temperature and atmospheric pressure. They are mercury (a metal) and bromine (a non-metal). The gases at room temperature and pressure are hydrogen, helium, nitrogen, oxygen, fluorine, neon, chlorine, argon, krypton, xenon and radon. These are all non-metals.

All elements are made up of tiny particles called atoms. These atoms are so small that they cannot be seen with a microscope. A block of iron is made up of iron atoms and a block of sulphur is made up of sulphur atoms. Iron and sulphur atoms are different.

5.2 Mixtures

Elements can be mixed together to form a **mixture.** The properties of the mixture are the same as the properties of the constituent elements. A mixture of iron and sulphur powders looks different from the separate elements but the mixture has the properties of iron and sulphur. A magnet attracts iron filings to it. If a magnet is put into a mixture of iron and sulphur all of the iron filings stick to the magnet and can be removed.

It is always possible to separate the elements in a mixture of elements providing you find a suitable method.

There are many mixtures in the world around us. Air, for example, is a mixture mainly of the elements oxygen and nitrogen. It still has the same properties as oxygen and nitrogen and can be separated (see Unit 12).

BELOW   An electromagnet being used to separate iron and steel from scrap in a scrapyard.

BELOW RIGHT   Separating a mixture of iron filings and powdered sulphur with a magnet.

5.3 Compounds

Certain mixtures of elements react together or **combine** to form compounds. Often it is necessary to heat the mixture of elements to get the reaction to start. When the reaction starts energy is given out and the mixture glows. The formation of a compound from its elements is called **synthesis.**

If a mixture of iron and sulphur is heated, the mixture starts to glow and a black solid is formed. This black substance is called a **compound** called iron(II) sulphide. Why is it called iron(II) sulphide rather than just iron sulphide? The reason is that there are two possible iron sulphides and this is a way of distinguishing them. They are called iron(II) sulphide and iron(III) sulphide.

Iron(II) sulphide has entirely different properties from the mixture of iron and sulphur. Pure iron(II) sulphide would not be attracted to a magnet. It is extremely difficult, if not impossible, to get iron and sulphur back from the iron(II) sulphide compound.

What has happened? The iron and sulphur atoms have joined together to form pairs of atoms. These pairs of atoms are called **molecules**. This process is summarised in Fig. 5.1.

Other common examples of synthesis are the formation of water and ammonia.

Formation of water

Hydrogen and oxygen are colourless gases. You might know that hydrogen burns and oxygen supports burning.

A mixture of hydrogen and oxygen is still a gas and you could find a method to separate the mixture.

Fig. 5.1 Formation of iron(II) sulphide

Fig. 5.2 FAR RIGHT Formation of water

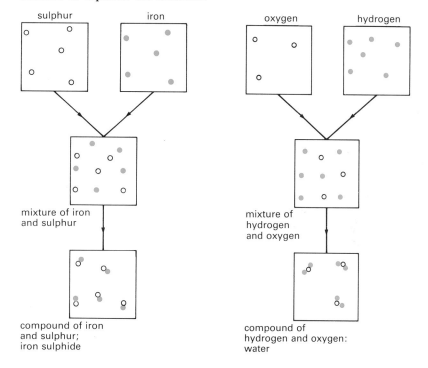

RIGHT The formation of aluminium and iodine. This is an exothermic reaction (see page 153). The purple vapour is iodine vaporised during the experiment. The resulting aluminium iodide is shown by the tripod.

FAR RIGHT Buildings made of Lego bricks. Everything in the world around us is made up from very tiny 'building bricks' which we call elements.

If a lighted splint is put into the mixture of gases, an explosion takes place and a few drops of colourless liquid are formed. The colourless liquid is water. This is a compound of hydrogen and oxygen. It has entirely different properties to hydrogen and oxygen. It does not burn and it does not support burning.

The formula of water is written as H_2O because two hydrogen atoms combine with one oxygen atom, not one-to-one as before. These three atoms joined together are called a water molecule. The process is summarised in Fig. 5.2 (see previous page).

Formation of ammonia   Ammonia is an important compound made from the elements nitrogen and hydrogen. It is not easy to get the elements to combine but it can be done in a factory in the Haber process (see page 120). One nitrogen atom combines with three hydrogen atoms to produce a molecule of ammonia. The formula for ammonia is NH_3.

Table 5.2 summarises some of the important differences between mixtures and compounds.

Table 5.2 Mixtures and compounds

Mixture	Compound
Proportions of different elements can be altered.	Different elements have to be present in fixed proportions.
Elements can be separated by simple methods.	Difficult to separate into its constituent elements.
Properties of the mixture are the same as the properties of the elements making it up.	Properties of the compound are different from the properties of the elements making it up.
No energy change when a mixture is made.	Energy is usually evolved or absorbed when a compound is formed.

5.4 Naming compounds

The following simple rules are used to name compounds correctly:

1. A compound whose name ends in **–ide** is a compound of only two elements. For example, sodium chloride is a compound of sodium and chlorine only. (Note the difference in the ending. This is important.)
   Hydroxides are an exception to this. The compound sodium hydroxide contains sodium, hydrogen and oxygen.

2. Compounds ending in **–ite** and **–ate** both contain oxygen. For example, sodium carbonate is a compound of sodium, carbon and oxygen. Sodium nitrite is a compound of sodium, nitrogen and oxygen.
   The compound ending in –ate contains more oxygen than the compound ending in –ite.

3. Compounds with a prefix **per–** contain extra oxygen. This extra oxygen is easily lost. For example, Na_2O sodium oxide and Na_2O_2 sodium peroxide.

4. A compound with a prefix **thio–** contains an extra sulphur atom in place of an oxygen atom. For example, Na_2SO_4 sodium sulphate and $Na_2S_2O_3$ thiosulphate.

QUESTIONS ON UNIT 5

Domain I: Knowledge and understanding

1.
    A. A pure element
    B. A mixture of elements
    C. A pure compound
    D. A mixture of compounds
    E. A mixture of elements and
        compounds

Which of the above best describes each of the following:

(a) Sea water?   (d) Petroleum?
(b) Air?   (e) Salt?
(c) Hydrogen?

2. How many elements are combined in each of the following compounds:

(a) Copper(II) oxide?
(b) Potassium hydroxide?
(c) Sodium sulphate?
(d) Sodium thiosulphate?
(e) Potassium chloride?
(f) Potassium chlorate?

3. Give the chemical names for each of the substances shown by the following chemical formulae:

(a) MgO (f) K_2O
(b) Mg_3N_2 (g) K_2SO_4
(c) $Mg(NO_3)_2$ (h) $K_2S_2O_3$
(d) K_2CO_3 (i) $NaCl$
(e) $KHCO_3$ (j) $NaClO_3$

Domain II: Handling information and solving problems

4. Which one of the diagrams below represents:

(a) An element?
(b) A pure compound?
(c) A mixture of elements?
(d) A mixture of compounds?
(e) A reaction between two elements which is not completed?

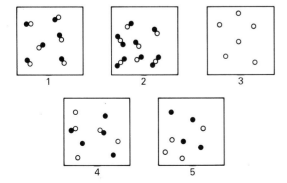

5. The table below contains some information about five substances labelled A–E. Use this information to decide whether each substance A–E is an element, a mixture or a compound. Give reasons for your answers.

Substance	Appearance	Changes on heating	Other information
A	Black liquid	Split up into other liquids with different boiling points	
B	White solid	Melts at a high temperature	Split up by electricity when molten, producing a metal and a gas
C	Silvery solid	Burns when heated in air producing a single oxide	
D	Colourless liquid	Liquid boils away leaving a white solid residue	
E	Colourless gas	Burns in air to form water and carbon dioxide	

6. Below is a bar graph giving the main elements present in the human body:

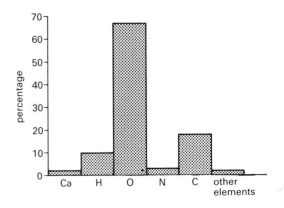

(a) List the elements present in the human body, in order of quantity, starting with the largest.
(b) Which metal is present in the human body in the largest amount?

UNIT 6 Metals, non-metals and the reactivity series

6.1 Metals and non-metals

We all have a good idea of what a metal is, based on common physical properties such as colour, lustre, density, etc.

Properties of metals

We expect metals to be high melting point solids. For example, the melting point of iron is 1540°C. However, mercury is a liquid metal at room temperature and lead, for example, has a melting point of only 327°C.

We also expect metals to have high densities. The density of iron, for example, is 7.87 g/cm^3. Sodium, however, has a density of only 0.97 g/cm^3.

Metals are usually shiny, although this may be disguised by surface corrosion.

Because metals contain electrons which can move around easily, metals are good conductors of heat and electricity.

Metals can be beaten into very thin sheets without breaking. Gold can be beaten into a sheet so thin that light will pass through it! Metals are said to be **malleable.**

Metals can also be drawn into fine wires. The filament inside an electric light bulb is an example of one of these fine wires. Metals are said to be **ductile.**

Metals usually make a ringing sound when struck. This is why metals are used for bells.

LEFT 'Native' copper. Unlike most other metals, copper is found uncombined or native in the Earth. This is because it is very unreactive.

ABOVE Copper pipes. These are made to carry hot and cold water. What properties of copper make it suitable for this purpose?

Properties of non-metals

We can contrast these properties with those of the non-metal elements sulphur, iodine, bromine, phosphorus and oxygen.

We can see that non-metals can be solid, liquid or gas at room temperature. We cannot say that all non-metals have low melting and boiling points because, of course, the melting points of diamond and graphite are very high.

Non-metals generally have low densities and are usually dull in appearance, but iodine crystals are shiny.

Non-metals are usually poor conductors of heat and electricity but graphite (carbon) is, of course, a good conductor of electricity.

Solid non-metals are brittle. This means they break into small pieces if struck with a hammer.

A silicon chip. Thin wafers of this metalloid are used to make microchips. This type is used widely in telecommunications systems.

The distinction between metals and non-metals is not easy when physical properties alone are considered. There are some elements (silicon is a good example) that really have properties between those of metals and non-metals. Silicon is a grey, shiny solid with a comparatively low density. It is a semi-conductor and is brittle. Elements like silicon and germanium are called **metalloids**. These elements, because of their semi-conductive properties, are used in transistors and microchips.

6.2 Classifying elements as metals or non-metals using chemical properties

Physical properties can be used to divide elements into metals and non-metals. Chemical properties can be tested more reliably:

1. Add dilute hydrochloric acid to the element. If hydrogen is produced the element is a metal. Not all metals will do this, so a negative result cannot be used to prove the element is a non-metal.

2. A piece of the element is burned in oxygen using the apparatus shown in Fig. 6.1. An **oxide** is produced.

   A few drops of Universal indicator is then added and the colour of the indicator noted. From this we can get the pH of the oxide, i.e. we can tell if the oxide is acidic, alkaline or neutral.

   If the oxide is neutral or alkaline (pH 7 or greater) the element is a metal. If the oxide is acidic (pH 6 or less) the element is a non-metal. This is a very reliable test.

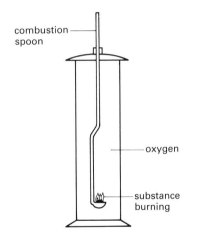

combustion spoon

oxygen

substance burning

Fig. 6.1 Burning a substance in oxygen

Different metals react with oxygen, water and dilute acids in different ways. We will now look at the reactions of some common metals with oxygen, water and dilute acids.

6.3 Reactions of metals with air or oxygen

Oxygen is a very active gas and reacts with most metals. Metals usually react in a similar way when they burn in air but, because the oxygen is diluted by nitrogen, they react less well.

The metals potassium, sodium, magnesium, aluminium and zinc all burn well in oxygen to form oxides. The metals iron and copper react only slowly with oxygen. Copper, in fact, forms only a surface coating of the oxide.

Fig. 6.2 below shows apparatus suitable for burning a small sample of metal in air. The lid prevents solid oxide escaping as smoke. The lid has to be lifted from time to time to allow the air to enter.

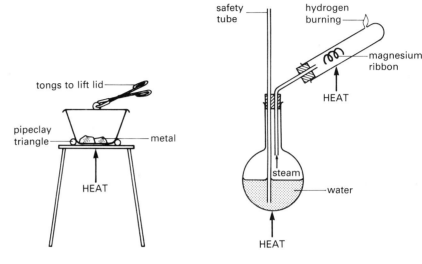

Fig. 6.2 Burning a metal in air   Fig. 6.3 Reaction of magnesium with steam

6.4 Reactions of metals with water and steam

Potassium and sodium react with cold water to produce hydrogen (see page 187). If a small piece of sodium is put onto water it floats, because it is less dense than water, and reacts quickly. A fizzing sound is heard as the sodium reacts and hydrogen is formed.

Magnesium, aluminium and zinc do not react with cold water but react with steam. Fig. 6.3 above shows apparatus suitable for the reaction of magnesium with steam. This is a vigorous reaction and the hydrogen produced burns as it leaves the test tube.

Iron reacts partly with steam. Copper does not react with water or steam.

6.5 Reactions of metals with dilute acids

Potassium and sodium react violently with dilute hydrochloric or sulphuric acids. Magnesium, aluminium, zinc and iron react with dilute hydrochloric or sulphuric acids. Copper does not react with dilute hydrochloric or sulphuric acids.

6.6 The reactivity series

Table 6.1 summarises the results of reactions of metals with oxygen, water and dilute acids:

Table 6.1 Reactivity of metals

Metal	Heated in oxygen	Reaction with water or steam	Reaction with acids
Potassium		React with cold water	Violent reaction
Sodium			
Magnesium	Burn to form oxide	React with steam	React with dilute acid
Aluminium			
Zinc			
Iron	Reacts slowly	Partial reaction	
Copper	Partial reaction	No reaction	No reaction

The reactivity series:

Potassium
Sodium
Magnesium
Aluminium
Carbon
Zinc
Iron
Hydrogen
Copper

The metals in Table 6.1 are arranged in order of their reactivity. They are called a **reactivity series.** The reactivity series can be very useful to you in your Chemistry course. You do not have to remember it. It will be given to you when you need it.

We frequently include carbon and hydrogen in the reactivity series although they are not metals. The reactivity series we use is therefore:

We frequently include carbon and hydrogen in the reactivity series although they are not metals. The reactivity series we use is shown on the left.

We could enlarge this reactivity series by including other metals.

6.7 Displacement reactions

Silver crystals being produced by a displacement reaction between copper and silver nitrate solution.

A displacement reaction is a reaction where one metal replaces another during a chemical reaction. For example, if an iron nail is put into copper(II) sulphate solution, a displacement reaction occurs. Brown copper is formed and the blue solution loses its colour.

This reaction can be summarised in words as:

copper(II) sulphate + iron → copper + iron(II) sulphate

This is called a **word equation.**

The reaction takes place because iron is more reactive than copper. Iron is higher than copper in the reactivity series.

No reaction takes place when zinc is added to magnesium sulphate solution. This is because zinc is not reactive enough. Magnesium is above zinc in the reactivity series.

Displacement reactions can take place when a metal is added to an aqueous solution of a metal compound (i.e. a metal compound dissolved in water). It can also occur when a mixture of powdered metal and metal oxide are heated.

If a mixture of aluminium powder and iron(III) oxide is heated a very violent reaction occurs. Aluminium, being more reactive than iron, replaces iron in the iron(III) oxide:

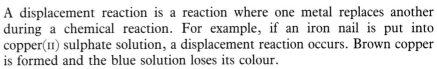

aluminium + iron(III) oxide → aluminium oxide + iron

This reaction, called the 'thermit' reaction, is used to weld lengths of rail together when re-laying railway tracks.

If a mixture of magnesium oxide and zinc are heated together, no reaction will take place.

The 'thermit' reaction used to weld lengths of railway track into a continuous length for the comfort of passengers. The photographs show (ABOVE RIGHT) the lengths ready for welding; (LEFT) the exothermic reaction between iron(III) oxide and aluminium powder producing *molten* iron, which is directed into the gap between the ends of the lengths of rail; (ABOVE) the finished welded rail after cleaning up.

NEWS BRIEF NEWS BRIEF NEWS BRIEF NEWS

The traditional method of extracting gold from a heap containing minute amounts of gold uses highly poisonous sodium cyanide. It produces a yield of less than 70%.

A new method of bioleaching involves breaking down the gold in the heap with microbes. This method produces nearly 100% yields.

QUESTIONS ON UNIT 6

Domain I: Knowledge and understanding

1. sodium, iron, copper, magnesium, silicon, sulphur

   Using only the elements in the list above, choose:

   (a) a metal stored in oil
   (b) a metalloid used to make transistors
   (c) a yellow coloured non-metal
   (d) a metal with strong magnetic properties
   (e) a metal which does not react with water, steam or dilute hydrochloric acid
   (f) a metal which hardly reacts with cold water but reacts well with steam

2. For each of the following pairs of chemicals state whether or not a displacement reaction would take place if the following were mixed. In some cases heat would be necessary. If a reaction would take place, name both of the products.

   (a) Zinc and copper(II) sulphate solution
   (b) Copper and silver nitrate solution
   (c) Copper and aluminium sulphate solution
   (d) Magnesium and copper(II) oxide
   (e) Iron and zinc oxide

Domain II: Handling information and problem solving

3. The table below summarises the results of some experiments where four metals − X, lead, copper and magnesium − were added to different salt solutions.

   Arrange the four metals in order of reactivity with the most reactive metal first.

4. Three metals X, Y and Z have the following properties:

   X does not react with water or dilute hydrochloric acid.
   Y reacts steadily with cold water and rapidly with dilute hydrochloric acid.
   Z does not react with cold water or steam but reacts slowly with dilute hydrochloric acid.

   Arrange the three metals in order of reactivity with the most reactive metal first.

5. The metal titanium occurs in the earth in the mineral called rutile which contains titanium dioxide, TiO_2. In order to extract titanium, the titanium dioxide is converted into titanium tetrachloride, $TiCl_4$. This is then heated with the metal sodium.

   (a) Write a word equation for the reaction producing titanium from titanium tetrachloride.
   (b) What does this information tell you about the position of titanium in the reactivity series compared to sodium?

6. The metal chromium can be extracted from the compound chromium(III) oxide by heating a mixture of chromium(III) oxide and aluminium.

   (a) Write a word equation for the reaction which takes place.
   (b) What does this reaction tell you about the position of chromium in the reactivity series compared to aluminium?
   (c) Describe how you would try to compare the position of chromium and iron in the reactivity series.

Metal salt solution	Metal X	Lead	Copper	Magnesium
Solution of X nitrate	No reaction	No reaction	No reaction	Metal X deposited
Lead(II) nitrate solution	Lead deposited	No reaction	No reaction	Lead deposited
Copper(II) sulphate solution	Copper deposited	Copper deposited	No reaction	Copper deposited
Magnesium nitrate solution	No reaction	No reaction	No reaction	No reaction

7. Magnesium ribbon reacts very slowly with cold water to produce hydrogen. The apparatus shown below can be used and about 3 cm³ of hydrogen would be collected after one week. A few drops of Universal indicator can be added to the water. The solution is green in colour at the start. Slowly, the liquid around the magnesium turns purple. This colour spreads slowly throughout the whole solution.

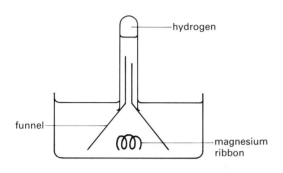

(a) Why does the solution turn purple first around the magnesium ribbon?
(b) Why does the purple colour spread through the solution?
(c) Apart from trying to heat the water, suggest one method of speeding up this reaction.
(d) A student suggested that magnesium ribbon will react quite quickly with hot water. Plan a simple experiment to find out if this is so.
  (i) List the apparatus and chemicals required.
  (ii) Outline the steps which should be taken making sure they are in the correct order.
  (iii) Suggest any problems which could be caused by the method you suggest.

8. As part of a long-term investigation into the reaction of iron with water, the apparatus shown below was set up:

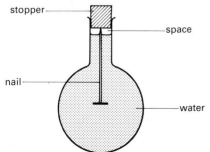

The flask was filled completely with boiling water. The rubber stopper was placed in the neck of the flask, care being taken to avoid trapping air between the water surface and the stopper. As the water cooled down, the stopper moved further into the flask. A small space was seen between the water surface and the stopper. For the first year, nothing but the water and the iron nail could be seen in the flask, but slowly a white powder collected in the bottom of the flask. As time went on, more of this powder was seen and it became greener in colour.

(a) Usually we expect an iron nail to rust. Rusting requires the presence of air and water. Why does rusting not take place in this case?
(b) Using the information in the question, identify the white solid formed and name the new substance collected in the space between the stopper and the water after a few years.

9. Metals can also be arranged in order of reactivity by carrying out a series of experiments to measure the voltages of simple cells using the apparatus shown below:

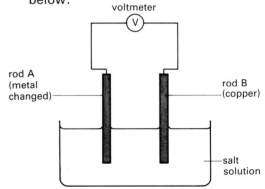

In each case a copper rod was used but the other metal rod was changed. The metals used for the other rod were, in turn, copper, W, X, Y and Z. The results are summarised below:

Rod A	Rod B	Voltage produced in volts
Copper	Copper	0.00
W	Copper	0.02
X	Copper	1.00
Y	Copper	−0.05
Z	Copper	0.60

Arrange the five metals (copper, W, X, Y and Z) in order of reactivity. The most reactive metal will be the metal which produces the largest positive voltage in a simple cell with copper.

UNIT 7 Atomic structure and bonding

7.1 Atoms

All elements are made from very tiny particles called **atoms.** The atoms in a lump of iron are different from the atoms in a lump of sulphur. Atoms are extremely small and cannot be seen with an ordinary microscope.

About five thousand years ago an ancient Greek called Democritus first suggested that matter was made up of atoms. But this idea was not accepted at that time. In 1808, John Dalton revived the idea. He proposed that matter was made up of tiny, indivisible particles called atoms, and that atoms of the different elements were different.

Later in the nineteenth century it became obvious to chemists and physicists that atoms were, in fact, made up of even smaller and simpler particles.

7.2 What are atoms made of?

Table 7.1 Particles which make up atoms

Particle	Charge	Mass
proton (p)	+1	1 mass unit
neutron (n)	0	1 mass unit
electron (e)	−1	negligible

All atoms are made up of three particles. These particles are called **protons** (p), **neutrons** (n) and **electrons** (e). Table 7.1 summarises the masses and charges of these particles.

All atoms are neutral. Therefore, an atom must contain an equal number of protons and electrons so that the positive and negative charges exactly cancel out. The number of neutrons does not affect the charge, only the mass. Electrons are so light that their mass can be ignored in anything that we do.

There are two 'vital statistics' about any atom which should be recorded. These are the atomic (or proton) number and mass number. The **atomic number** (Z) is the number of protons in an atom. It is also, of course, the number of electrons in the atom. Any carbon atom must contain 6 protons and 6 electrons because the atomic number is 6.

The **mass number** (A) is the number of protons plus neutrons in an atom. If a carbon atom has a mass number of 12 and an atomic number of 6, it contains 12 minus 6 neutrons.

In the case of a carbon-12 atom there are 6 protons, 6 electrons and 6 neutrons. It is unusual for all three types of particle to be present in equal numbers.

The element, atomic number and mass number are often represented as follows:

$$^{12}_{6}\text{C} \qquad \text{i.e.} \qquad ^{\text{mass number}}_{\text{atomic number}}\text{SYMBOL}$$

From the atomic number and mass number of an atom you should now be able to work out the number of protons, neutrons and electrons in an atom. Table 7.2 over the page gives some examples. Check that you can do this before you move on further.

Table 7.2 Composition of some elements

Atom	Atomic number (Z)	Mass number (A)	Number of:		
			Protons	Neutrons	Electrons
$^{24}_{12}Mg$	12	24	12	12	12
$^{31}_{15}P$	15	31	15	16	15
$^{23}_{11}Na$	11	23	11	12	11
$^{27}_{13}Al$	13	27	13	14	13

John Dalton (1766–1844)

John Dalton was the son of a poor Quaker handloom weaver who lived at Eaglesfield near Cockermouth in Cumberland.

He loved the countryside and especially the weather. He was very bright and went to the local Quaker school – where he took over as teacher when he was only 12 years old.

When Dalton was 27, he decided teaching was getting in the way of his scientific studies. So when the Manchester Academy, where he now taught, moved to York in 1799 he resigned. He joined the Manchester Literary and Philosophical Society and devoted much of the rest of his life to it.

From his early childhood he had made a daily note of the weather and collected over 200 000 observations on it. That interest developed into a study of atmosphere and gases, and led to him forming several laws, including **Dalton's Law of Partial Pressures** which applied Boyle's Law to mixtures of gases.

Unlike Boyle, Dalton did not rely on the help of others to form *his* laws! But, also unlike Boyle, Dalton's experiments were rather inaccurate and some have since been disproved.

His greatest claim to fame, however, was through his **atomic theory** which says that all matter is made up of elements, or atoms.

Dalton also studied colour-blindness, probably because he was a sufferer.

In 1822 he was elected a Fellow of the Royal Society, and four years later he became its first Royal Medallist.

He lived a simple life with regular patterns of work and play – he went on holiday to the Lake District once a year . . . and played bowls every Thursday!

Manchester loved Dalton. At his funeral 40 000 people filed past his coffin, and the public paid for a statue which can still be seen in Manchester Town Hall.

Dalton collecting marsh fire gas.

A computer representation of an atom. Notice on the left how the electrons move around the nucleus. On the right, the nucleus is enlarged to show the protons and neutrons.

7.3 Arrangement of particles in an atom

electrons travelling around the nucleus in certain energy levels

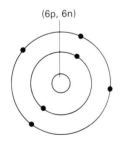

protons and neutrons packed together in the nucleus

Fig. 7.1 The structure of atoms

(6p, 6n)

Fig. 7.2 A carbon-12 atom

There are similarities in the arrangement of particles in atoms. The protons and neutrons are always tightly packed together in a positively charged **nucleus**. Unless the atom is radioactive and undergoes decay, the nucleus never changes during chemical reactions.

The electrons move around the nucleus. They move rapidly and at relatively great distances from the tiny nucleus. It is impossible to trace electrons closely as they move around the nucleus. What we can say is that they occupy certain available energy levels. Each energy level is capable of holding only a certain number of electrons. A simple representation of this is given in Fig. 7.1. The positively charged nucleus is shown in the centre of the atom. The first energy level (sometimes called the K shell and labelled 1 in Fig. 7.1) is the lowest energy level but can hold only two electrons. This energy level is filled first.

The second energy level (sometimes called the L shell and labelled 2) can hold only eight electrons. This energy level is filled only when energy level 1 is full.

The third energy level (sometimes called the M shell and labelled 3) can hold a maximum of 18 electrons. However, when eight electrons are in the third energy level it gives it some stability and the next two electrons go into the fourth energy level. Then the extra electrons enter the third energy level until it contains the maximum of 18 electrons.

There are further energy levels containing larger numbers of electrons.

A carbon-12 atom with six electrons has two electrons in the first shell (the maximum), and then four electrons in the second. Its electron arrangement can be represented as '2,4' and a simple drawing of the atom can be made, as shown in Fig. 7.2.

The electron arrangement of the first twenty elements needs to be understood. Table 7.3 over the page gives the numbers of protons, neutrons and electrons in the atoms of the first twenty elements, and the electron arrangement in these atoms.

Electron arrangement is extremely important in Chemistry as we are going to see later. The chemical properties of an element very much depend on the number of electrons in the outer energy level. For example, sodium and potassium are very similar metals. Their electron arrangements are 2,8,1 and 2,8,8,1 respectively. In each case there is one electron in the outer energy level.

Table 7.3 The first twenty elements

Element	Atomic number (Z)	Mass number (A)	Number of: p	n	e	Arrangement of electrons
Hydrogen	1	1	1	0	1	1
Helium	2	4	2	2	2	2
Lithium	3	7	3	4	3	2,1
Beryllium	4	9	4	5	4	2,2
Boron	5	11	5	6	5	2,3
Carbon	6	12	6	6	6	2,4
Nitrogen	7	14	7	7	7	2,5
Oxygen	8	16	8	8	8	2,6
Fluorine	9	19	9	10	9	2,7
Neon	10	20	10	10	10	2,8
Sodium	11	23	11	12	11	2,8,1
Magnesium	12	24	12	12	12	2,8,2
Aluminium	13	27	13	14	13	2,8,3
Silicon	14	28	14	14	14	2,8,4
Phosphorus	15	31	15	16	15	2,8,5
Sulphur	16	32	16	16	16	2,8,6
Chlorine	17	35	17	18	17	2,8,7
Argon	18	40	18	22	18	2,8,8
Potassium	19	39	19	20	19	2,8,8,1
Calcium	20	40	20	20	20	2,8,8,2

7.4 Relative atomic mass

In the information about elements on pages 248–9 you will find relative atomic masses given. You will also see them on examination papers for you to use. For example, you may see either O = 16 or A_r (O) = 16. These mean that the relative atomic mass of oxygen is 16. But what is the relative atomic mass?

Because atoms are very small they are impossible to weigh. The mass of an atom can, however, be compared with the mass of a standard atom. This can be done in an expensive piece of apparatus called a **mass spectrometer** (Fig. 7.3).

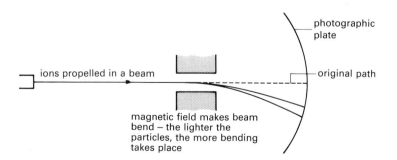

Fig. 7.3 How a mass spectrometer works

Atoms in a stream are stripped of their outside electrons, making them positively charged. They are then subjected to strong magnetic fields. Their pathway is bent by the magnetic field and from this bending calculations about the mass of the atoms can be made. To understand this better, try to imagine an exposed motorway in a strong wind – the light vehicles are more likely to be blown off the road than the heavy vehicles.

What is used as the standard atom? Originally, a hydrogen atom was chosen. Now, a carbon–12 atom (remember: 6p, 6n and 6e) is the standard and we compare the mass of all other atoms with **one twelfth** of the mass of a carbon–12 atom.

7.5 Isotopes

Table 7.4 Hydrogen isotopes

No. of protons	No. of electrons	No. of neutrons
1	1	0
1	1	1
1	1	2

Not all of the atoms in a sample of hydrogen, for example, will be identical. There are three types of hydrogen atom. These are summarised in Table 7.4. They all contain the same number of protons and electrons but different numbers of neutrons. These different types of atom of the same element are called **isotopes.** Most, but not all, of the elements contain more than one isotope.

There are two chlorine isotopes – chlorine–35 and chlorine–37. A sample of chlorine gas consists of 75% chlorine–35 and 25% chlorine–37. The average mass of chlorine atoms, bearing in mind the different amounts of the two isotopes present, would be 35.5. This is the relative atomic mass of chlorine. The relative atomic mass is the mass of an 'average' atom compared to one twelfth of a carbon–12 atom.

Isotopes of the same element have identical chemical properties but slightly different physical properties.

Other elements contain mixtures of different isotopes, sometimes quite complicated mixtures! For example, there are six possible isotopes of calcium. A sample of calcium will consist of five of them:

calcium–40	96.9%
calcium–42	0.64%
calcium–43	0.14%
calcium–44	2.1%
calcium–46	0.0032%

A few elements contain only a single isotope, e.g. fluorine–19 is the only isotope of fluorine.

7.6 Joining atoms together

Joining atoms together is called **bonding.** There are three common types of bonding – ionic, covalent and metallic.

When the atoms are joined together they produce a **structure.** The properties of a substance, i.e. how it behaves under certain conditions, depends on the bonding and structure.

7.7 Ionic bonding

Ionic bonding (sometimes called electrovalent bonding) is a common method of joining atoms together. It involves a metal atom and a non-metal atom (or group of non-metal atoms) joining together. The atoms involved lose or gain electrons to form **ions.**

An ion is a particle which is positively or negatively charged because it has lost or gained electrons. If an atom loses one electron it forms an ion with a single positive charge. Losing two electrons forms an ion with a 2+ charge and so on. Negatively charged ions are formed when atoms gain electrons.

Examples   Ionic bonding is best explained using an example, and the one most commonly given is sodium chloride. The electron arrangements in sodium and chlorine atoms are:

$$\textbf{Na} \quad 2,8,1 \qquad \textbf{Cl} \quad 2,8,7$$

A sodium atom has one more electron than a neon atom. Also a chlorine atom has one less electron than an argon atom. Neon and argon belong to the family called the 'noble gases'. These are extremely unreactive and stable gases. It has been assumed that, because they are unreactive, they must have stable electron arrangements. Other atoms, it is suggested, attempt to get the same electron arrangements as these noble gases.

If a sodium atom loses an electron, it forms a sodium ion (Na^+):

$$Na \rightarrow Na^+ + e^-$$

The sodium ion now has the same electron arrangement as the stable neon atom. It is not a neon atom, however, because it still has 11 protons and 12 neutrons and neon atoms contain 10 protons and 10 electrons.

If a chlorine atom gains an electron it forms a chloride ion (Cl^-):

$$Cl + e^- \rightarrow Cl^-$$

The chlorine ion has the same electron arrangement as an argon atom, which again is a stable arrangement.

The positive and negative ions are held together by strong electrostatic forces.

Another example of ionic bonding is magnesium oxide. Magnesium and oxygen have the following electron arrangements:

$$\textbf{Mg} \quad 2,8,2 \qquad \textbf{O} \quad 2,6$$

A magnesium atom has two electrons more than a neon atom and oxygen two electrons less. The magnesium atom loses two electrons and forms a magnesium ion (Mg^{2+}) while the oxygen atom gains two electrons and form an oxide ion (O^{2-}):

$$Mg \rightarrow Mg^{2+} + 2e^- \quad \text{and} \quad O + 2e^- \rightarrow O^{2-}$$

The magnesium and oxide ions are held together by strong electrostatic forces.

Ionic bonding is sometimes called **electrovalent bonding.**

Crystals of sodium chloride seen magnified many times under a scanning electron microscope. Notice their regular, cubic structure.

7.8 Covalent bonding

Covalent bonding involves a sharing of electrons, and the atoms being joined are non-metals. An example of covalent bonding is a chlorine molecule. A chlorine molecule can be represented by:

$$\overset{\text{xx}}{\underset{\text{xx}}{\overset{\text{x}}{\underset{\text{x}}{\text{x}}}\text{Cl}}} \; \overset{\text{xx}}{\underset{\text{xx}}{\overset{\text{x}}{\underset{\text{x}}{\text{x}}}\text{Cl}\overset{\text{x}}{\underset{\text{x}}{\text{x}}}}}$$

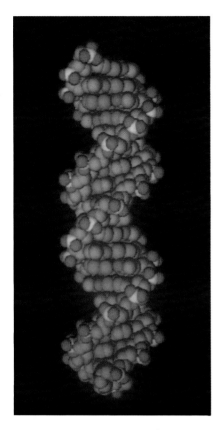

A computer representation of a very large and complex molecule called DNA. Notice how the atoms are bonded together in spirals.

Each cross represents an electron in the outer (3rd) energy level. A chlorine atom has one less electron than the noble gas argon, which has a stable electron arrangement of 2,8,8.

In a chlorine molecule, Cl_2, each chlorine atom gives a single electron to form an **electron pair**. This pair of electrons holds the two atoms together and can be represented by ' — '.

The chlorine molecules produced are separate from one another and they are said to be **discrete**.

Another example of covalent bonding is an oxygen molecule, O_2. Each oxygen atom (electron arrangement 2,6) has two electrons less than the noble gas neon. Each oxygen atom gives two electrons, making four electrons altogether. These form two electron pairs and they hold the atoms together:

$$O \quad O \qquad\qquad O = O$$

In a nitrogen molecule, each nitrogen atom supplies three electrons and three electron pairs are formed between the two atoms:

$$N \quad N \qquad\qquad N \equiv N$$

Methane, CH_4, is a compound containing covalent bonding. Each hydrogen has a single electron and the carbon atom has an electron arrangement of 2,4. One electron from the carbon atom and an electron from a hydrogen atom form an electron pair and a single covalent bond. A methane molecule consists of four single covalent bonds:

$$H \quad C \quad H \qquad\qquad H-C-H$$

Other common examples of covalent bonding are shown below:

O = C = O
carbon dioxide

water

H – C – C – H
ethane

Cl – C – Cl
tetrachloromethane

H – H
hydrogen

H – Cl
hydrogen chloride

7.9 Metallic bonding

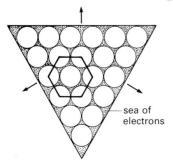

—sea of electrons

The bonding of atoms together in a metal is very complicated and we need only a very simple understanding of this type of bonding. In a metal, the ions are tightly packed together in layers and around these ions there is a 'sea' of electrons which holds the ions together. This is shown in Fig. 7.4. There are alternative methods of stacking these layers. Around any ion in a layer there are six ions arranged hexagonally.

Fig. 7.4 Part of a metal layer

7.10 Effects of bonding on the properties of substances

o Na
● Cl

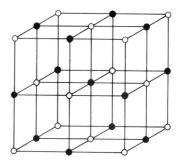

Fig. 7.5 Sodium chloride

Substances containing ionic bonding have high melting points and boiling points. They are, therefore, usually solids at room temperature. The ions are usually held together in a regular arrangement called a **lattice**. Fig. 7.5 above shows a lattice for sodium chloride. Each sodium ion in the lattice is surrounded by six chloride ions. Also, each chloride ion is surrounded by six sodium ions.

Substances containing ionic bonding usually dissolve in water. The solutions formed conduct electricity. These substances do not dissolve, however, in other solvents such as hexane or methylbenzene.

Substances containing covalent bonding may be solids, liquids or gases. They are usually soluble in solvents such as hexane but insoluble in water. They do not conduct electricity in any form.

Metals generally have high melting and boiling points because there are strong forces between the ions holding them together. The ions being closely packed produce a high density. The free electrons in the structure explain why metals are good conductors of electricity.

7.11 Types of structure

The three solids iodine, silicon(IV) oxide and sodium chloride have different structures and behave differently when heated.

If a crystal of dark-grey iodine is heated it quickly melts to form a dark-coloured liquid, and then at a temperature, still below 200°C, the liquid boils to form a purple gas. The purple gas is made up of iodine I_2 molecules. The covalent bond between the two iodine atoms is strong.

However, the forces between the iodine molecules in the crystal are very weak and these break down with only gentle heating. Iodine has what is called a **molecular structure.**

Silicon(IV) oxide is commonly called sand. If silicon(IV) oxide is heated there is no change even at high temperatures. Similarly, there is no change when sodium chloride is heated up to 700°C. In both cases the forces between the particles in the solid are very strong and are not easily broken. These structures are called **giant structures.** There can be two sorts of giant structure. In the case of silicon(IV) oxide the structure is made up of atoms of silicon and oxygen covalently bonded to form a single structure (Fig. 7.6). When sodium chloride is heated strongly, to a temperature above 800°C, the giant structure breaks down and forms **free ions.**

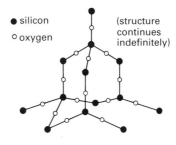

Fig. 7.6 Silicon(IV) oxide

The three types of structure are summarised below:

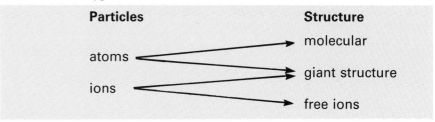

QUESTIONS ON UNIT 7

Domain I: Knowledge and understanding

1. protons, neutrons, electrons, atoms, nucleus, ion, isotopes

   Use the words in the list above to complete the following passage:

   An atom must contain equal numbers of positively charged . . . . and negatively charged . . . . The number of . . . . in an atom is of less importance. Different . . . . of the same element may contain different numbers of . . . . They are called . . . .

   Protons and . . . . are tightly bound together in the positively charged . . . . of an atom. The . . . . move rapidly around the nucleus.

   When an atom gains or loses electrons an . . . . is produced.

2. Complete the table below, which summarises information about the three particles which make up an atom:

Particle	Charge	Mass
. . . .	+1	1 a.m.u.
neutron	. . . . . .	. . . .
. . . .	. . . . .	negligible

3. Below is a simple representation of a carbon atom:

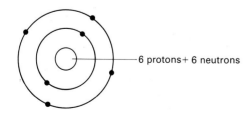

6 protons + 6 neutrons

   Draw similar diagrams of lithium, magnesium, fluorine and sodium atoms.

4. Unit 7 describes three types of bonding – ionic, covalent and metallic. Which of the three following descriptions best describes each type of bonding?

Description 1:
   This consists of a regular arrangement of positively charged ions held together by a 'sea' of electrons.

Description 2:
   This consists of atoms held together by one or more pairs of shared electrons.

Description 3:
   Atoms gain or lose electrons. The particles produced are held together by strong electrostatic forces.

Domain II: Handling information and solving problems

5. Below is a diagram representing an atom:

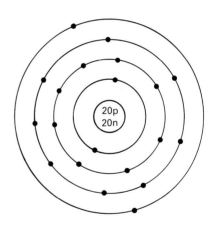

20p
20n

   (a) How many particles are there in the nucleus of this atom?
   (b) How many protons are there in the nucleus of this atom?
   (c) Complete the electron arrangement of this atom: 2, −, −, −.
   (d) The atom loses two electrons to form an ion. What is the charge on the ion produced and what is the electron arrangement in this ion?

6. Atoms and ions which have the same number of electrons are said to be isoelectronic. Using the elements sulphur, chlorine, potassium and calcium, write the formulae of three ions which are isoelectronic with an argon atom.

7. The element europium contains equal quantities of two isotopes. These are:

$$^{151}_{63}\text{Eu} \qquad\qquad ^{153}_{63}\text{Eu}$$

(a) Complete the following table:

	Number of electrons per atom	Number of protons per atom	Number of neutrons per atom
$^{151}_{63}\text{Eu}$			
$^{153}_{63}\text{Eu}$			

(b) What would you expect the relative atomic mass of naturally occurring europium to be?

(c) Europium forms an ion Eu^{2+}. Would you expect europium to be a metal or a non-metal? Explain your answer.

8. Complete the table below by putting in the correct numbers of protons, neutrons and electrons:

Particle	Number of		
	electrons	neutrons	protons
Magnesium atom Mg	12	12	12
Magnesium ion Mg^{2+}			
Sulphur atom S			
Sulphide ion S^{2-}	18	16	

9. The following list contains six elements with their atomic numbers:

hydrogen (1)
fluorine (9)
sodium (11)
magnesium (12)
phosphorus (15)
chlorine (17)

Using this information, complete the table on the right:

10. Lithium fluoride (LiF) has a melting point of 877°C and a boiling point of 1667°C. Molten lithium fluoride conducts electricity.

(a) What type of bonding is present in lithium fluoride?
(b) What is the structure of lithium fluoride at room temperature?
(c) Explain the changes of electron arrangement which take place when lithium fluoride is formed from lithium and fluorine atoms.

11. Complete the following table using information from the data section on pages 250–1:

Compound	Melting point	Boiling point	Solubility in water
Sodium chloride			
Silicon tetrachloride			
Potassium iodide			
Silicon dioxide			
Phosphorus trichloride			

From the table above select:

(a) two substances which contain ionic bonding;
(b) two substances which are made up from small molecules containing covalent bonding;
(c) one substance which exists as a giant structure of atoms held together by covalent bonding.

Elements in the compound	Formula of the compound	Type of bonding	Electrical conductivity	
			when solid	when liquid
Magnesium and chlorine	$MgCl_2$	ionic	non-conductor	good
Phosphorus and hydrogen				
Sodium and fluorine				

UNIT 8 The Periodic Table

8.1 Introduction

It is possible to arrange elements into families and other groups. During the nineteenth century, chemists tried to find a better way of classifying the elements. Finally, in 1869, the Russian chemist Dimitri Mendeléev devised the **Periodic Table** which is still widely used today. This classification was more difficult for Mendeléev to understand than for modern chemists, because many of the elements we know today had not been discovered when he devised his table. He left gaps where he knew elements would go. This pointed the way for other chemists to look for, and find, these elements. In this unit we are going to look at the modern Periodic Table and how it can help us.

Dimitri Ivanovich Mendeléev (1834–1907)

Mendeléev was a man of contradictions. He had two wives at the same time – a contradiction which brought him into conflict with the Russian Church. He also argued with the Education Minister so vehemently that he had to resign his job, but later went on to become the Russian Government's Foreign Minister and one of the most important scientists of his age. Throughout his life he pursued a greater understanding of Chemistry.

Mendeléev was born in Siberia in 1834, the 14th child of the Director of a college at Tobolsk. When his father went blind, the 16-year-old Dimitri was taken by his mother to St Petersburg – which is now called Leningrad – for further education. After much study and training he became the Professor of Chemistry at St Petersburg University in 1861, at the age of 27.

For 29 years he dedicatedly studied his subject. But then he fell into a vehement argument with the Minister of Education and resigned. Three years later, in 1893, he became Director of the Bureau of Weights and Measures – a post which he held until he died.

Throughout all these ups and downs he produced over 300 books and learned papers, mainly on Chemistry, but some on art, education and economics. He began his most important book, *Principles of Chemistry*, back in 1868. In order to state those chemical principles he needed to classify the chemical elements, so worked out the **Periodic Law** to explain how elements with similar properties could be grouped together in a logical order. He presented a paper on the subject to the Russian Chemical Society later in 1868, and it was this great paper which led to the formulation of the Periodic Table which we all use today.

Ironically, however, there was unknown to Mendeléev another chemist, Newlands, working along the same lines and reaching similar conclusions in London at the same time. Even so, Britain's Royal Society awarded Mendeléev the Davy Medal in 1862, and the Copley Medal in 1905, two years before he died at the age of 73.

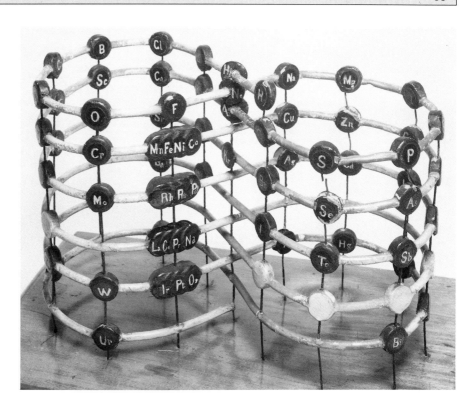

A 3-dimensional representation of the elements. This model is known as Crooke's Spiral. It was devised in 1888 as a way of classifying the elements in a logical order.

8.2 The Periodic Table

The Periodic Table is an arrangement of elements in order of increasing atomic number, with elements having similar properties in the same vertical column of **group.** The horizontal rows are called **periods.** Fig. 8.1 shows a simplified version of the Periodic Table. You should also refer to the more detailed version on pages 246–7.

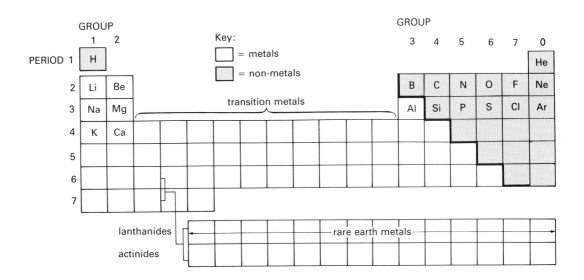

Fig. 8.1 The first 20 elements in the Periodic Table.

The elements shown in groups 1 to 0 are called the **main block** elements. Between groups 2 and 3 a block of **transition metals** is found. Transition metals generally:

(a) have high melting points, boiling points and densities
(b) are not very reactive
(c) form coloured compounds
(d) form more than one ion; for example, iron can form Fe^{2+} and Fe^{3+} ions – iron(II) compounds are often green in colour and iron (III) compounds are often yellow or brown.

The rare earth metals or lanthanides occur in very small quantities in some minerals. They have chemical properties similar to aluminium.

Hydrogen has no obvious place in the Periodic Table. It has some similarities with the elements in group 1 and the elements in group 7.

8.3 What information can you get from the Periodic Table?

1. Metals are on the left-hand side of each period. Non-metals are on the right-hand side. In Fig. 8.1 the bold line divides metals from non-metals. The properties of the elements in a group become more metallic as the atomic number increases (i.e. down a group).

2. Elements which are gases at room temperature and atmospheric pressure are in the top right-hand corner of the Periodic Table.

3. In any group of the Periodic Table, the atoms of the different elements increase in size down the group. In any period, the atoms of the different elements decrease in size across the period from left to right.

4. Metals in groups 1, 2 and 3 form positive ions by losing electrons. The number of positive charges on the ion is the same as the group number of the metal.

5. Non-metals in groups 5, 6 and 7 form negative ions by gaining electrons. The number of charges on the ion formed is the same as the number of the group subtracted from eight. For example, oxygen in group 6 gains two electrons and forms an O^{2-} ion.

6. The number of electrons in the outer shell of any atom of an element is the same as the group in which the element is placed. For example, a carbon atom has 4 electrons in the outer shell and carbon is in group 4 of the Periodic Table. Noble gases (group 0) are an exception to this.

QUESTIONS ON UNIT 8

Domain I: Knowledge and understanding

1. Neon, sodium, chlorine, magnesium, oxygen, aluminium, silicon, phosphorus, sulphur.

   From the list of elements above, choose:

   (a) two elements in the same group of the Periodic Table
   (b) three metallic elements
   (c) an element in group 4 of the Periodic Table
   (d) a halogen element
   (e) a noble gas
   (f) an alkali metal.

2.

List A	List B
neon	chlorine
sodium	sulphur
oxygen	calcium
bromine	silicon
magnesium	potassium
carbon	argon

   Choose an element in list B which most closely resembles each element in list A. You will finish up with six pairs of elements.

Domain II: Handling information and solving problems

3. Below is a skeleton Periodic Table with only some of the elements inserted. Using only the elements in this Periodic Table, give the symbols for:

   (a) two elements in the same group
   (b) two elements in the same period
   (c) an alkali metal
   (d) a transition metal
   (e) a noble gas
   (f) a metal usually stored under oil
   (g) the element whose atoms contain the largest number of protons
   (h) the element which would contain the largest number of atoms in a 10 g sample.

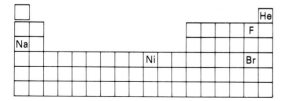

4. When Mendeléev devised the Periodic Table many of the elements that are now known had not been discovered. The following account refers to such an element. It is represented by the symbol X but this is not the usual symbol for this element:

   X is an element with a melting point of 30°C and a boiling point of 2440°C. It conducts electricity at room temperature.

   It burns in oxygen to form an oxide which has a pH of 7. The oxide is a colourless solid with a formula X_2O_3.

   X forms a compound with fluorine which is a high melting point solid that conducts electricity when molten. The similar compound with bromine has a formula XBr_3 but is a low melting point solid.

   The approximate relative atomic mass of X is 70.

   (a) Is X a solid, liquid or gas at room temperature (20°C)?
   (b) Predict the formula for the fluoride of X.
   (c) In which group and period of the Periodic Table would you place the element X?

5. Look at the Periodic Table on pages 246–7 and especially at the first ten elements (hydrogen to neon).

   (a) Which one of these ten elements:
      (i) would diffuse fastest?
      (ii) is the lightest (least dense) element whose atoms have a complete outer shell of electrons?
      (iii) is the heaviest (most dense) element whose atoms have one electron in their outer shell?

   (b) X, Y and Z represent three of the first ten elements in the Periodic Table. They each form compounds with hydrogen. These compounds are XH_4, YH_3 and HZ. Give the names of X, Y and Z.

UNIT 9 Extraction of metals

9.1 Introduction

The reactivity series:

Potassium
Sodium
Magnesium
Aluminium
Carbon
Zinc
Iron
Hydrogen
Copper

In Unit 6 a list of metals was given called the **reactivity series** (see left). Also the differences in reactivity were used to explain displacement reactions. In this unit we are going to consider the methods used to obtain metals from their ores. An ore is a rock which contains a compound of the required metal along with unwanted impurities.

The method used to obtain or extract a metal from its ore depends on the position of the metal in the reactivity series.

Metals such as potassium, sodium, magnesium and aluminium cannot be extracted using carbon. (This is because carbon is below them in the reactivity series.) Compounds of these metals are very difficult to split up and **electrolysis** has to be used. This is a method which provides a lot of energy but is expensive to carry out.

Zinc and iron, in the middle of the reactivity series, can be extracted by reduction with carbon.

Metals low in the series, such as gold and mercury, are very unreactive. They may be found as free metals in the earth. Otherwise the compounds containing them are easily split up by heating.

In this unit the extraction of iron and aluminium will be examined in detail. Methods used to make steel will also be explained.

9.2 Extraction of iron in the blast furnace

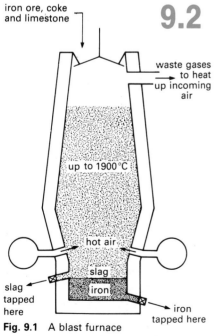

Fig. 9.1 A blast furnace

Iron is extracted from iron ore in a blast furnace. A modern blast furnace can be 70 metres high, made of steel and lined with insulating bricks.

The blast furnace is loaded with iron ore, coke (carbon, C) and limestone (calcium carbonate, $CaCO_3$). There are many forms of iron ore including haematite, Fe_2O_3. The iron ore is 'sintered' before loading. This involves roasting the ore and making it into pellets.

The furnace (Fig. 9.1) is heated with blasts of hot air – hence its name.

A series of chemical reactions take place. Firstly, coke burns in the oxygen in the air forming carbon dioxide:

$$carbon + oxygen \rightarrow carbon\ dioxide$$

This is an exothermic reaction and raises the temperature in the furnace. This can reach 1900°C.

The carbon dioxide is then reduced to carbon monoxide by more coke. Carbon monoxide, CO, is the important chemical in the furnace:

$$carbon\ dioxide + carbon \rightarrow carbon\ monoxide$$

The carbon monoxide reduces the iron(III) oxide to iron:

$$iron(III)\ oxide + carbon\ monoxide \rightarrow iron + carbon\ dioxide$$

The iron sinks to the bottom of the furnace. The iron can be tapped off at the bottom of the furnace as molten iron. It is run into moulds and, on cooling, forms 'pig iron'.

The waste gases escape through the top of the furnace.

The iron ore contains impurities including silicon dioxide (sand, SiO_2). If this is not removed it would clog up the furnace and prevent it operating continuously. The limestone is added to remove these impurities.

The limestone is decomposed to form calcium oxide and carbon dioxide:

$$\text{calcium carbonate} \rightarrow \text{calcium oxide} + \text{carbon dioxide}$$

Incidentally, the carbon dioxide produced will react with more carbon, making more carbon monoxide and hence more iron.

The calcium oxide (basic oxide) reacts with silicon dioxide (acidic oxide) to form calcium silicate, which we commonly call 'slag':

$$\text{calcium oxide} + \text{silicon dioxide} \rightarrow \text{calcium silicate}$$

The slag is used as a cheap phosphorus fertiliser or for road surfacing.

The furnace runs continuously. Fresh iron ore, coke and limestone are added and molten iron and slag are tapped off. A modern blast furnace can produce 10 000 tonnes of iron every day. To produce this, 20 000 tonnes of iron ore, 8000 tonnes of coke, 5000 tonnes of limestone and 40 000 tonnes of hot air are required.

9.3 Converting iron into steel

The pig iron from the blast furnace contains a number of impurities – up to 7% of carbon, silicon, phosphorus and sulphur are examples. Most of the pig iron is converted into steel. Steel contains up to 1.7% carbon. Undesirable impurities have to be removed from the iron and a controlled amount of carbon, and possibly other elements, have to be added.

There are many variations on the way in which this can be done. You are not expected to know the details of these processes, only the principles.

Molten pig iron is put into the furnace and scrap iron and limestone are added. Crushed motor car bodies can be used here and this recycling of steel saves precious resources (see photographs on page 62).

Oxygen is then blown through the molten iron (Fig. 9.2, page 60) and this oxidises the impurities. The gaseous impurities such as sulphur dioxide and carbon dioxide are blown out of the furnace. Silicon dioxide and other solid oxides react with the limestone to form calcium silicate (slag) and other impurities, which can be scooped off the surface of the molten iron. Finally, the exact required amounts of carbon and other elements are added to give the type of steel required.

9.4 Types of iron and steel

Steel is an **alloy** of iron (i.e. a mixture of iron and other metals). It is extremely important for many different uses.

Cast iron is an impure form of iron used to make engine blocks, man-hole covers, etc. It contains up to 4% carbon and is very brittle.

Wrought iron is pure iron. It is soft and bends easily. It is used for garden gates, chains, etc.

METALS FROM OLD MINES

In the Northern Pennine hills of England there are numerous sites where 'heavy' metals have been mined. Two of the most abundant ores are galena (lead sulphide) and sphalerite (zinc sulphide.) The industry was at its peak in the early 19th century, but the richest two mines continued to be worked until the 1930s. At an even later date, some mines were reworked for zinc ore, which had been ignored by earlier lead miners. Extracting fluorspar (calcium fluoride) for use in steel-making has since taken over as the most important mining activity in the area.

The many years over which lead and zinc were mined have led to widespread contamination of the surrounding land and watercourses. Polluted water drains out of old mine shafts, particles of ore are washed into streams from old spoil heaps and soil remains poisoned around old smelters.

Having developed test tube methods for extracting and analysing lead and zinc, a group of students decided to explore part of the North Pennine orefield, Upper Weardale in the West of County Durham.

On the left is a map summarising their results. On the facing page is part of their report.

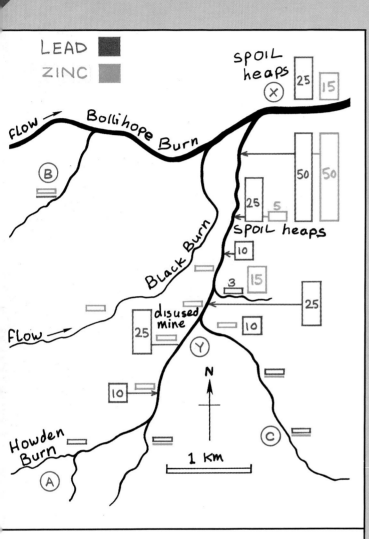

KEY:

On this map the amounts of lead and zinc found in the stream sediments are represented by columns (red for lead and green for zinc). The height of each column is proportional to the amount of metal found, as in a histogram (i.e. the taller the column, the larger the amount). The numbers in the columns correspond to values on our colour indicator charts. Where there is no number, only the lowest detectable amount was found. Where none was found, a simple horizontal line — is shown.

ACTIVITIES ▼

Here are some of the questions which arose from the students' discussions during the trip:

1. Why were the highest concentrations of both metals found in the lowermost reaches of the Howden Burn, rather than upstream or in the main Bollihope Burn itself?

2. Why were both metals virtually absent from sediments in the uppermost reaches of all the streams?

3. What must have been the major occupation of the mine in this valley — lead mining or zinc mining?

4. What explanation might there be for the 15 result for zinc in the tributary half-way up the Howden Burn (the lead result there was only 3)?

5. In the light of this high result, how can you explain the low zinc result in the Howden Burn just downstream of the tributary?

6. In view of the large amounts of lead and zinc found in some of the sediments, why do you think the concentrations of lead and zinc ions in the water were so low as to be undetectable?

Here are some further questions which arose out of trips to other mining sites:

7. What sorts of living things might be affected by lead and zinc in streamwater?

ACTIVITIES ▼

8. The Northern Pennines is an area which now relies heavily on sheep farming. What dangers might there be for sheep grazing near old lead and zinc mining sites?

9. Extracting the metals from the ores by smelting involved a two-stage treatment:
(a) roasting the ore in air to obtain the oxide:

zinc sulphide + oxygen → zinc oxide + sulphur dioxide

$$2ZnS + 3O_2 \rightarrow 2ZnO + 2SO_2$$

(b) reducing the metal oxide with carbon monoxide produced by adding coke or another carbon-containing fuel:

zinc oxide + carbon monoxide → zinc + carbon dioxide

$$ZnO + CO \rightarrow Zn + CO_2$$

Sometimes the two stages were combined in one process:

lead sulphide + oxygen → $\underbrace{\text{lead sulphide + lead oxide}}$ + sulphur dioxide

$\downarrow$ lead + sulphur dioxide

$$3PbS + 3O_2 \rightarrow \underbrace{PbS + 2PbO} + 2SO_2$$

$$\downarrow 3Pb + SO_2$$

Zinc metal has a particularly low boiling point and both metal oxides are produced as very tiny particles during the reactions.

i) What do you think might have been the three main types of pollutant released by the smelters?

ii) What problems might these pollutants have caused?

iii) What three 'carbon-containing fuels' might have been most easily obtained by the miners from their Pennine surroundings?

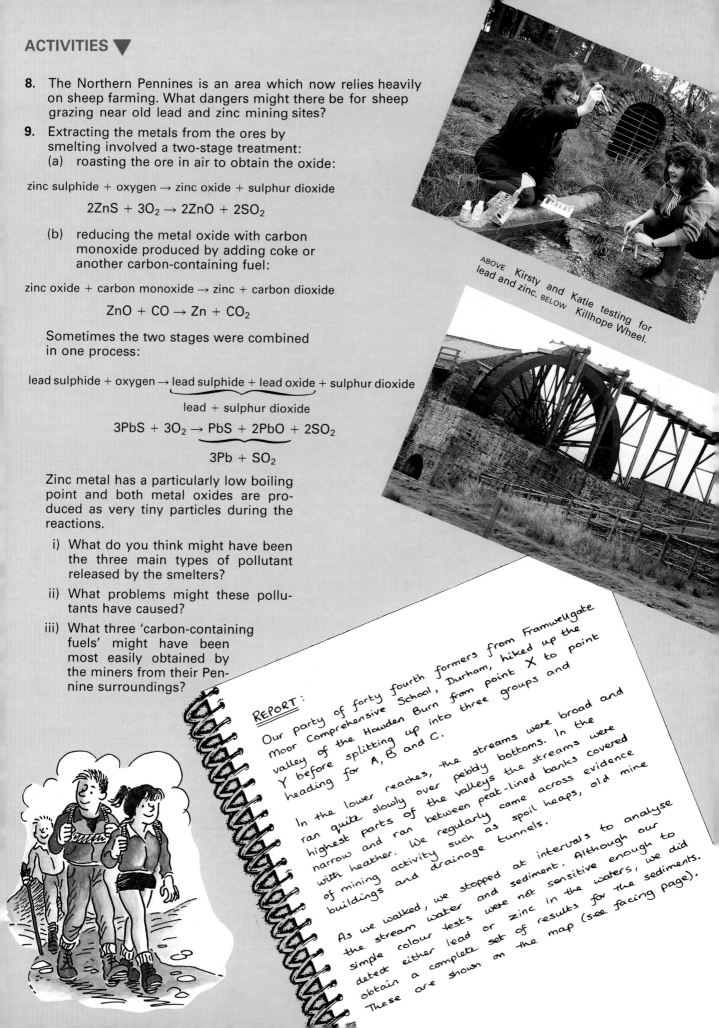

ABOVE *Kirsty and Katie testing for lead and zinc.* BELOW *Killhope Wheel.*

REPORT:

Our party of forty fourth formers from Framwellgate Moor Comprehensive School, Durham, hiked up the valley of the Howden Burn from point X to point Y before splitting up into three groups and heading for A, B and C.

In the lower reaches, the streams were broad and ran quite slowly over pebbly bottoms. In the highest parts of the valleys the streams were narrow and ran between peat-lined banks covered with heather. We regularly came across evidence of mining activity such as spoil heaps, old mine buildings and drainage tunnels.

As we walked, we stopped at intervals to analyse the stream water and sediment. Although our simple colour tests were not sensitive enough to detect either lead or zinc in the waters, we did obtain a complete set of results for the sediments. These are shown on the map (see facing page).

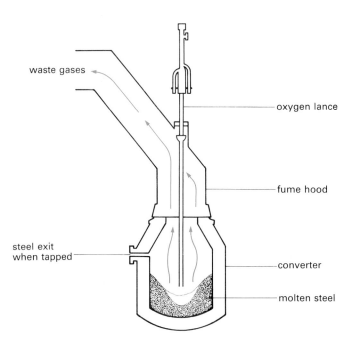

waste gases

oxygen lance

fume hood

steel exit
when tapped

converter

molten steel

Fig. 9.2 Basic oxygen process for steel-
making

Stainless steel is steel which contains other metals such as nickel, chromium, manganese and cobalt. Stainless steel is more resistant to rusting. It is used for making knives, scissors, magnets and high-speed drills.

9.5   Siting of an iron and steel works

A blast furnace uses large amounts of raw materials. It also produces a very heavy product. It is important to site the works near to the source of the raw materials and near to customers.

Unfortunately, in Great Britain we have used up all of the best iron ores, which contained the highest percentage of iron compounds. Low-grade ores from this country are mixed with high-grade ores from Sweden, USSR, Australia and Africa. It is therefore wise to site the works on the coast, preferably on an estuary with good port facilities. Also, deposits of suitable coal and limestone close-by will reduce transport costs.

Many of Britain's traditional markets for steel have declined – ship-building, car-making, tin plate, etc. For this reason, and because of highly competitive imports of steel, iron and steel-making capacity has been greatly reduced.

An inland iron and steel works such as the one at Corby in Northamptonshire was at a big disadvantage. The alternative to using low-grade local ores, which require enormous fuel costs, is to import high-grade ores – but then transport costs become very high. Corby, along with other small or inefficient iron and steel works, has now been closed and iron and steel-making is confined to one or two centres.

There are other considerations when siting an iron and steel works. The quarrying of iron ore is a very unsightly and dusty business. After the iron ore is removed the land must slowly be returned to a natural state and landscaped. There are often restrictions to places where quarrying is acceptable. Air pollution is produced from the iron and steel works. The main pollutants are:

1. Sulphur dioxide (Unit 13). This is produced during the burning of fossil fuels, sintering of the ore and from the limestone used. It is also produced during the steel-making process.
2. Black smoke from the coal-burning plant.
3. Grit and dust from ash, slag, sinter and iron ore.
4. Very fine particles of iron oxide suspended in the waste gases during steel-making. These give rise to reddish-brown fumes.

Dust and grit are filtered out and every effort is made to remove sulphur dioxide before the waste gases are let out of a tall chimney. Modern plants are much cleaner than older iron and steel works, where air pollution was not as seriously considered as it is today. Because of air pollution it is wise to site the works so that prevailing winds blow any pollution away from residential areas.

Iron and steel works also use large amounts of water. About 200 tonnes of water are needed to produce one tonne of steel. However, much of this water can be recovered and re-used. About 37 tonnes of recycled water are actually used up to produce one tonne of steel. Therefore, an iron and steel works has to be sited close to a river or estuary for a plentiful supply of water.

Effluents from an iron and steel works can range from slightly contaminated cooling water to highly toxic wastes from acid pickling. Waste water has to be treated before it can enter public sewers or be discharged into waterways.

9.6 Extraction of aluminium

Aluminium is the most common metal in the Earth's crust. It occurs in the ore called bauxite, so called because it was first found near the town of Les Baux in the South of France.

Bauxite is hydrated aluminium oxide, $Al_2O_3.3H_2O$. The ore is found close to the surface and can be obtained by open-pit mining. Deposits of bauxite are found in Brazil, Australia, Guinea, Jamaica and India.

In the ore there is a great deal of waste material including sand, iron(III) oxide and titanium oxide. Before aluminium is extracted the ore has to be purified using sodium hydroxide solution. The product is pure alumina, Al_2O_3.

Aluminium is too high in the reactivity series to be obtained by reduction with carbon. Electrolysis has to be used for extraction on an industrial scale.

In 1825 Hans Christian Oersted extracted aluminium by reduction, but until the electrolysis was developed in 1886 large-scale aluminium production was impossible.

The problem with the extraction centres around aluminium oxide. This is a solid with a very high melting point. It is very insoluble in water. Finding a suitable solvent to make electrolysis possible was very difficult. In 1886, two men independently solved the problem – Charles Hall in the USA and Paul Héroult working in France. (Incidentally, both men discovered this when they were 22 years old and they both died in 1914!) The method they developed, sometimes called the Hall-Héroult method, involves the electrolysis of alumina dissolved in molten cryolite and fluorspar (calcium fluoride, CaF_2). Cryolite is a complex sodium aluminium fluoride (Na_3AlF_6) found naturally in Greenland.

Fig. 9.3 shows a cell used to extract aluminium from aluminium oxide.

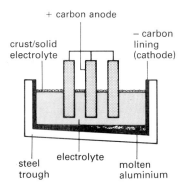

+ carbon anode

crust/solid electrolyte

– carbon lining (cathode)

steel trough

electrolyte

molten aluminium

Fig. 9.3 Extracting aluminium by electrolysis

ABOVE Molten iron being poured into a steel-making furnace. Oxygen is then blown through the iron to oxidise the impurities.

ABOVE RIGHT The Port Talbot Steel Works.

RIGHT Each metal cube is a crushed car! These are ready for melting down to produce new steel.

The cell is lined with carbon which acts as the cathode (negative electrode) of the cell. Carbon anodes are lowered into the cell. The electrolyte is aluminium oxide dissolved in cryolite and fluorspar. Passage of an electric current causes the following overall reaction:

$$\text{aluminium oxide} \rightarrow \text{aluminium} + \text{oxygen}$$

Aluminium is deposited at the cathode and oxygen is produced at the anode. The anodes burn away in the oxygen and form carbon monoxide and carbon dioxide. The anodes have to be replaced from time to time.

The cryolite is unchanged and fresh alumina is added as required.

Molten aluminium is tapped off from the cell from time to time.

Making 1 tonne of aluminium requires 5 tonnes of bauxite, 0.6 tonnes of carbon anodes, 0.45 tonnes of fuel oil, 0.08 tonnes of caustic soda and 0.05 tonnes of cryolite/fluorspar. The electricity required to produce 1 tonne of aluminium is 17 000 kW – the total consumption of a good-sized power station for nearly an hour.

9.7 Siting of an aluminium works

The original aluminium works were built next to the Niagara Falls in the USA to use the cheap electricity generated there – and cheap electricity is certainly an important factor when siting an aluminium works.

It is usual to purify the bauxite in the country where it is mined. This reduces the cost of transporting the bauxite and unwanted wastes. Both the mining and the waste products of purifying the bauxite can be unsightly. A red iron(III) oxide mud is produced during the purifying and this can be toxic when dumped.

A factory producing aluminium from alumina needs:

1. A large supply of electricity. This can be provided by surplus power from a hydroelectric project such as the Volta Dam in Ghana. Alternatively, it can be provided by a coal- or oil-fired power station. Although the electricity may be more expensive, the factory can perhaps be built closer to sources of raw materials or markets for aluminium.
2. A large supply of cooling water;
3. Raw materials – alumina, coke, cryolite and fluorspar;
4. A good transport system to bring in raw materials and take out products;
5. A workforce;
6. Finance for the project from private funds, Government or EEC grants;
7. To be built so pollution produces the minimum of problems. Water from an aluminium works may contain fluorides from the cryolite. This can blight vegetation and cause cattle to go lame. Air pollution can be produced from the burning of fossil fuels to produce electricity.

ABOVE RIGHT   Open cast mining of bauxite. Notice the very orange colour of the mineral caused by the presence of iron(III) oxide. What are the problems associated with open cast mining of bauxite?

LEFT   The Lynemouth Aluminium Smelter. In the distance you will see a power station which produces electricity from coal mined alongside. The electricity is conveyed by overhead cables to the smelter in the foreground. What do you think happens to any surplus electricity produced by the power station?

ABOVE LEFT   Adding fresh electrolyte to one of the electrolysis cells at the Lynemouth Aluminium Smelter. The photograph gives you some idea of the scale of the operation.

QUESTIONS ON UNIT 9

Domain I: Knowledge and understanding

1. (a) Complete the diagram on the right, which summarises the method used to extract iron from iron ore.

(b) Name a common iron ore and the chief chemical constituent of the ore.

(c) Name the major gas present in the waste gases leaving the blast furnace.

(d) Complete the following word equations taking place in the blast furnace:

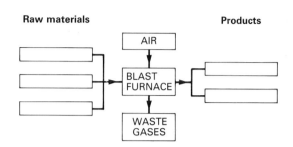

Raw materials   **Products**

AIR

BLAST FURNACE

WASTE GASES

---

carbon + ... → carbon dioxide

---

carbon dioxide + carbon → . . . .

---

iron(III) oxide + ... → iron + ...

---

calcium carbonate → . . . . + ...

. . . . + silicon dioxide → . . . .

(e) molten, oxygen, oxidised, carbon, limestone, slag, reduced

Use the words above to complete the following passage about steel-making:

In order to make steel . . . . is blown through . . . . iron from the blast furnace. The impurities are . . . . Gases such as carbon dioxide, phosphorus oxide and sulphur dioxide escape from the furnace. . . . . is added to the furnace to remove silicon dioxide as . . . . This can be scooped off the surface of the molten iron.

In order to make steel of the required specification, exactly the correct amount of . . . . is added.

(f) In the blast furnace iron is made continuously. Steel is, however, usually produced in batches. Explain why continuous production is better for iron-making, and batch production better for steel-making.

2. alumina, cryolite, oxygen, anode, cathode, bauxite, fluorspar

Use the words in the list above to complete the following passage:

The usual aluminium ore is called . . . . It contains many impurities including iron(III) oxide. The ore is purified and pure . . . . (aluminium oxide) is produced.

Aluminium is produced by electrolysis of . . . . dissolved in molten . . . . and . . . .

The . . . . and cathode are made of carbon.

Aluminium metal is produced at the . . . . and can be tapped off as a liquid. . . . . is first produced at the anode but the anode burns in this gas. Therefore, it is necessary to replace the anodes from time to time.

Domain II: Handling information and solving problems

3. You are working in the research laboratories of a firm producing metal cans for food. You are asked to compare the properties of aluminium with tin-coated steel for a new range of cans for a supermarket 'own-brand' contract. Your results are summarised in the table below.

Write a brief report to your Managing Director (who is not a chemist) comparing the merits of the two materials for this use. You should conclude your report by making recommendations about which one of the materials should be used. Bear in mind that you may be required to can lager (containing ethanol), shellfish in brine, very alkaline products like health salts and some products which are slightly acid (e.g. fruit juice).

Table 9.1

	Aluminium	Steel coated with tin
Reaction with water	No reaction even on heating	No reaction even on heating
Reaction with acid	Bubbles given off slowly. Vigorous reaction on heating	Little reaction on heating. Few bubbles given off
Reaction with alkali	Vigorous reaction without heating. Gas evolved	No reaction on heating
Reaction with salt	No reaction even on heating	No reaction on heating
Reaction with ethanol	No reaction	No reaction
Mass of can	35.9 g	59.7 g
Relative hardness	Soft	Quite hard
Price per tonne	£1100	£800

NEWS BRIEF NEWS BRIEF NEWS BRIEF NEWS BRIEF NEWS BRIEF NEWS BRIEF NEWS BRIEF

Brazil is the second largest producer of iron ore in the world. Since 1950 it has been turning some of this iron ore into iron and steel using coke. The coke has to be made from coal and Brazil has few coal deposits.

Now there is a plan to step up iron and steel production using charcoal, in place of coke. This would be made from the tropical rain forests. The pig iron produced in this way is cheaper to transport than iron ore, fetches a much higher price and contains much less undesirable sulphur than iron ore produced using coke. Money for this project has been obtained in the form of loans from America, the EEC and Japan.

Environmentalists are deeply concerned about the problems caused by the burning of the rain forest. (See Case Study 5.)

An aluminium smelter in Greece

Greece is a country in Southern Europe bordering the Mediterranean sea. Most of the country's income comes from agriculture and tourism. The Greek government is anxious to develop industry and has co-operated with overseas companies such as Philips, Pirelli and Benz.

The country has few valuable mineral deposits. Deposits of bauxite (the ore for extracting aluminium) are probably most important, being some of the largest in Europe. They are found at Elevsis and Distomon. A small aluminium smelter was built some years ago at Distomon and this produces enough aluminium for use in Greece – about 100 000 tonnes each year. Most of the unpurified bauxite ore is sold to the USSR.

There is a little brown coal (lignite) mined at Megalopoli but this is needed for making electricity.

A new large aluminium smelter is proposed close to the town of Delphi. This will produce 600 000 tonnes of aluminium a year using bauxite mined in Greece. A large coal-fired power station would be built close to the smelter. This would use imported coal which is available at reasonable prices. The power station would produce more electricity than is required by the smelter. The plan is proposed by a joint consortium from the USSR and Poland. They would provide finance, the latest equipment and they promise to buy all of the aluminium at a guaranteed price.

The proposed smelter would not be seen from the ancient monuments at Delphi. The passage from a travel brochure will give you some idea of the area in which the smelter and power station would be built.

GREECE

Area
131 944 km² (50 943 sq miles)

Location
34°50' – 41°45' N
19°20' – 28°15' E

Population
8 960 000

Population density
68 per km² (176 per sq mile)

Capital and largest city
Athens: 2 540 240

Language
Greek

Major imports
machinery, transport, equipment, iron, steel, petroleum, meat, dairy products, pharmaceuticals and textiles

Major exports
tobacco, fresh and processed fruit and vegetables, olive oil, aluminium, cotton, minerals and handicrafts

Currency
drachma

Gross National Product
19 860 million US dollars

Status
republic

DELPHI

The town of Delphi is about 100 miles from Athens and is one of the most popular destinations for tourists in Greece. Every day people arrive by road and sea and many of them stay in hotels in Delphi.

Delphi is built in a deep valley with mountains rising above 2000 metres surrounding it. On these mountain slopes there are millions of olive trees and some of the best vineyards in Greece.

The Ancient Greeks believed that Delphi was the point where earth touched the divine. The remains at Delphi date back many thousands of years. In the middle of the monuments is the large Doric Temple of Apollo dominating the entire landscape. The original temple was destroyed by fire and rebuilt in 548 BC, larger and more luxurious than the original.

Delphi ▶

Olives ▶

Olive trees are very slow-growing. They are used to produce olive oil and also the olive wood is used for making many decorative objects sold to tourists. Each olive tree receives a subsidy from the EEC each year.

ACTIVITY ▼

Divide into groups of three. One person in each group should assume the role of each of the following people in Greece:

1. Minister of Employment and Economics
2. Minister of Tourism and Culture
3. Minister of Agriculture and Environment

Each person should go away and write a report not longer than 300 words summarising the advantages and disadvantages of the proposed smelter and power station development **in the view of their Ministry.**

Then each group of three should sit down and discuss the three conflicting reports. Before starting, you should appoint a chairperson and a reporter. Each group should write one agreed report to the President of Greece, either recommending or turning down the proposals with clearly explained reasons.

(All reports should be handed to the teacher at the end of the lesson.)

You must reach a decision. You cannot suggest alternative sites or delay the project.

UNIT 10 Recycling

10.1 Introduction

The amounts of important raw materials in the earth are limited. Over many centuries man has used up these minerals, often with little thought for generations to follow. These raw materials include metal ores and fossil fuels.

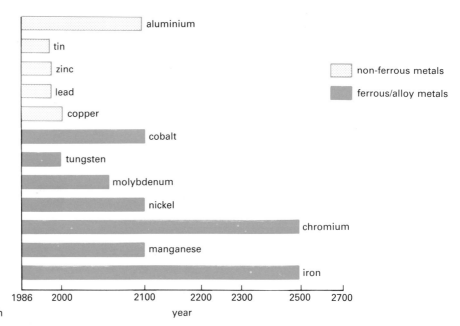

Fig. 10.1 Supplies of metals in the earth

Fig. 10.1 shows approximately when different raw metals will run out. Natural sources of raw metals may last longer if we find new supplies in the earth. We can make them last longer if we use them more slowly. One way of doing this is to re-use materials – a process we call **recycling.**

At present we recycle some metals, such as aluminium, lead and copper, as well as glass, rubber, paper and some plastics. The pressure to recycle materials becomes stronger as prices rise and supplies of raw material run out.

10.2 Recycling of metals

Since the Second World War the amount of copper used each year has increased threefold and the amount of aluminium sixfold. With this increasing demand, supplies will not last long.

Aluminium is now recovered from soft drink cans, kitchen containers, etc. Tin is removed from scrap tin cans and re-used. Copper is recovered

Making coins at the Royal Mint. The machine on the left punches coins out of a continuous sheet of metal. The remaining metal is then melted down and recycled to make more coins.

NEWS BRIEF NEWS BRIEF

A recent report has estimated that Britain burns or dumps 41 million tonnes of materials each year, which could be worth £750 million if recycled.

from scrap electrical wires and water pipes. Scrap steel from used car bodies, ships and other vehicles is re-used in steel works.

Household refuse is a valuable source of metals but the separation of metals from household refuse is not easy. A magnet can be used to extract iron and other ferrous metals. If household refuse is put into a suitable detergent bath, paper and plastics will float and can be scooped off from the heavier materials such as metals. The mixture of paper and plastic will separate because, after a time, the paper will sink when it becomes thoroughly soaked.

Fig. 10.2 shows a new method for separating metals from refuse.

1. X-ray detector identifies metal

2. Computer relays instructions to air jets

3. Air jets blow metal into appropriate bin

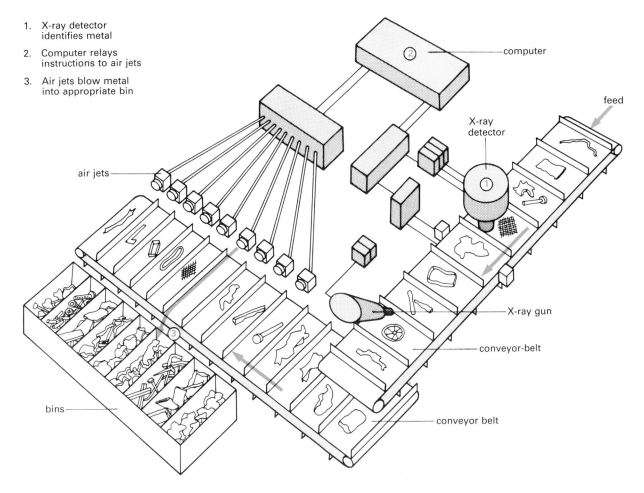

Fig. 10.2 A new way of extracting metals from household rubbish

About 10% of the refuse, after paper and plastic have been removed, consists of valuable metals such as copper, aluminium and brass (an alloy of metals). At present these metals have to be picked out of household refuse by hand. This is a very wasteful (and unpleasant!) method which recovers only about 40% of the valuable materials. A team of scientists have devised a new system to separate metals. A vibrator arranges the lumps of scrap metal in a neat, evenly spaced row on a conveyor-belt. The pieces of metal are scanned with X-rays. Different metals re-emit X-rays at different frequencies – a microprocessor can identify up to 14 metals by this process. A swinging arm or a blast of air can then be used to separate the metals into different containers. The system separates five lumps of metal per second.

Scrap metals can be very valuable but scrap paper and plastics are less important. The problem with scrap plastics is that the composition of the mixture is very variable, and it is impossible to separate individual plastics. If the mixture could be separated, then these plastics could be used more widely.

TOP　Disposing of empty bottles in bottle banks. The crushed glass is re-used by the glass-making industry. Why are there two sorts of bottle banks in this picture?

ABOVE RIGHT　Waste paper to be used for making recycled paper.

ABOVE　The inside of an incinerator where domestic rubbish is burned. Water in the boiler tubes overhead is heated to steam, which is used to drive the turbo alternators (RIGHT). These generate electricity which is fed into the National Grid.

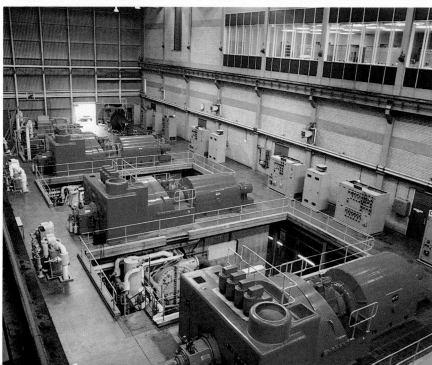

UNIT 11 Acidity and salt formation

11.1 Acids and alkalis in the everyday world

Lemon juice turning blue litmus paper red. What does this tell you?

We are familiar with acids and alkalis in the world around us. The sharp taste we get when we bite into an apple is malic acid. Acids always have a sour taste, although we would be unwise to taste some of them! Acids are present in lemons, oranges, limes (i.e. citrus fruit – citric acid). The sourness in sweet-and-sour chicken comes from vinegar – ethanoic or acetic acid.

Natural rain water containing no pollution is slightly acidic because carbon dioxide, in the air, dissolves to form carbonic acid. Soda water is a solution of carbon dioxide in water under pressure, and so it contains carbonic acid. Other fizzy drinks contain carbonic acid.

Air pollutants such as sulphur dioxide and oxides of nitrogen also dissolve in water to form acids (Unit 16). Acid rain causes all sorts of problems to stone buildings, to trees and plants and to metal structures. Also, acid rain makes inland lochs more acidic and farmland very acidic. If soil becomes too acidic, plants will not grow well. Farmers neutralise their land by putting lime or other alkalis on it.

Every adult has several hundred cubic centimetres of hydrochloric acid in the gastric juices of the stomach. This is used, along with biological catalysts called enzymes, to digest the food. The food is broken down into usable chemicals. This acid is usually no problem. However, for about one person in ten at some time in their life, the stomach wall breaks down and an ulcer is produced. Minor problems of indigestion caused by too much acid can be corrected by taking antacids. These are substances like sodium hydrogencarbonate or milk of magnesia (a suspension of magnesium hydroxide). These alkalis will neutralise excess acid.

A collection of everyday products. Can you decide which contain acids and which contain alkalis? One product contains both.

Insect bites and stings involve the injection of a small amount of chemical into the skin. This causes irritation. Stinging nettles and ants inject methanoic acid (formic acid) into the skin. Bee stings also involve the injection of an acid. The sting or bite should be treated with calamine lotion (a suspension of zinc carbonate) or bicarbonate of soda (sodium hydrogencarbonate) to neutralise the acidity and remove the irritation.

Wasp stings are different, however. The wasp injects an alkali into the skin. These stings are treated by neutralising with a weak acid, such as vinegar (ethanoic or acetic acid).

11.2 Acids

How can we test for an acid? Usually they are dissolved in water (i.e. in an **aqueous** solution) and they look like other liquids. There are three tests that can be used to show that an acid is present.

1. Indicators

The simplest indicator to use to detect an acid, or an alkali for that matter, is litmus. This is a solution made from a lichen which grows in Arctic areas. It is normally purple in colour and you can get it either in a solution or soaked up and dried on a piece of paper. We call this **litmus paper** (see photograph on page 71).

If litmus is added to an acid, the litmus turns red. If it is added to an alkali it turns blue. This can be summarised as:

ALKALI　　ACID
BLUE　　　RED

Litmus gives you no idea about the strength of the acid. Both vinegar and sulphuric acid turn litmus red.

Universal indicator is a better test for acids and alkalis. Universal indicator is a mixture of simple indicators and it changes through several colours. From the colour you can get the pH (see page 78).

pH is a number on a scale which shows whether a substance is acid, neutral or alkali (see Table 11.1).

You will note that the colours Universal indicator turn are in the same order as the colours of the rainbow. If a solution is slightly acidic it would turn Universal indicator yellow and have a pH of 6. An exactly neutral substance has a pH of 7 and turns Universal indicator green.

Table 11.1 Colour changes with Universal indicator

pH	Colour	Acidity/alkalinity
1 2 3 4	red	acid
5 6	orange yellow	
7	green	neutral
8 9 10 11	blue indigo (blue/purple)	alkali
12 13	purple	

2. Magnesium (or zinc)

Magnesium and zinc are reactive metals which react with acids to form hydrogen gas. These reactions can be used to test if an acid is present. If magnesium is added to an acid solution, bubbles of colourless gas are produced. If a lighted splint is put into the gas, the gas burns with a squeaky pop and the splint goes out. The gas is hydrogen. For example:

magnesium + sulphuric acid → magnesium sulphate + hydrogen

zinc + hydrochloric acid → zinc chloride + hydrogen

3. Sodium carbonate crystals

If sodium carbonate crystals are added to an acid solution, colourless bubbles of carbon dioxide gas are produced. The gas puts out a lighted splint and turns limewater milky. The gas is carbon dioxide. For example:

sodium carbonate + hydrochloric acid → sodium chloride + carbon dioxide

The three common acids derived from chemicals obtained from the ground or from the air are called **mineral acids.** They are:

sulphuric acid, H_2SO_4
hydrochloric acid, HCl
nitric acid, HNO_3

Many other acids are obtained from natural products, e.g. citric acid from citrus fruits. These are sometimes called **organic acids.**

All acids contain the element hydrogen but not all compounds which contain hydrogen are acids. Compounds show acid properties only when water is present.

In acids the element hydrogen can be replaced by a metal or an ammonium ion. The substance formed when hydrogen is replaced is called a **salt.** For example:

hydrochloric acid	$\rightarrow$	sodium chloride
HCl	$\rightarrow$	NaCl
sulphuric acid	$\rightarrow$	sodium sulphate
H_2SO_4	$\rightarrow$	Na_2SO_4
nitric acid	$\rightarrow$	sodium nitrate
HNO_3	$\rightarrow$	$NaNO_3$

Sodium chloride, sodium sulphate and sodium nitrate are all salts.

11.3 Bases and alkalis

A **base** is any metal oxide, e.g. copper(II) oxide, CuO, or sodium oxide, Na_2O. Some bases dissolve in water to form alkalis.

Sodium oxide dissolves in water to form sodium hydroxide but copper(II) oxide does not dissolve in water.

The common alkalis are:

sodium hydroxide, NaOH
potassium hydroxide, KOH
calcium hydroxide, $Ca(OH)_2$

Fig. 11.1 Relationships between acids, bases and alkalis

Fig. 11.1 shows the relationships between acids, bases and alkalis. There are two tests to show that an alkali is present:

1. Indicators

Litmus and Universal indicator can be used to test for an alkali (see Table 11.1 opposite).

2. Ammonium chloride

If an alkali is heated with ammonium chloride, a strong-smelling gas is produced. This gas smells like wet babies' nappies and is called ammonia.

11.4 Methods of preparing salts

The method used to prepare a salt depends on whether the salt is soluble or insoluble in water.

DUSTBIN POWER

Every year, we dump 30 million tonnes of rubbish. This could produce heat and power for 2½ million homes, factories, schools, swimming pools and hospitals. Many countries have harnessed this source of energy for years, but in Britain we have largely failed to use it.

At present 90% of our household refuse is just tipped into suitable 'landfill' sites. Only 10% is incinerated. As suitable landfill sites run out and people realise the amount of energy being thrown away, there is a move away from tipping.

Remember – 2½ bins of household rubbish have the same energy content as 1 bag of coal.

Landfill sites
Suitable landfill sites are becoming increasingly difficult to find. Residents in an area where a landfill site is proposed object to the unsightly appearance, the increased traffic, possible smells and dangers to health. Also, when refuse is tipped and left it starts to decompose and produce the gas methane. This can lead to explosions such as the one in Loscoe, in Derbyshire where explosion of methane from a landfill site demolished a bungalow and threatened other properties. Old landfill sites are possible sources of natural gas in the future.

This bungalow was demolished when methane gas from a landfill site exploded.

Incinerating or burning our refuse
This is becoming an increasingly popular solution to the problem of disposal of household refuse especially in towns. Lorries deliver household refuse directly to specially designed combustors. The refuse is burnt and boilers can recover the heat to produce steam, electricity and hot water. (See page 70.) In places like Nottingham these are used in local houses and factories. In other places such as Stoke-on-Trent no effort is made to use the energy produced. Burning here is just a way of solving the refuse problem.

The ash produced contains metals which are extracted before the ash is safely tipped or used for construction. The ash has only 5% of the volume of the original refuse and is sterile.

Burning rubbish to generate power.

Making fuel pellets

At the Byker Reclamation Plant in Tyne-and-Wear household refuse is converted into fuel pellets which can be sold. The process used is summarised by the following flow diagram. The pellets are made from the light fraction. Approximately 8000 tonnes of pellets are made each year and there is no difficulty selling them.

 INPUT **DOMESTIC REFUSE**
▼

Primary pulverisation
▼

Initial screening
Rotary screen — material larger than 150 mm and smaller than 12 mm discarded
▼

Air classification
Light and heavy fractions separated; heavy fractions discarded after ferrous metal removed
▼

Secondary pulverisation
Light fraction shredded in horizontal mill
▼

Densification
Light fraction densified in pellet press
▼

Cooling
Formed pellet cooled before stock-piling
▼

◀ OUTPUT ■ **WASTE-DERIVED FUEL PELLET**

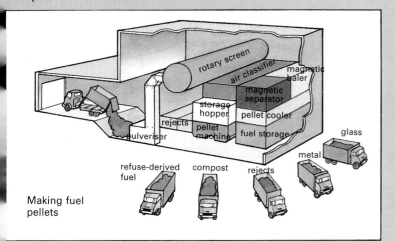

Making fuel pellets

ACTIVITIES ▼

1. Find out who is responsible in your area for:
   i) collecting household refuse;
   ii) disposal of the refuse.
   Often it is a different body. Perhaps your teacher can organise somebody to come in and discuss the disposal of refuse in your area.

2. Choose an area around school, perhaps a housing estate. Make an estimation of the amount of refuse to be collected and some estimate of the amount of fuel wasted.

3. Suppose you live in the imaginary town of Brainford which has traditionally disposed of refuse by landfill using disused claypits about ten miles away. Your town is rapidly expanding due to the building of new housing estates and new industry. Write a letter to the local council suggesting the policy that should be formulated for disposal of household refuse in the new town. Local industry is not interested in purchasing steam, hot water or electricity from any new incinerator unless there is a continuous supply. Suggest to the council any alternatives that they have.

4. The economics of a refuse disposal plant at Doncaster in 1980 were as follows:

Expenditure	
salaries	£70 000
capital repayments	£180 000
running costs	£140 000
	£390 000

Income	
4900 tonnes tin cans @ £16 per tne	£78 400
5600 tne glass @ £15 per tne	£84 000
1400 tne paper @ £15 per tne	£21 000
14000 tne fuel pellets @ £8 per tne	£112 000
	£295 400

In addition the 25 900 tonnes of material recovered will not require dumping. There is a saving of £3.25 per tonne, i.e. £84 175.

(a) Calculate the profit or loss of this plant at these prices.
(b) In some areas of Great Britain the cost of tipping can be £12 per tonne. Calculate the profit or loss with this price.
(c) At what price does the plant just make a profit?

Preparation of soluble salts

One of the following reactions can be used to prepare a soluble salt:

metal + acid → salt + hydrogen

metal oxide + acid → salt + water

metal hydroxide + acid → salt + water

metal carbonate + acid → salt + water + carbon dioxide

Examples

zinc + hydrochloric acid → zinc chloride + hydrogen

copper(II) oxide + sulphuric acid → copper(II) sulphate + water

sodium hydroxide + hydrochloric acid → sodium chloride + water

calcium carbonate + nitric acid → calcium nitrate + water + carbon dioxide

If you are making a chloride, hydrochloric acid should be used. Sulphuric acid should be used when making a sulphate and nitric acid for a nitrate.

In each salt preparation, a solid is reacted with an acid. The choice of which solid to use to react with an acid depends on various factors:

1. The cost and availability of the different solids. Calcium carbonate is cheaper and more readily available than calcium. It is better for reacting with hydrochloric acid to produce calcium chloride.
2. The rate of reaction of the solid and the acid. Sodium chloride is not made from sodium and hydrochloric acid because the reaction would be too dangerous.

The method used to prepare a soluble salt (for example copper(II) sulphate from copper(II) oxide and sulphuric acid) is summarised in Fig. 11.2 below.

The acid is warmed to speed up the reaction between copper(II) oxide and dilute sulphuric acid. The copper(II) oxide is added in small amounts until no more will react and the unreacted black solid remains. (NB The solution is not saturated with copper(II) oxide. All of the acid has been used up and the solid remaining is **excess** copper(II) oxide.)

The excess copper(II) oxide is removed by **filtering**. The solution left consists of blue copper(II) sulphate solution dissolved in water. Heating the solution makes sure that all of the copper(II) sulphate remains dissolved.

Fig. 11.2 Preparation of copper sulphate

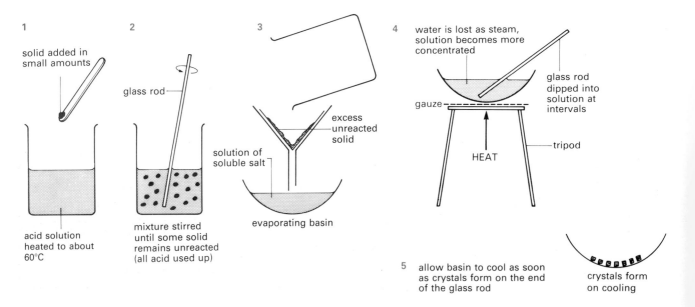

1
solid added in
small amounts

2
glass rod

mixture stirred
until some solid
remains unreacted
(all acid used up)

acid solution
heated to about
60°C

3
excess
unreacted
solid

solution of
soluble salt

evaporating basin

4   water is lost as steam,
solution becomes more
concentrated

glass rod
dipped into
solution at
intervals

gauze

HEAT

tripod

5   allow basin to cool as soon
as crystals form on the end
of the glass rod

crystals form
on cooling

The salt is obtained from the solution by **evaporation.** It is important not to evaporate the solution to dryness as it would decompose the salt. The solution can be tested, during evaporation, to find the stage at which the solution will crystallise on cooling to room temperature. If a glass rod is dipped into the solution from time to time, eventually crystals will form on the end of the glass rod when cooled in the air. At this stage the solution can be left to cool and crystallise.

Sodium, potassium and ammonium salts are often prepared by a slightly different method. This is summarised in Fig. 11.3.

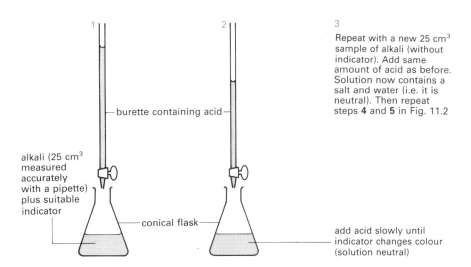

Fig. 11.3 Preparation of alkali metal and ammonium salts

Preparation of insoluble salts

Insoluble salts can be prepared by **precipitation.** If lead(II) sulphate is to be made, two suitable solutions are prepared and mixed. Suitable solutions would be lead(II) nitrate (a soluble lead salt) and sodium sulphate (a soluble sulphate). When they are mixed a white precipitate of lead sulphate is formed:

lead(II) nitrate + sodium sulphate → lead(II) sulphate + sodium nitrate

The lead(II) sulphate is removed from the solution by filtering. Then it is washed with distilled water and dried to produce pure lead(II) sulphate.

11.5 Important soluble and insoluble salts

Table 11.2 gives the names, formulae and uses of some common soluble salts:

Table 11.2 Useful soluble salts

Chemical name	Formula	Common name	Use
Sodium chloride	NaCl	Common salt	Flavouring food
Sodium carbonate	$Na_2CO_3.10H_2O$	Washing soda	Chemical raw material Softening water
Sodium sulphate	$Na_2SO_4.10H_2O$	Glauber's salt	Medicine
Magnesium sulphate	$MgSO_4.7H_2O$	Epsom salt	Laxative

One of the most important use of insoluble salts is as pigments for making paints. A typical gloss paint is made by grinding together a hardening oil (such as linseed oil), a pigment, driers, extenders and solvent.

The paint dries partly by evaporation of the solvent. The important process, however, is the reaction of the oil with oxygen to form a hard film. Driers are compounds of lead or cobalt. They act as catalysts and speed up the hardening. The pigment is an insoluble substance (often a salt) which gives the paint its colour and covering power. Lead(II) chromate is a yellow pigment used for making paint for painting yellow lines on roads.

Pigments – insoluble salts – are used in many everyday products such as printing inks, fabric dyes and make up.

In the control of water pollution, precipitation of insoluble salts is used to remove toxic substances from the water. Cyanides dissolved in water can be removed by precipitation with iron(II) sulphate.

The label on a Universal indicator bottle. These photographs show the colour you will see when using the indicator. What is the pH of a solution which has the colour shown above?

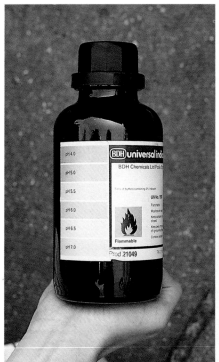

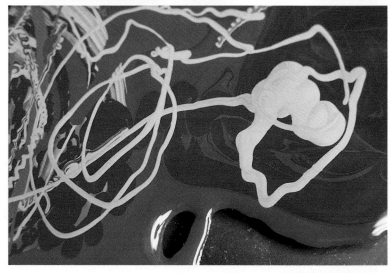

Insoluble salts in the form of pigments, used in the cosmetics industry to make face rouge.

QUESTIONS ON UNIT 11

Domain I: Knowledge and understanding

1. base, acid, alkali, salt, less than 7, exactly 7, greater than 7, neutral

   Complete the passage on the right by putting in words from the list above:

   Copper(II) oxide is a . . . . Some bases are soluble in water. When a base dissolves in water it forms an . . . . When tested with Universal indicator, the pH is . . . .

   When a non-metal oxide is dissolved in water an . . . . is produced, which has a pH . . . .

   When an acid and an alkali react together in the correct proportions, a . . . . is produced.

2. Complete the following word equations:

   (a)
   | zinc + dilute sulphuric acid → . . . . + ... |

   (b)
   | zinc + dilute hydrochloric acid → . . . . + ... |

   (c)
   | potassium hydroxide + hydrochloric acid → . . . . + ... |

   (d)
   | potassium hydroxide + sulphuric acid → . . . . + ... |

   (e)
   | potassium hydroxide + nitric acid → . . . . + ... |

   (f)
   | sodium carbonate + hydrochloric acid → . . . . + ... + ... |

   (g)
   | sodium carbonate + sulphuric acid → . . . . + ... + ... |

   (h)
   | sodium carbonate + nitric acid → . . . . + ... + ... |

   (i)
   | magnesium oxide + hydrochloric acid → . . . . + ... |

   (j)
   | magnesium oxide + sulphuric acid → . . . . + ... |

   (k)
   | magnesium oxide + nitric acid → . . . . + ... |

3. ammonium chloride, copper(II) sulphate,
   sodium chloride, sodium hydroxide, barium
   chloride, silver chloride, magnesium chloride,
   barium sulphate, hydrochloric acid

   Using only the substances in the list above,
   name:

   (a) a substance which is an alkali;
   (b) a salt which does not contain a metal;

   (3) (c) the salt which is the chief chemical present
   in table salt;
   (d) two salts which are insoluble in water;
   (e) the salt which will form as a white
   precipitate when dilute hydrochloric acid is
   added to a solution of silver nitrate;
   (f) two salts which can be made by mixing
   together substances in the list (see left).

4. Complete the following:

   Dilute acids have four general reactions:

   (a)
   > dilute acid + fairly reactive metal → . . . . + ...

   (b)
   > dilute acid + metal oxide → . . . . + ...

   (c)
   > dilute acid + metal carbonate → . . . . + ... + ...

   (d)
   > dilute acid + alkali → . . . . + ...

Domain II: Handling information and solving problems

5. The table below contains information about
   the solubility of salts in water. Use the
   information in the data section on pages 245–
   259 to complete this table. Then use the table
   to answer the questions which follow.

	chloride	nitrate	sulphate	carbonate
ammonium				s
barium		vs		i
calcium			ss	
copper(II)				i
lead(II)				i
magnesium			s	i
silver			ss	i
sodium				
zinc		vs		i
potassium			s	s

Key: i = insoluble, ss= slightly soluble, s = soluble,
vs = very soluble.

(5) (a) Decide whether each of the following
statements is true or false on the basis of
the information given in the table:
   (i) Nitrates are generally more soluble in
   water than chlorides, sulphates or
   carbonates.
   (ii) All salts of sodium, potassium and
   ammonium are soluble in water.
   (iii) Most carbonates are insoluble in
   water.
   (iv) Barium sulphate, lead(II) sulphate,
   silver chloride and barium chloride are
   all insoluble in water.

   (b) Name the precipitate formed when each of
   the following pairs of solutions are mixed:
   (i) Sodium chloride and silver nitrate.
   (ii) Sodium carbonate and lead(II) nitrate.
   (iii) Potassium sulphate and barium
   chloride.

   (c) Explain why a white precipitate is formed
   when concentrated solutions of calcium
   nitrate and zinc sulphate are mixed
   together but no precipitate is formed when
   dilute solutions of these chemicals are
   mixed.

6. Magnesium sulphate crystals, $MgSO_4.7H_2O$, can be made by adding excess magnesium oxide, MgO (which is insoluble in water), to dilute sulphuric acid.

   (a) Write a word equation for the reaction taking place.
   (b) Why was the magnesium oxide in excess?
   (c) The apparatus shown below could be used to separate the excess magnesium oxide from the solution. Label the diagram below.

   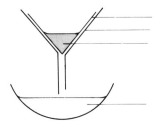

   (d) Describe clearly how crystals of magnesium sulphate could be obtained from the solution passing through the filter.
   (e) Why is it important not to evaporate the solution of magnesium sulphate in water to dryness?

7. Using the information below, correctly place substances A, B and C in the Venn diagram:

   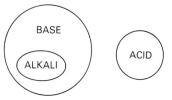

   Substance A is a black solid metal oxide which is completely insoluble in water.

   Substance B dissolves in water to form a solution with a pH of 7. It gives a lilac coloured flame when put into a hot Bunsen burner flame.

   Substance C is a white solid which dissolves readily in water to form a solution with a pH of 13.

   (You are not expected to identify these three substances.)

UNIT 12 The air

12.1 Composition of air

Because air is always around us we tend to take it for granted, but it is not as simple as it seems. Air is a mixture of gases. Its composition varies from place to place. A typical sample of air has the following composition, by volume:

Nitrogen	78%
Oxygen	21%
Carbon dioxide	0.03%
Argon	0.9%
Helium	0.0005%
Neon	0.002%
Krypton	0.0001%
Xenon	0.000001%

In addition, air contains water vapour in varying amounts.

Argon, helium, neon, krypton and xenon belong to the family of noble gases (group 0 in the Periodic Table).

The percentage of oxygen in a sample of air in the laboratory can be found using the apparatus in Fig. 12.1.

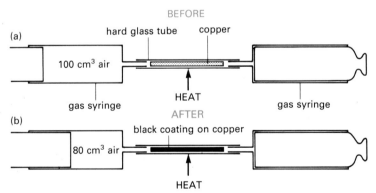

Fig. 12.1 Finding the percentage of oxygen in air

Oxygen is the active gas in the air. Heated copper can be used to remove oxygen from air. Oxygen combines with copper forming copper(II) oxide:

$$\text{copper} + \text{oxygen} \rightarrow \text{copper(II) oxide}$$

100 cm^3 of air is trapped in one of the gas syringes. The air is passed over the heated copper into the other syringe. The air is passed backwards and forwards over the copper until no further change takes place.

On cooling to room temperature, only about 80 cm^3 of gas will remain. 20 cm^3 of the air is removed. This means that 20% of the air consists of oxygen.

During the experiment the hard glass tube and contents increase in mass by the same amount as the air decreases in mass.

12.2 Separating air into its constituent gases

Separating air into its constituent gases is a very difficult process. It cannot be done satisfactorily in the laboratory. However, it is an important process in industry because all of the gases are valuable as pure gases.

Industrial separation of air involves the fractional distillation of liquid air. The air is first cooled in a refrigeration plant to separate carbon dioxide and water vapour. Both of these gases solidify in the cooler and the solid can be removed. If these gases were not removed at this stage, they would later solidify in the pipes and block them.

The air is compressed to about 150 times atmospheric pressure. Compressing a gas causes it to heat up. Remember that your bicycle tyre gets hot when you pump it up. The compressed air is cooled, then allowed to expand through a small hole. This expansion causes the gas to cool rapidly. The compressing and expanding cycles are repeated until the temperature is about $-200°C$. At this temperature most of the air has liquefied.

The liquid air is then allowed to warm up slowly. The boiling points of the different liquids present in liquid air at $-200°C$ are given in Table 12.1.

In fractional distillation the liquid with the lowest boiling point boils off first. Nitrogen, therefore, boils off first from the liquid air. As the liquid warms up the different gases boil off separately. Each gas can be stored separately in gas cylinders.

A fractional distillation plant can separate about 100 tonnes of air a day. Because about four-fifths of the air is nitrogen, fractional distillation of liquid air produces much more nitrogen than other gases.

Table 12.1 Constituents of liquid air

Gas	Boiling point in °C
Nitrogen	−196
Oxygen	−183
Helium	−269
Neon	−249
Argon	−189
Xenon	−108

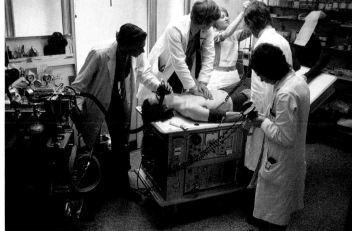

ABOVE One of the most modern air separation plants, at Fawley near Southampton. The photograph shows the air-separation columns and the pipes which supply the separated gases directly to the customers.

ABOVE RIGHT Oxygen being used in a hospital to help a patient whose breathing has failed.

RIGHT Pizzas frozen by a spray of liquid nitrogen as they pass through the tunnel on a conveyor belt.

12.3 Uses of gases from the air

Oxygen

Pure oxygen is very important for helping breathing. 'Medical grade' oxygen, the purest grade, can often revive a patient who is having problems breathing, perhaps after an accident or during an operation (see previous page). Climbers going to climb high mountains, pilots of high-flying fighter planes and divers require cylinders of oxygen for their breathing.

Less pure oxygen can be used in industry in large amounts. Oxygen is used in steel-making (Unit 9) to oxidise unwanted impurities. Ethyne (still called acetylene) is a hydrocarbon which burns in air. This burning, however, produces a higher temperature if oxygen is used in place of air. Oxy-acetylene flames produce high temperatures sufficient to cut metals or weld them together (see page 162).

Oxygen in the form of a liquid is carried in rockets to enable the rocket fuel to burn. Oxygen is also used in sewage treatment. Blowing air through raw sewage helps to break it down.

Oxygen is supplied in cylinders that are black in colour.

Nitrogen

Much of the nitrogen from the air is used to make ammonia, nitric acid and fertilisers (Units 17 and 18).

Unlike oxygen, which is an active gas, nitrogen is an inactive gas. Many of its uses rely upon its inactive nature. Nitrogen is used to fill food packages (e.g. crisps). Oxygen spoils food and so air in contact with food has to be avoided. Light bulbs also contain gases including nitrogen.

Liquid nitrogen (boiling point $-198°C$) is an inexpensive liquid that is used for a wide range of 'cooling' uses. Small quantities of food can be 'deep-frozen' by dipping into liquid nitrogen (see previous page). It is also useful for transporting biological tissue for transplant surgery and samples of semen to a farm for artificial insemination.

Noble gases

The noble gases (helium, neon, argon, krypton and xenon) are extremely unreactive and their uses rely upon this.

Helium is the second lightest of all the gases. Hydrogen is the lightest gas and was widely used for airships. However, hydrogen is highly flammable. Airships filled with hydrogen were involved in fires in the 1930s and it looked as though airships would never be built again. However, in recent years helium has been produced cheaply and now helium-filled airships are flying (page 86). A helium-filled airship can provide slow but cheap transport for heavy objects. An airship can carry out many of the tasks of a helicopter for a fraction of the cost. It has a useful military role because it is difficult for an enemy to detect on radar. Hydrogen is still used to fill weather balloons.

Helium and argon are used to protect pure metals during heat-treatment. Many metals will burn in air or oxygen but cannot burn when heated in an atmosphere of helium or argon.

Argon is used for filling light bulbs. Neon is used for filling the light-tubes used for advertising signs (page 86). Krypton and xenon are used for filling special bulbs, e.g. lighthouse and projector bulbs.

12.4 Processes involving the air

Burning (or combustion)

The burning or combustion of a substance is the combination of the substance with oxygen. Loss of heat and/or light usually accompanies combustion.

The term combustion is sometimes used in reactions not involving oxygen. For example, the combustion of sodium in chlorine gas produces sodium chloride.

Substances which burn are said to be **combustible**. Some substances like petrol and paper burn very easily and are said to be **highly flammable**.

A substance which is burned to produce heat is called a **fuel**. Fuels are considered in Unit 21.

Substances burn better in oxygen than they do in air. If the oxygen or air supply is cut off, burning will stop.

Although it does not always seem so, the combined mass of all of the substances produced during combustion is always greater than the mass of substance burned.

Respiration

Respiration is very closely related to combustion. In the human body, 'food' burns in oxygen to form carbon dioxide and water. The oxygen is obtained from the air breathed in. Oxygen is transported to the muscles by the blood. The 'burning' takes place in the muscles. Carbon dioxide is transported to the lungs by the blood and breathed out. The air breathed out contains much less oxygen and much more carbon dioxide than the air breathed in. Heat produced in this process helps to keep the body temperature constant.

Rusting

Rust is a flaky, red-brown solid formed when iron or steel is left exposed to the atmosphere. Rust is a form of hydrated iron(III) oxide. For rusting to take place, both oxygen and water vapour must be present. Rusting is a corrosion process and is dealt with fully in Unit 14.

Photosynthesis

Combustion, respiration and rusting are all processes which use up oxygen from the air. The percentage of oxygen in the air, however, remains approximately constant. Photosynthesis is a process which puts oxygen back into the atmosphere to replace the oxygen being used up.

NEWS BRIEF NEWS BRIEF NEWS BRIEF NEWS BRIEF NEWS BRIEF NEWS BRIEF NEWS BRIEF

American scientists are developing a new plane which will speed up air travel around the world and will also launch satellites. The journey from California to Japan will take one hour instead of the present 15 hours, with the plane cruising at 90 000 feet at a speed three times the speed of Concorde.

The plane will be powered by liquid hydrogen which gives more energy than any other non-nuclear fuel. The exhaust will be a plume of harmless steam instead of kerosene and carbon dioxide which could harm the environment.

The plane would require no heavy heat shield for re-entry into the atmosphere. Liquid hydrogen boils at $-253°C$. At this temperature, just $20°C$ above absolute zero, liquid hydrogen would be circulated around the plane to keep it cool.

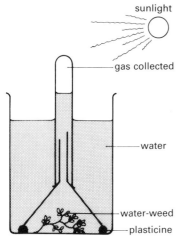

sunlight

gas collected

water

water-weed

plasticine

Fig. 12.2 Demonstrating photosynthesis

The leaves of a green plant act as 'chemical factories' (Fig. 12.2). The plant takes in water through the roots and carbon dioxide from the atmosphere. In the leaves, in the presence of the green substance chlorophyll, these raw materials are converted into sugars and oxygen gas which escapes into the atmosphere. This change only takes place in sunlight with the chlorophyll acting as a **catalyst**.

The sugars in the plant are either used to produce cellulose, which is needed for the plant to grow, or put into store as starch.

The process can be summarised as follows:

$$\text{carbon dioxide} + \text{water} \rightarrow \text{sugars} + \text{oxygen}$$

South American tropical forests play an important role in putting oxygen back into the atmosphere. If they are destroyed it could have a significant effect on the composition of the Earth's atmosphere.

Table 12.2 summarises these processes which involve the air.

Table 12.2

Components of air	Combustion	Rusting	Respiration	Photosynthesis
Nitrogen	Usually not involved	Not involved	Not involved	Not involved
Oxygen	Usually necessary	Necessary	Necessary	Produced
Carbon dioxide	Formed if substances containing carbon burn	Speeds up rusting but it is not necessary	Produced	Necessary
Noble gases	← Not involved →			
Water vapour	Formed if substances containing hydrogen burn	Necessary	Produced	Necessary

RIGHT   The helium-filled Goodyear Airship. What are the advantages and disadvantages of using helium rather than hydrogen?

BELOW   A forest in Peru. Oxygen is produced by trees during photosynthesis. If tropical rain forests are destroyed there could be far-reaching environmental effects.

BOTTOM RIGHT   Bright lights in Las Vegas. These advertising signs are made of neon-filled light tubes.

QUESTIONS ON UNIT 12

Domain I: Knowledge and understanding

1. oxygen, nitrogen, carbon dioxide, hydrogen, argon, helium, neon

   Use the gases in the list above to answer the following questions. You can use each gas more than once. Name:

   (a) the gas present in largest quantities in the air
   (b) the gas not normally in the air
   (c) a compound present in air
   (d) the 'active' gas in the air
   (e) the gas produced when fuels containing carbon are burned
   (f) the commonest noble gas in the air
   (g) two gases used to produce ammonia in the Haber process
   (h) the gas used in advertising signs
   (i) the gas used for filling weather balloons
   (j) the gas used to help ill patients to breathe in hospital
   (k) the gas removed when air is passed over heated copper
   (l) the gas removed when air is passed through an alkali solution

2. oxygen, nitrogen, carbon dioxide, liquid, solid, gas

   Complete the following passage about the industrial separation of oxygen and nitrogen from air:

   .... and water are first removed from the air. The air is then cooled and compressed. The ...... is then allowed to expand and it cools further as it expands. After repeating this a number of times, the air becomes ....

   The .... air is allowed to warm up. .... boils off first because it has a lower boiling point. Then .... boils off.

   More .... is produced during the fractional distillation of .... air because there is much more of it in the air.

3. Which of the following (i) use up oxygen and/ or (ii) produce carbon dioxide:

   (a) combustion of fossil fuels?
   (b) rusting of iron?
   (c) photosynthesis in plants?
   (d) souring of wine?
   (e) fermentation of sugars to produce ethanol?
   (f) combustion of a metal such as magnesium?
   (g) burning sodium metal in chlorine gas?

Domain II: Handling information and solving problems

4. An experiment was carried out to compare the time it took for a candle flame to go out when it was covered with beakers of different sizes. The results are shown in the graph below:

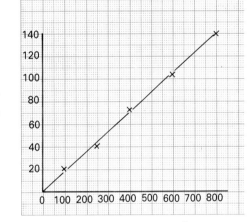

volume of beaker (cm^3)

   (a) How long would it take for a candle to go out if it were covered with a 500 cm^3 beaker?
   (b) The results plotted do not fall exactly on the line drawn. Why do you think this is so?
   (c) What can be concluded from the results shown in this graph?
   (d) If a very large beaker (e.g. 2000 cm^3) is used the time is much less than expected. How would you explain this?

5. Mrs Evans, the teacher, is trying to show the class that when a candle burns there is an increase in mass. Even though she explains that this is true only if all of the substances produced are collected and weighed, they do not seem convinced.

 She sets up the apparatus shown below.

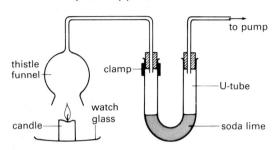

 The U-shaped tube contains soda lime which absorbs both carbon dioxide and water vapour. She weighs the whole apparatus including the candle and watch glass before the experiment.

 Air is drawn through the apparatus for a few minutes, with the candle alight. The apparatus is allowed to cool to room temperature and is then re-weighed.

 The results were:

 Mass of apparatus before experiment = 132.35g

 Mass of apparatus after experiment = 132.65g

 (a) Calculate the increase in mass during the experiment.
 (b) Explain how there came to be an increase in mass.
 (c) A particularly doubting girl called Claire pointed out that the increase of mass could have been caused by the presence of two gases in the air and have nothing to do with the burning of the candle. To which two gases was Claire referring?
 (d) How could Mrs Evans show the class that the increase in mass was due to the products of the burning of the candle and not to gases already in the air?

6. The table on the right gives you some information about five different types of fire extinguishers. From the list **A** to **E**, choose the one which:

 (a) is the cleanest to use;
 (b) works by just cooling the fire;
 (c) could produce toxic gases.

7. Photosynthesis takes place in green plants when they are in strong light. Chlorophyll has an important part to play in the process and oxygen gas is produced.

 (a) What part does chlorophyll play in the process?
 (b) The graph below shows the amount of sugar produced by a green plant over several days under normal conditions.

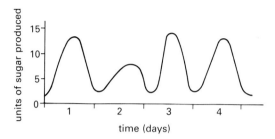

 i) Suggest one factor in the environment to explain why less sugar is produced during day 2.
 ii) Draw a line on the graph to show how much light would be produced if the plant was kept under bright light all of the time.

8. The table below shows the approximate percentages of oxygen and nitrogen in 'ordinary' air and in the air which is dissolved in water:

Percentage of:	oxygen	nitrogen
'ordinary' air	21	79
air dissolved in water	35	64

 (a) Draw a pie diagram to show composition of the two gases in the air which is dissolved in water.
 (b) Summarise the difference in composition of 'ordinary' air and the air dissolved in water.

	Type	How it works	Other information
A	Soda-acid	Makes a jet of water which cools the fire	Should not be used on electrical equipment
B	Sand	Stops air getting to the fire	Quick acting but does not stop hot things relighting
C	Foam	Stops air getting to the fire	Stays in place long enough for natural cooling
D	Carbon dioxide	Stops air getting to the fire	Blows away easily leaving nothing behind
E	Halon	Stops air and cools the fire	Safe on electrical equipment but can make poisonous fumes

UNIT 13 Air pollution

London fog in the 1950s before efforts were made to clean up the atmosphere in cities.

13.1 Introduction

Apart from the gases normally found in air, other gases such as sulphur dioxide, oxides of nitrogen and carbon monoxide can be present. These gases can cause **air pollution** and are called **pollutants.** Pollutants can cause a variety of problems to the environment.

13.2 Sulphur dioxide

Sulphur dioxide is a major cause of air pollution. Coal and fuel oil contain about 2% sulphur. When they are burnt this sulphur is turned into sulphur dioxide. Sulphur dioxide is a colourless gas with a strong smell. It dissolves in water to form sulphurous acid, H_2SO_3:

$$\text{sulphur dioxide} + \text{water} \rightarrow \text{sulphurous acid}$$

Sulphurous acid is closely related to sulphuric acid, H_2SO_4. Sulphurous acid can change to the more harmful sulphuric acid in the air.

In the early 1950s sulphur dioxide, and the smoke which is always with it, caused great problems. Apart from blackening buildings and producing long-term fogs, they caused serious health problems. In 1952, for example, there were over 4000 deaths thought to be caused by air pollution in London alone. Most of these deaths were due to lung illnesses including bronchitis.

The Clean Air Act of 1956 set up 'smokeless zones' in large towns and cities. Within these areas coal cannot be burned and smokeless fuels must be used. The result of this Act, and other measures taken, has been to improve greatly the conditions in towns and cities.

The burning of coal in household fires was regarded as the major problem. Even today considerable quantities of sulphur dioxide are lost

Destruction of the ozone layer

Ozone is a reactive allotrope of oxygen. Unlike ordinary oxygen, which has two atoms in each molecule, ozone has three. We write its formula as O_3. It is a gas found in the Earth's atmosphere some 10 to 30 km above the Earth. If all the ozone molecules in the atmosphere were gathered together, they would form a layer no thicker than a one pound coin!

Why is the ozone layer so important?

The main reason is that this fragile layer soaks up harmful ultraviolet (UV) rays from the sun and prevents lethal levels of radiation from reaching us on the ground. If the ozone layer is broken down there is likely to be a large increase in the number of skin cancers. Americans have estimated that even a small increase in UV reaching the Earth could cause a million extra cancers over the lifetime of people living today and 20 000 of these cancers would lead to death.

What evidence have we that the ozone layer is breaking down?

Above the Antarctic, the layer of ozone is shattered. Scientists have for many years measured the Antarctic ozone with instruments on the ground and aboard balloons, aircraft and satellites. The amount of ozone in the air seems particularly low in spring. Similar studies are now being carried out in other parts of the world, especially in the Arctic.

What is causing the breakdown of the ozone layer?

Chlorofluorocarbons are normally called CFCs. These are compounds of carbon, chlorine and fluorine. There are many, the commonest being dichlorodifluoromethane, CF_2Cl_2, and trichlorofluoromethane, $CFCl_3$. These are commonly called F-12 and F-11 respectively. They are low boiling point liquids under pressure but vaporise rapidly under normal conditions. In the early 1970s three-quarters of all CFCs made went into aerosol cans as the propellant (see left). When the button on top of the aerosol is pressed the pressure inside the can is reduced, the propellant vaporises and forces out the liquid contents of the container. The propellant escapes also. These CFCs then escape into the atmosphere. Now, because of more understanding of the problems, only 25% of the CFCs are used in aerosols.

CFCs are also used to form foam-polystyrene cartons for the take-away food market, in foam-filling cavity walls, in some types of fire extinguisher and as the refrigerant in a refrigerator. Recycling fluids from old refrigerators is not viable and the gas is allowed to escape into the atmosphere.

In the upper atmosphere CFCs are broken down by sunlight to form chlorine atoms, which break down the ozone by a series of chain reactions. In fact, one chlorine atom can break down 100 000 molecules of ozone.

Can CFCs be replaced by other chemicals?

In 1978 the United States banned CFCs in aerosols and used alternative chemicals. Other countries are following their example. The replacement of CFCs for other use is progressing more slowly.

push valve releases pressure inside the container

propellant vaporises when pressure is released

contents (insecticide, deodorant, etc.)

contents forced out

The workings of an aerosol can.

Aerosol cans and fast-food containers. These products can contain CFCs.

ACTIVITIES ▼

1. Draw out structural formulae for the two CFCs mentioned on the facing page. Draw out structural formulae for other CFCs based on methane.

2. Below is a simplified diagram of a refrigerator which contains a CFC as refrigerant. Explain the working of a refrigerator.

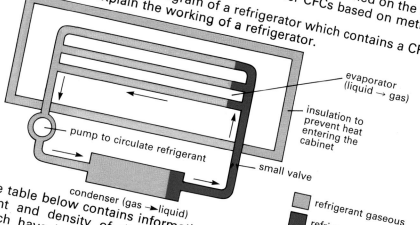

evaporator (liquid → gas)

insulation to prevent heat entering the cabinet

pump to circulate refrigerant

small valve

condenser (gas → liquid)

refrigerant gaseous

refrigerant liquid

3. The table below contains information about the melting point, boiling point and density of dichlorodifluoromethane and several alkanes which have been suggested as alternatives to CFCs. Complete the information by using the information in the Data Section on page 252.

Name	Formula	Melting point in °C	Boiling point in °C	Density g per cm³ when liquid
dichlorodifluoromethane	CF_2Cl_2	−158	−30	1.40
ethane				0.57
propane				0.58
butane				0.60
pentane				0.62

(a) It is important that the alternative to CFC chosen liquefies below room temperature. Which of the alternatives in the table would be suitable?

(b) One alternative would be suitable but perhaps would fail in car de-icers which are used at temperatures below freezing. Which substance is this?

(c) Have these alternatives any disadvantages?

4. Dinitrogen monoxide, N_2O, is used as a propellant in cans of whipped cream. It has a melting point of −91°C and a boiling point of −88°C. It has a density of 1.65 g per cm³ when liquid, and a price of £650 per tonne. Explain the advantages and disadvantages of dinitrogen mon-oxide as a propellant compared to alkanes.

5. What warnings are given on an aerosol container about storage and disposal of aerosol cans? Why do these warnings make sense?

6. You can get further information about CFCs and the aerosol problem along with other environmental information from Friends of the Earth Trust Ltd, 26–28 Underwood Street, London N1 7JQ.

from factories and power stations. The chimneys of factories and power stations are much higher than household chimneys and this gives more chance for the sulphur dioxide to disperse. Even today there are links between emission of sulphur dioxide and **acid rain** (section 13.6).

13.3 Oxides of nitrogen

About 30–40% of the oxides of nitrogen in the air come from car exhausts. In the car engine nitrogen and oxygen combine together to form oxides of nitrogen. Other sources of pollution are factories and fires. Often oxides of nitrogen are formed when the fuel is burnt at a low temperature.

Even small concentrations of oxides of nitrogen can cause serious environmental problems. Like sulphur dioxide, oxides of nitrogen dissolve in water to form acids.

13.4 Carbon monoxide

Carbon monoxide is a poisonous gas produced on the partial combustion of fuels. Much of the carbon monoxide comes from the incomplete combustion of petrol in the car engine.

Close to heavy traffic the concentration of carbon monoxide in the air can reach 10–20 parts per million (p.p.m.). Levels as high as 200 p.p.m. have been recorded. Levels above 50 p.p.m. can be harmful to adults. Carbon monoxide is poisonous because it forms a stable compound called carboxyhaemoglobin which prevents the blood transporting oxygen around the body. Low concentrations are still harmful as they affect the proper working of the brain.

13.5 Lead compounds

A lead compound called tetraethyl lead is usually added in small quantities to petrol. This increases the octane number of petrol (the number of stars on the petrol pump), lubricates the valves in the engine and enables more litres of petrol to be made from a given amount of petroleum.

A car covering 9000 miles per year consumes about 200 g of lead and most of this is lost into the air through the exhaust system. Recent studies have emphasised how serious the emission of lead into the air can be. Lead is an intoxicant in much the same way as alcohol, and some studies have linked it with antisocial behaviour. A study in a London school has shown that children with high lead levels in their blood had lower intelligences and found it difficult to concentrate. There is also considerable evidence that vegetables such as lettuces and cabbages grown near busy roads contain higher levels of lead than normal.

Making 'lead-free' petrol is possible, and it is now produced. It costs about 2p per litre more to make than normal petrol, however it is cheaper at the pump because less tax is paid. Some cars cannot use it without expensive changes. In the long-term only lead-free petrol will be produced. New cars will have to be built with engines which can run on lead-free petrol.

13.6 Problems caused by air pollution

Exhaust gases from motor cars are causing problems throughout the world. Strong sunlight acting on a mixture of oxides of nitrogen, carbon monoxide and hydrocarbon vapour (unburnt petrol) produces new and more unpleasant substances. These acrid fumes collect in valleys and cause many problems. Apart from health problems, these fumes cause the breaking down of rubber and plastics, and can also fade dyes.

Much of the problems of air pollution could be minimised by cleaning up car exhausts. A converter containing a platinum catalyst (Fig. 13.1) fitted to the exhaust system would convert all of the harmful gases into carbon dioxide, nitrogen, oxygen and water vapour. These gases are all normally present in air and therefore do not cause pollution.

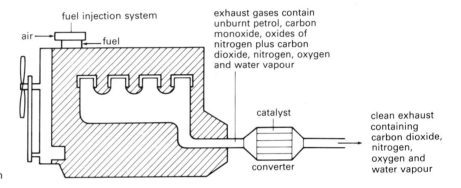

Fig. 13.1 An improved exhaust system for cars to reduce air pollution

Acid rain

Pure rain water has a pH of approximately 5. Oxides of nitrogen and sulphur dioxide dissolve in water to form acids. The presence of these pollutants reduces the pH, making the rain water more acidic and causing certain problems.

The effects of 'acid rain' include:

- Damage to stonework on buildings. St Paul's Cathedral and Westminster Abbey are just two of the buildings that show the damage caused by acid rain. A black skin first appears on the surface of the building. This then blisters and cracks, causing the stonework to be disfigured seriously.

- Rivers and lakes over a wide area become more acid. This is said to be killing wild life, such as otters. There are many lakes in Sweden and Norway that now have no life.

- Forests are seriously damaged. Forests in Scandinavia and Germany especially are being damaged by acid rain. Trees are stunted, needles and leaves drop off and the trees die. It has been estimated that acid rain is costing the German forestry industry about £150 million each year.

- Human life can be affected. Acid conditions can alter levels of copper, lead and aluminium in the body. These changes have been linked with diarrhoea in small babies, breathing disorders and senile dementia.

- Damage to metalwork. Acid rain can speed up corrosion of metals. Wrought iron railings in city areas can show considerable damage.

NEWS BRIEF NEWS BRIEF

Russian scientists have suggested two ways of 'patching up' holes in the ozone layer in the upper atmosphere. The Earth could be ringed with vast electric motors which produce ozone from liquid oxygen. Alternatively, pellets of frozen ozone could be fired into the upper atmosphere. Both ideas border on science fiction.

CFCs in the upper atmosphere could be destroyed by infra red laser beams fired from Earth.

The main cause of acid rain today is undoubtedly factories, especially coal-fired power stations. Coal contains up to 2% sulphur and, in fact, coal from Britain contains more sulphur than coal from other parts of the world. Removing the sulphur from the coal by burning is impractical. Efforts are being concentrated on removing all of the sulphur dioxide produced when the coal is burnt. This can be done by treating the waste gases by passing them over limestone (calcium carbonate). However, the waste product calcium sulphite, in the form of a slurry (mixture of solid and water), is extremely difficult to dispose of and causes more environmental problems. By more careful treatment, the slurry can be converted into calcium sulphate which can be used to make plasterboard.

Experiments have been carried out using a fluidised bed furnace. Here the powdered coal is burnt at a high temperature in a stream of air. The gases produced contain less pollution.

RIGHT   An aerial view of a complex motorway system called Spaghetti Junction near Birmingham. Notice the houses nearby affected by noise and the pollution produced by motor vehicles. There is considerable concern about the effects of lead and carbon monoxide on people living nearby.

BELOW LEFT   Comparison of the growth rates of two 30-year-old Sitka spruce trees. The two cross sections come from a healthy tree (bottom) and a tree stunted by the effects of acid rain (top).

BELOW RIGHT   The cause and effect of acid rain.

UNIT 14 Corrosion and rusting

14.1 Oxidation and reduction

The terms oxidation and reduction are frequently used in Chemistry and they are, in fact, opposites.

Oxidation is any reaction where oxygen is added. For example, the burning of magnesium or the burning of sulphur:

sulphur + oxygen → sulphur dioxide

magnesium + oxygen → magnesium oxide

In fact, any combustion or burning reaction is an oxidation. In these two examples magnesium and sulphur are said to be oxidised.

Joseph Priestley (1733–1804)

Joseph Priestley was a church minister with an interest in breweries – or more accurately the carbon dioxide they gave off.

He was born in Fieldhead near Leeds, and following his parents' teaching became a church minister when he was 27. Three years later he began teaching classics and literature in a private school at Warrington.

He wrote a history of electricity, and was admitted to The Royal Society in 1766.

At this time Priestley lived next to a brewery. He became interested in the 'heavy air' which lay over the fermentation vats as they brewed their liquor. He was also studying the gas given off when acid was added to chalk, and from both sets of observations identified carbon dioxide. That work led to him being awarded the Copley medal by The Royal Society in 1773.

A year earlier he discovered nitrogen . . . but called in 'Phlogisticated Air', and two years later identified oxygen, which he called 'De-phlogisticated Air'. However, unlike Lavoisier (see page 97), he still believed in the existence of Phlogiston – a substance later proved never to have existed!

In 1780 Priestley became the minister of a church in Birmingham, which brought his science and religion into conflict. On the one hand people respected his scientific writings, but on the other some disliked his religious writings so much that in 1791 a mob burned down his church and house, and he was forced to flee to Worcester in disguise.

Later he settled at Hackney in London, but was very unhappy there, so emigrated to America where three of his sons already lived.

He became a minister and a professor there, and died in that country when he was 71 having discovered, but failed to fully understand, the existence of nitrogen and oxygen, as well as greatly advancing ways of handling gases.

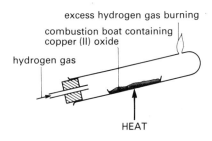

Fig. 14.1 Reduction of copper(ii) oxide with hydrogen

Reduction is any reaction where oxygen is lost. For example, oxygen was first produced when Joseph Priestley heated mercury(ii) oxide:

mercury(ii) oxide → mercury + oxygen

This is a reduction of mercury(ii) oxide to mercury. The mercury(ii) oxide is said to be reduced.

Often oxidation and reduction take place together. A reaction in which both oxidation and reduction occur is sometimes called a **redox** reaction.

An example of a redox reaction is when dry hydrogen gas is passed over heated copper(ii) oxide in the apparatus shown in Fig. 14.1. Excess hydrogen is burnt at the jet.

copper(ii) oxide + hydrogen → copper + water

The copper(ii) oxide loses oxygen and is therefore reduced. The hydrogen gains oxygen and is therefore oxidised. The hydrogen, which causes the copper(ii) oxide to be reduced, is sometimes called the **reducing agent**. Similarly, copper(ii) oxide can be called the **oxidising agent.**

14.2   Corrosion of metals

Sodium and potassium are very reactive metals, at the top of the reactivity series (Unit 6). They corrode very easily because of their reactions with air and water. For this reason they are stored under paraffin oil to reduce this corrosion.

Generally, the higher a metal is in the reactivity series the more rapidly it will corrode. Corrosion is an oxidation process.

Some metals such as aluminium do not corrode as rapidly as you would expect from their position in the reactivity series. This is because they form very tough oxide films on the surface which prevent further corrosion.

Only very unreactive metals like gold and platinum do not corrode. This is one reason why they are highly prized.

It is the corrosion of iron and steel which is so important economically. This is given a special name – rusting.

14.3   Rusting

Rusting of iron and steel costs many of millions of pounds each year and a great deal of research has been carried out into ways of reducing it.

Fig. 14.2 shows a simple experiment to show what causes rusting. Four test tubes are set up:

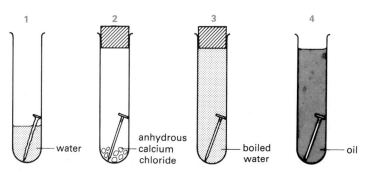

Fig. 14.2 Rusting of iron

Test tube 1   An iron nail is put into water. The nail is in contact with air and water. This tube is being used as a **control.**

Test tube 2   Anhydrous calcium chloride removes all of the water vapour from the air. The nail is in contact with air but not with water.

Test tube 3   The distilled water is boiled before use to remove any dissolved air. The nail is in contact with water but not with air.

Test tube 4   The nail is in an oil. It is out of contact with air and water.

Antoine Laurent Lavoisier (1743–1794)

Lavoisier was one of the greatest figures of Chemistry, who put much work into using Science to help everybody. Even so, he ended up on a guillotine during the French Revolution.

He was born in Paris and was given an excellent education by his wealthy parents. He studied Mathematics, Astronomy, Chemistry and Botany at the College Nazarin.

In 1766 he received a gold medal from the French Academy of Sciences for an essay on the best method of lighting a large town.

Lavoisier graduated in Law, but was appointed Director of the Academy of Sciences in 1768. His scientific work continued, through a succession of experiments, some of which resulted in an improved way of making gunpowder.

Above all he killed off the old misconception that Phlogiston existed and was produced when substances burned. In its place Lavoisier proved, by following the theories of Priestley, that oxygen was crucial to burning, breathing and oxidisation – or rusting.

In 1778 he proved the benefits of a scientific approach to farming by setting up an entire experimental farm.

His involvement in politics led to him being elected to the Assembly of Orleans in 1787, where he made many attempts to improve the living conditions of ordinary people.

In 1790 he was appointed Secretary of the Commission set up to make sure weights and measures were the same across France – work which led to the introduction of the metric system.

However, it was his wealth which people remembered, and he became a target during the French Revolution. In 1794 he was arrested, tried by a revolutionary court in just a few hours and sentenced to death along with 27 others.

That evening the man who did so much to improve the lives of ordinary people was guillotined before the masses and buried in a common grave.

The 'greenhouse' effect

Read the article from the Daily Telegraph dated 14th March 1988.

A touch of the tropics is coming our way

ENVIRONMENT

Charles Clover

THIS MONTH a group of Government-sponsored scientists began an unpublicised and sensitive project. Their brief: to make informed guesses about what would happen to the economy, agriculture and ecology of Britain if, by the year 2050, the global climate has been drastically altered by the heating process known as the greenhouse effect.

Assume, the scientists were told, that the global average temperature rises by 1·5 to 4·5°C in 60 years — a lightning shift in the life of the Earth since only 5°C separate us from the last Ice Age. Assume, too, a rise in sea level of 0·2 to 1·4 m and variations in rainfall of 50 cms a year.

What would happen? Would Britain be able to grow the same crops, the same trees? Could we use the same water supplies? Would the country sustain the same wildlife? We may assume that the answer is probably not.

For some years environmental Cassandras have been ringing alarm bells by predicting, for example, the gradual melting of the polar icecaps — but the evidence of a speedy onset of global warming has been less than firm.

Britain's £250,000 "desktop" project, which is to report in six months, is one of many indications that the greenhouse effect has begun to trouble Western governments. "The effect is real, there is no doubt of that," a senior Government scientist told me last week.

It seems that having looked into the projections of, among others, the University of East Anglia's climate research unit and the Met Office computer models, the Government has decided to take precautions.

What the "desk top" studies now commissioned are likely to predict is, as expected that whenever the warming happens, many of our sea defences would need to be rebuilt much higher. Water supplies might become salinated. New planning regulations might be needed to prevent houses flooding.

Unpredicted until recently are some of the possible climatic changes. In the next century central England could acquire a climate rather like Bordeaux. Red wine-growing would become possible. Forests would be the least likely to adapt, bringing devastation to cold-weather loving conifer plantations. Many wildlife species would be forced to move northwards to find a more temperate climate. Many plant species, from crocuses to apple trees, would die out.

Some evidence suggests higher average temperatures might actually mean more extremes: harsher frosts and hotter summers, more storms.

Britain, however, looks to be lucky. For low-lying countries such as Bangladesh rising sea levels could mean

— principally carbon dioxide from the burning of wood and fossil fuels. These gases are likely to form a layer of "double glazing" through which radiation from the sun will be able to enter, but reflected warmth from the earth will not be able to escape — so the Earth's atmosphere will heat up. Other "greenhouse" gases are the ozone-depleting chemicals CFCs and methane.

Few scientists believe there is yet definite evidence that it has begun to happen. But, for one reason or another, global average temperatures have risen by 0·5°C since the middle of the 19th century. Four of the hottest years on record occur in the 1980s, the hottest of all being 1987.

Huge assumptions have to be made about how fast we will reach the worrying doubling of carbon dioxide, since such questions depend on the energy needs of developing countries.

Research needs to be done into how any carbon dioxide increase would heat the climate, taking into account the buffering effect of oceans absorbing carbon dioxide. But our best guess brings us back to the above brief — given to the biologists and scientists doing the desk-top studies.

Department of the Environment scientists believe we are still five years away from an understanding of temperature rise, 15 years away from predicting climatic effects in, say, Britain; 30 years away from having the greenhouse effect "tied down" in accurate computer models.

That is a long time considering the carbon dioxide the world's energy industries are likely to generate in that time — and the greenhouse effect is not reversible, at least for thousands of years.

Some optimism now exists, that a global agreement might perhaps be reached to limit worse floods than those which already regularly devastate

the Ganges basin.

Changed rainfall patterns could mean new deserts in Africa and dustbowls in the Mid-Western states of America, the Soviet Union, and perhaps the thickly populated Nile delta.

The greenhouse effect is caused by the build-up in the Earth's atmosphere of gases carbon dioxide levels in time — as a result of last year's first global anti-pollution agreement to reduce CFCs. An international meeting to discuss the greenhouse effect takes place in Montreal this July.

Nuclear power, which creates no CO_2, but is expensive, together with energy conservation, is likely to be discussed. Britain is inclined to criticise certain Western countries who want action on the greenhouse effect — but still subsidise electricity use.

The biggest priority of all is research into climate modelling and, particularly, the oceans. Such research in Britain has been under strict spending limits, according to the perenially empty begging bowls of the Natural Environment Research Council. When the results of the "desk-top" reports flood in, that may change.

ACTIVITIES ▼

1. Summarise the reasons for the rise in temperature in Great Britain.

2. List as many important social, economic and environmental problems caused by this rise in temperature. The article will give you some, but you may be able to think of others.

3. Is there anything that can be done to stop or reverse those predictions?

Sea defences in Holland. Before these were built all of the low-lying land was flooded from time to time. If the sea-level rises many parts of the world will need expensive defences.

BRITAIN BY AD 2050

A global greenhouse effect may produce a temperature rise of 1.5 to 4.5°C and a climate like the Gironde Valley or a climate with wider temperature changes, storms and floods. Sea level rises 20-140 cms. Rainfall varies by 20 inches.

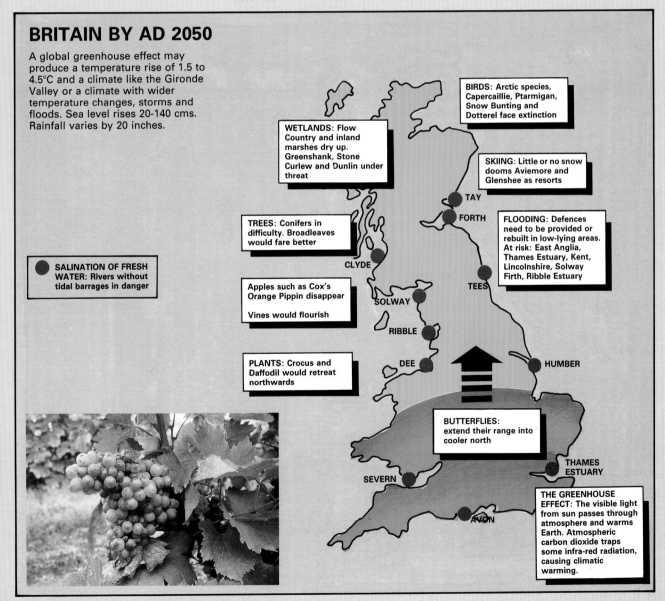

BIRDS: Arctic species, Capercaillie, Ptarmigan, Snow Bunting and Dotterel face extinction

WETLANDS: Flow Country and inland marshes dry up. Greenshank, Stone Curlew and Dunlin under threat

SKIING: Little or no snow dooms Aviemore and Glenshee as resorts

TREES: Conifers in difficulty. Broadleaves would fare better

FLOODING: Defences need to be provided or rebuilt in low-lying areas. At risk: East Anglia, Thames Estuary, Kent, Lincolnshire, Solway Firth, Ribble Estuary

● SALINATION OF FRESH WATER: Rivers without tidal barrages in danger

Apples such as Cox's Orange Pippin disappear

Vines would flourish

PLANTS: Crocus and Daffodil would retreat northwards

BUTTERFLIES: extend their range into cooler north

THE GREENHOUSE EFFECT: The visible light from sun passes through atmosphere and warms Earth. Atmospheric carbon dioxide traps some infra-red radiation, causing climatic warming.

TAY
FORTH
CLYDE
TEES
SOLWAY
RIBBLE
DEE
HUMBER
THAMES ESTUARY
SEVERN
AVON

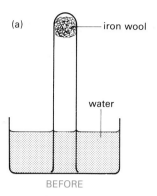

(a) — iron wool

water

BEFORE

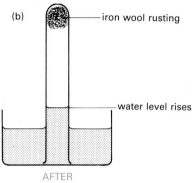

(b) — iron wool rusting

water level rises

AFTER

Fig. 14.3 Demonstrating that oxygen causes rusting

The results obtained are summarised in the table below:

Table 14.1

Test tube number	Observations
1	Rust seen
2	No rusting
3	No rusting
4	No rusting

From this experiment we can conclude that air and water must be present for rusting to take place.

Fig. 14.3 shows an experiment which demonstrates that it is the oxygen in air which causes rusting. In (a) we can see the situation at the start of the experiment. Some iron wool is being left to rust in contact with water vapour and a fixed volume of air. In (b) we can see that after one week the water level has risen by one-fifth, showing that one-fifth or 20% of the air is used up in rusting, i.e. the oxygen.

Other substances such as carbon dioxide, sulphur dioxide and salt can speed up the rusting process.

Rust is a very complex compound and is best considered to be a hydrated iron(III) oxide.

14.4 Ways of preventing rusting

You can see one of the problems with rusting if you look at any rusty panel on a car. When the steel corrodes, the rust formed is flaky and when it flakes away it produces a new surface to corrode. Eventually the whole panel will rust away.

There are many ways of preventing rusting. One of the most common methods of preventing rust is painting. A film of paint covers the iron or steel and prevents air and water vapour coming in contact with the metal. Unfortunately, if the paint film is broken rusting will take place under the paint and the paint will lift away. A good primer paint is used under any final coating.

Parts of a car engine or woodworking tools which cannot be painted are often coated with a thin layer of oil or grease.

Iron and steel can be coated with plastic to prevent air and water vapour coming in contact with the metal. A kitchen washing-up rack, for example, may be coated with plastic. Vulnerable parts of the underbody of a car can be coated with pvc (polyvinyl chloride). This provides a hard surface which is not easily chipped by flying stones.

Iron can be coated with a layer of the metal zinc in a process called galvanising. The zinc can be scratched but the iron still does not rust. Zinc-based paints are used in the primer paints.

Food cans are often made of steel coated with a thin layer of tin. We call this tin-plating. If the tin coating is scratched, the steel continues to rust under the coating.

A steel pier is very prone to rusting. Its legs rest in sea-water and often it is impossible to paint them. Rusting is prevented by fixing blocks of the reactive metal magnesium to the legs of the pier. The magnesium corrodes in preference to the steel. As long as magnesium is there, no rusting will take place. This is called 'sacrificial protection' – the magnesium is being sacrificed to save the steel. Magnesium is an extremely expensive metal but the costs of replacing the pier would be much greater. A similar method is used to prevent the rusting of underground steel pipes and steel hulls of ships.

14.5 Corrosion when metals are in contact

The corrosion of a steel pier is reduced by having blocks of magnesium in contact with the steel legs of the pier.

There is often a corrosion problem when two different metals are in contact. If copper and steel are in contact, the steel will corrode faster than normal. It would be unwise to use a copper washer in joining two lengths of steel exhaust pipe together.

NEWS BRIEF NEWS BRIEF NEWS BRIEF NEWS BRIEF NEWS BRIEF NEWS BRIEF NEWS BRIEF

Hi-fi owners have been alarmed by reports that compact discs are rusting. A compact disc is pressed out of polycarbonate plastic. On the disc is a series of flats and pits — about 45 000 per second — which store sounds as numbers. The disc is then coated with aluminium. The aluminium reflects the laser beam used to read the information on the disc. The laser beam is reflected from the flat but not from the pit. The reflected laser beam is changed by a photoelectric cell into a series of on-off electrical signals. This digital information is then converted into the final sounds.

For protection, the aluminium coated disc is further coated with a thin protective lacquer which should seal the aluminium from any corrosion. Finally the label is printed on top of the lacquer. When compact discs were first introduced it was claimed that the sound quality would never spoil. Recent studies have shown that this is not so.

Some corrosion of the aluminium does take place and this, if it reaches a certain stage, can prevent the reflection of the laser beam and alter the sound. How can corrosion take place? This is not certain. It may be that air and water are trapped in the polycarbonate during moulding. Alternatively, tiny cracks can occur in the surface if the disc is cooled quickly during manufacture. Finally, the ink used to print the label may eat into the protective lacquer and allow air and water in. However it happens, the life of an aluminium-coated disc may be limited

and experiments have been carried out to find a more suitable (i.e. less reactive) metal.

Nickel seems a reasonable alternative because it is not too expensive. It does not, however, reflect the laser beam. Platinum works very well but becomes too hot in use and melts the polycarbonate disc. Gold plated discs certainly work well and may provide an alternative. They would, however, be very expensive.

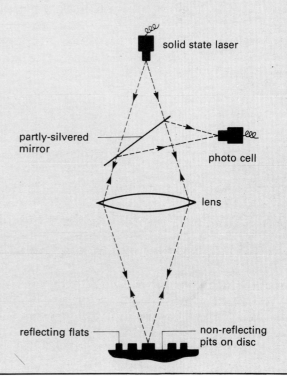

solid state laser

partly-silvered mirror

photo cell

lens

reflecting flats

non-reflecting pits on disc

A storm-battered oil platform in the North Sea, where waves can reach 23 metres to the underside of the deck. Corrosion is a constant problem.

BELOW An old steam locomotive which has been rusting away in a railway scrap yard since it was withdrawn from service in the mid-1960s.

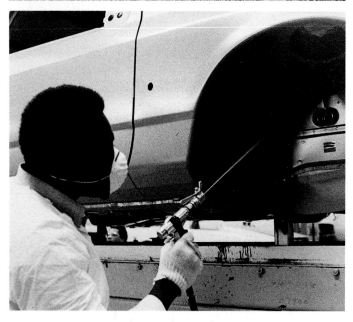

ABOVE LEFT The legs of the West Pier at Brighton showing corrosion. Why do pier legs corrode faster than other ironwork?

LEFT The underside of a car being sprayed with a PVC based material during manufacture to reduce corrosion.

QUESTIONS ON UNIT 14

Domain I: Knowledge and understanding

1. oxidation, reduction, oxidising agent, reducing
agent, oxygen, water, paraffin oil

   Complete the following passage by inserting
words from the list above.

   > Many metals corrode on standing in air.
Corrosion is an . . . . reaction.
Metals high in the reactivity series are most
prone to corrosion. They are stored under
. . . . to prevent corrosion.
>
> The corrosion of iron and steel is usually
called rusting. Iron and steel react with
. . . . in the air and water to produce
rust. If rust is heated in a dry test tube, drops
of . . . . are condensed on the cool part
of the tube. If dry hydrogen gas is passed
over heated rust in a combustion tube, iron
is produced. This is a . . . . reaction
and hydrogen is called the . . . .
. . . . The conversion of rust back into
iron by . . . . is an important process in
restoring the ship *The Mary Rose,* recovered
recently from underwater.

2. Give three ways of preventing iron and steel
from rusting.

3. What is meant by sacrificial protection? Give an
example of where it is used.

4. Aluminium is a fairly reactive metal and quite
high in the reactivity series. It does not corrode
rapidly. Why does aluminium not corrode
rapidly?

5. Why are metals such as gold and platinum so
often used for making jewellery?

Domain II: Handling information and solving problems

6. In each of the following reactions oxidation
and reduction are taking place. In each case
identify which substance is oxidised:

   (a) magnesium + oxygen → magnesium oxide

   (b) copper(ii) oxide + hydrogen → copper + water

   (c) methane + chlorine → carbon + hydrogen chloride

7. Antifreeze used in the cooling systems of
motor car engines can cause the dissolving of
metal parts in the engine.

   An investigation was made into the speed of
dissolving of iron in antifreeze at different
temperatures. The following procedure was
used on five pieces of iron foil:

   Step 1. Five pieces of iron foil of similar size
were rubbed with wire wool, dipped
into detergent solution, rinsed with
distilled water and dried.

   Step 2. The mass of each piece was found.

   Step 3. The pieces of foil were placed in
100 cm³ of 25% antifreeze solution
kept at different temperatures.

   Step 4. After one week the pieces of corroded
iron were removed from the antifreeze
solutions, washed with detergent,
rinsed with distilled water and dried.
The masses of each sample were
found.

   The results of the experiment carried out at
20°C were:

   > mass of foil at the start = 25.11 g
   > mass of foil at the end = 24.95 g

   The results of the other experiments are
shown below:

Temperature in °C	Mass loss of iron foil in g
20	—
30	0.24
40	0.34
50	0.40
60	0.48

7. continued on next page

(7) (a) Work out the mass loss at 20°C.
(b) What is the effect of temperature on the speed of dissolving of iron in antifreeze?
(c) Predict the mass loss when a similar piece of foil is left in 25% antifreeze solution at 80°C for one week.
(d) Outline how you would find out the way the mass loss changes with changing concentrations of antifreeze.
(e) A further investigation was made into the effects of various treatments on the speed of corrosion of iron in antifreeze. Three similar samples of iron were treated in the ways shown in the table opposite and left in 25% antifreeze solutions for one week at 40°C.

Treatment	Mass loss in g
copper coating	0.48
zinc coating	0.00
painting	0.11

What is the effect on the speed of corrosion of:
i) copper coating?
ii) zinc coating?
iii) painting?

8.

Nail	Treatment	Cost of treatment	Mass of nail + coating before exposure to the atmosphere in g	Mass of nail + coating after exposure to the atmosphere in g
A	Waxed	Low	5.0	5.3
B	Oiled	Low	5.0	4.1
C	Chromium plated	High	5.0	5.0
D	Painted	Low	5.0	5.4
E	Untreated	—	4.9	6.1
F	Galvanised	Fairly high	5.0	5.1
G	Dipped in salt solution	Low	5.0	6.7

The corrosion of iron was investigated by giving six identical iron nails certain treatments. One nail was left untreated. All seven nails were then left for several weeks exposed to the atmosphere. The results of the experiments are given in the table above. One of the results contains an error.

(a) Which nail is the control?
(b) Which nail was best protected against corrosion?
(c) Which nail received a treatment which made the corrosion worse than it would have been if it was untreated?
(d) In which of the experiments was there an obvious mistake made in the weighing of the nail and the coating after the experiment?
(e) Which treatment would be most suitable for iron railings?

UNIT 15 Water

15.1 Introduction

Water is an essential compound for all living things. Without it no life on Earth would be possible. Every day each one of us uses approximately 120 litres (26 gallons) of water. The amount of water we use is increasing all the time.

Ensuring that we have a safe supply of water to our homes and cleaning up the waste water we produce are just two of the jobs entrusted to the Regional Water Authorities.

15.2 Water as a solvent

Water will dissolve a very wide range of substances, probably more than any other solvent. The substances dissolved are called **solutes.** For this reason, it is extremely difficult to get pure water.

A solution which contains as much solute as can be dissolved at a particular temperature is called a **saturated solution.** If more solute is added to a saturated solution, the extra solute remains undissolved. The **solubility** of a solute is the mass of solute (in grams) which dissolves in 100 g of solvent at a particular temperature to form a saturated solution.

Water, as a **polar** solvent, dissolves substances containing ionic bonding (Unit 7). Generally, the solubility of ionic compounds in water increases with rise in temperature. A graph of solubility versus temperature for a solute is called a **solubility curve.** Fig. 15.1 shows solubility curves for some common solutes.

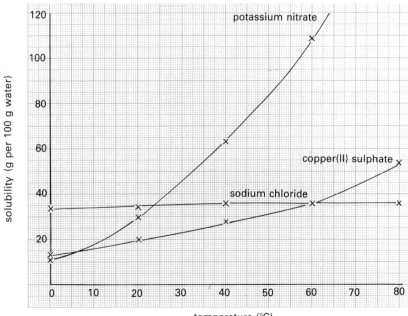

Fig. 15.1 Solubility curves

The annual well-dressing ceremony at Endon, Stoke-on-Trent. This well has provided a continuous supply of water for centuries. In the ceremony, the well is decorated with fresh flowers as a thanksgiving for the water.

15.3 Our water supply

The water cycle

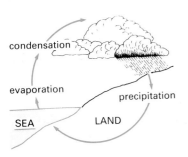

Fig. 15.2 The water cycle

Water evaporates from seas, rivers and lakes and the water vapour rises into the atmosphere. When this water vapour cools it forms clouds. The clouds travel on the air currents. The water vapour condenses and the droplets of water fall as rain. Much of the rain that falls runs into rivers and back into the sea. Fig. 15.2 summarises the evaporation and condensation of water, which we call the water cycle. Because it is a cycle, we will never run out of rain!

In some places the rain-water soaks into the ground and collects in spongy or porous rocks. We can get water from these rocks simply by drilling down and pumping the water to the surface.

Where there are no suitable porous rocks, water can be taken from a clean river or lake. Surplus water may be stored in a reservoir. Usually

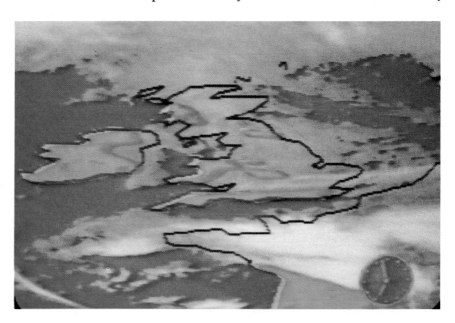

A computerised weather map used on television. Information is collected by radar and a computer produces a continuously changing rainfall forecast.

more rain falls in the winter and more water is used in the summer. A reservoir is often formed by damming one end of a valley. Water from the surrounding hills collects in the reservoir and can be used as required.

Water that is drawn from rivers, lakes, reservoirs or underground rocks is not pure. All sorts of substances will be dissolved in the water, so it has to be treated before it can be used for tap-water.

Water treatment

The most undesirable features of the water may be:

- *Colour:* An unpleasant colour may be caused by dissolved organic matter. This may be so if the water has come from peaty soil.
- *Suspended matter:* This is probably caused by mineral or vegetable matter.
- *Cloudiness:* This may be caused by fine mineral matter, e.g. clay.
- *Harmful germs and bacteria.*
- *Hardness* (page 109).
- *Taste and odour:* This may be due to sewage, decayed vegetation or lack of oxygen in the water.

Various methods may be used to treat the water to make it suitable for use as tap-water. These methods include:

1. Storage

Water can be stored in lakes or reservoirs. During the storage, suspended matter sinks to the bottom and harmful bacteria die out. The colour is bleached out by sunlight and some impurities are removed when they come into contact with oxygen in the air.

2. Air

Air may be bubbled through water. This will remove odours and oxidise mineral salts to make their removal easier.

3. Precipitation

Chemicals such as alum (potassium aluminium sulphate) or iron(II) sulphate may be added to water to precipitate out mineral salts.

4. Filtration

Precipitates can be removed from water by filtration (Unit 2). Rather than use a filter paper as we would in the laboratory, the filtering is done using a sand filter (Fig. 15.3).

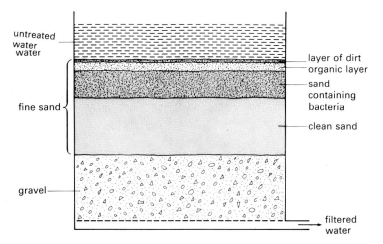

Fig. 15.3 A sand filter

5. Disinfection   The last stage in treatment is to kill any harmful bacteria by treating the water with the poisonous gas chlorine in carefully controlled amounts. This process is called chlorination.

At the end of the treatment process the tap-water produced is safe and suitable for household use. It should be clear, colourless and odourless with no unpleasant taste. It should not contain harmful bacteria or dissolved minerals. It is not pure, however, and will contain dissolved solids and dissolved gases. These impurities will vary from place to place.

15.4 Treatment of waste water

Fig. 15.4 Various stages in the water cycle

Safe disposal of waste water is essential for the health of the public. Fig. 15.4 summarises the ways in which water can be treated to make it safe to return to a river. This treatment is carried out in a sewage works.

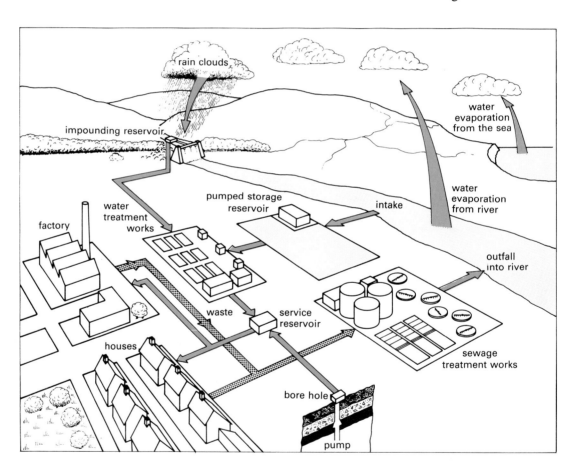

15.5 Tests for water

Water is frequently produced during chemical reactions. You cannot assume that any colourless, odourless liquid you come across is water. Either anhydrous copper(II) sulphate or cobalt(II) chloride paper can be used to show that water is present in a liquid.

Anhydrous copper(II) sulphate is a white powder produced when blue copper(II) sulphate crystals are heated. When a liquid containing water is added to anhydrous copper(II) sulphate, the mixture goes blue and becomes very hot.

Cobalt(II) chloride paper is produced by dipping a piece of filter paper into an aqueous solution of cobalt(II) chloride and then drying the paper thoroughly. During the drying process the paper turns from pink to blue. If a piece of cobalt(II) chloride paper is dipped into liquid containing water the paper turns from blue to pink.

Neither of these tests show that pure water is present. The presence of pure water is proved by doing melting and boiling point tests. If the liquid freezes at 0°C and boils at 100°C it is pure water.

15.6 Hard and soft water

As rain-water trickles through the ground it dissolves different rocks and minerals. These dissolved materials are not removed completely during water treatment and so the tap-water we receive is not pure and varies from place to place.

If calcium and magnesium compounds are dissolved in water, the water is said to be **hard**. When soap is added to hard water it does not lather well but forms scum. If water does not contain calcium and magnesium compounds, the water is said to be **soft** and will lather well without forming scum.

Fig. 15.5 shows areas in England and Wales where water is hard and where water is soft.

Fig. 15.5 Hard and soft water in England and Wales

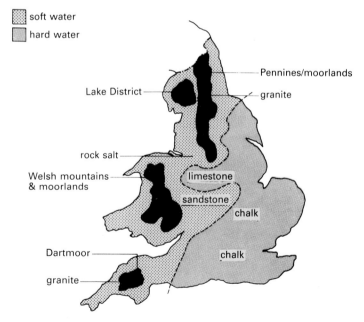

Hardness in water can be divided into two types – temporary and permanent hardness.

Temporary hardness is caused by dissolved calcium hydrogencarbonate. Rain-water, containing dissolved carbon dioxide, dissolves calcium carbonate in rocks forming calcium hydrogencarbonate:

calcium carbonate + water + carbon dioxide ⇌ calcium hydrogencarbonate

NB The sign ⇌ shows that the reaction is reversible.

Temporary hardness is easily removed from water. The simplest method is boiling, which decomposes the calcium hydrogencarbonate forming calcium carbonate. It is this calcium carbonate which causes 'furring' or 'scaling' on the inside of a kettle or in boilers and hot-water pipes.

Stalagmites and stalactites, found in underground caverns in limestone areas, are formed by decomposition of temporary hardness in water. Stalagmites grow up from the floor and stalactites hang down from the ceiling. They are made of calcium carbonate.

Permanent hardness is caused by dissolved calcium sulphate or magnesium sulphate. It is not removed by boiling and can only be removed by more expensive treatment.

The advantages and disadvantages of hard and soft water are shown in Table 15.1 (see opposite).

RIGHT   Ashford Common Water Treatment Works. During the process waste water is allowed to settle in the large rectangular tanks.

BELOW   Stalagmites and stalactites. These are formed in underground caves when hard water decomposes. If it decomposes before it drips it forms a stalactite and if it decomposes afterwards it forms a stalagmite.

BELOW RIGHT   An electron micrograph of kettle fur produced in a hard water area (Norwich).

Table 15.1 Advantages and disadvantages of hard water

Advantages	Disadvantages
• Supplies calcium compounds required by the body for bones and teeth.	• Wastes soap because some of the soap forms scum with the impurities in the water.
• Has a better taste than soft water.	• Scum formed leaves marks on clothes and baths.
• Better for brewing beer.	• Causes a layer of 'fur' in kettles and scale in boilers and pipes. Scale in pipes may block pipes and radiators may be less efficient.
• Lead compounds in the pipes are less soluble in hard water.	• Spoils special finishes on fabrics.

15.7 Softening hard water in industry and the home

hard water containing calcium & magnesium compounds

resin containing sodium compounds

soft water

Fig. 15.6 An ion exchange column

Any water sample can be softened (i.e. have its hardness removed) by distillation (Unit 4). This, however, would not be an economic process unless very cheap sources were available.

Usually the problems caused by hard water are overcome by the adding of suitable water-softening chemicals or by using an ion-exchange column.

The cheapest water-softening chemical which is used is washing soda – hydrated sodium carbonate, $Na_2CO_3.10H_2O$. This will precipitate out insoluble calcium carbonate and magnesium carbonate from the water and so remove the hardness. The resulting solution, however, is quite alkaline (at least pH 10). Sodium sesquicarbonate is a mixture of sodium carbonate and sodium hydrogencarbonate. It acts in a similar way but does not produce such an alkaline solution. Bath salts often contain sodium sesquicarbonate, along with suitable colouring and perfume.

Other substances such as *Calgon* (sodium metaphosphate) are also used in water softening.

Where hardness has to be removed from large quantities of water, an ion exchange column (Fig. 15.6) is probably advisable. This is a column filled with a complex resin. The resin contains a large surplus of sodium ions.

BELOW Household products containing detergents (page 112). Look at the products and decide for what purpose each should and should not be used.

RIGHT Part of the paper-making process (page 113.) Wood pulp fibres and large amounts of water are projected at high speed onto a wire mesh where the paper is formed.

When the hard water passes through the column, the calcium and magnesium ions are replaced by sodium ions from the resin. The resulting water, containing no calcium or magnesium compounds, is no longer hard. When the sodium ions on the resin are used, salt (sodium chloride) is added to the column to replace them.

15.8 Soaps and soapless detergents

Until about forty years ago, washing products usually contained soaps. Soaps were made from natural fats and oils, such as palm oil and olive oil. These fats and oils were boiled with an alkaline solution:

$$\text{fat or oil} + \text{sodium hydroxide} \rightarrow \text{soap} + \text{glycerol}$$

Salt solution was added to the resulting mixture and the soap precipitated out.

Soap caused problems in hard water areas, producing scum instead of lather. Soap has gradually been replaced in many cleaning products by soapless detergents. One reason for this change was the increasing costs of natural fats and oils.

Soapless detergents are made by treating liquid hydrocarbons – by-products of petroleum refining (Unit 21) – with concentrated sulphuric acid. Soapless detergents lather equally well in hard and soft water and do not form scum.

Fig. 15.7 shows the way that particles of soap or soapless detergent clean soiled materials. Soap and soapless detergent particles resemble tadpoles. The head of the particle likes being in water and the tail likes being in oil and grease.

Fig. 15.7 Cleaning action of detergents (note the 'heads' and 'tails' of the detergent molecules)

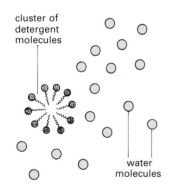

cluster of detergent molecules

water molecules

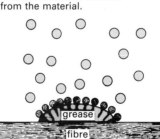

Tails of detergent molecules stick into the grease. Attraction between heads of detergent molecules and water molecules. Grease is lifted from the material.

grease

fibre

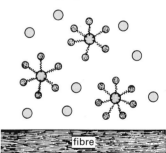

Grease is suspended in the solution. Repelling forces between droplets of grease prevent them from coming together.

fibre

15.9 Importance of water to industry

Many industries use large quantities of water. For this reason many factories are built alongside rivers or on the coast.

Water can be used by industry for various reasons. These include:

1. As an essential ingredient in the product (e.g. beer-making, whisky production).

2. For water to cool parts of the process (e.g. making electricity in an oil- or coal-fired power station).
3. As a source of energy (e.g. making electricity in a hydroelectric power station).
4. As a raw material which is removed during the process (e.g. paper-making).

Sea water, however, is not suitable for all industrial uses, such as cooling in a factory. This is because it is highly corrosive and leaves deposits of salt.

Fig. 15.8 shows the quantity of water required to produce some everyday items.

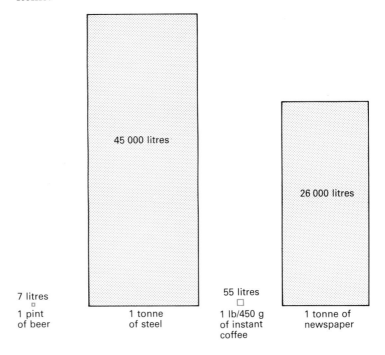

7 litres   45 000 litres   55 litres   26 000 litres

1 pint   1 tonne   1 lb/450 g   1 tonne of
of beer   of steel   of instant   newspaper
                                       coffee

Fig. 15.8   Quantities of water required to make some everyday items

NEWS BRIEF NEWS BRIEF NEWS BRIEF NEWS BRIEF NEWS

Millions of people around the world never have to worry about drinking bad tap water because their homes have no taps. Reports have come in that residents of the Lima suburb of San Juan De Dios, Peru, for example, get their water from an ancient lorry which delivers water twice a week. For a price three times as high as water through the mains, the driver will pump 200 litres of water into a rusty oil drum on the doorstep.

If someone wants to wash they dip a saucepan in the drum, flicking away floating insects and trying to avoid the thin coating of scum on the surface. Water for cooling or drinking must be strained and then boiled if residents want to avoid catching typhoid.

QUESTIONS ON UNIT 15

Domain I: Knowledge and understanding

1. increases, remains the same, mixture, compound, aqueous, oxygen, hydrogen, solvent, soluble, insoluble, saturated

   Complete the following passage by including words from the above list:

   Water is a .... of hydrogen and oxygen. In every water molecule there are two .... atoms and one .... atom. The formula of water is written as H_2O.
   Water is a very good .... since it dissolves a wide range of solutes. The resulting solutions are called ....
   solutions. A solution which contains the maximum amount of dissolved solute at a particular temperature is called a
   .... solution.
   Copper(ii) sulphate, salt and sugar all dissolve readily in water. They are said to be
   .... in water. The solubility of solids in water generally .... with increasing temperature.
   Sand does not dissolve in water. It is said to be .... in water.

2. Which of the chemicals in list B best fits each of the descriptions in list A? You must use the chemicals in list B only once.

   List A
   - Used to test for water
   - Used to soften hard water
   - The scale inside a kettle
   - Used to kill the germs, in water
   - Causes permanent hardness in water
   - Causes temporary hardness in water
   - Hardens the enamel on children's teeth

   List B
   - Sodium carbonate
   - Sodium fluoride
   - Anhydrous copper(ii) sulphate
   - Calcium hydrogencarbonate
   - Chlorine
   - Calcium carbonate
   - Calcium sulphate

Domain II: Handling information and solving problems

3. An experiment was carried out to compare the hardness of four water samples labelled A, B, C and D.
   $25\ cm^3$ of water sample A was transferred to a conical flask. Soap solution was then added to the flask in small portions using a burette until a lasting lather was formed.
   The experiment was repeated with water samples B, C and D. Fresh samples of each water sample were boiled and tested again with soap solution. The results are shown in the table below:

Water sample	Volume of soap solution required before boiling in cm^3	Volume of soap solution required after boiling in cm^3
A	5.0	5.0
B	1.0	1.0
C	11.0	6.0
D	9.0	1.0

   (a) Which of the four water samples:
   i) could be distilled water?
   ii) contains only temporary hardness?
   iii) contains only permanent hardness?
   iv) contains both temporary and permanent hardness?

   (b) Washing soda was added to fresh samples of each type of water. What volume of soap solution would you expect to be required in each case to produce a lasting lather?

   (c) Refer to the information on page 254 comparing the hardness of water samples in different places in England. Which one of the water samples could have come from Bath?

4. Two pupils were carrying out, separately, experiments to find the solubility of sodium chloride at room temperature. The procedure they took was as follows:

A beaker is half filled with water at room temperature. Sodium chloride is added to the water in small portions. After each addition, the solution is stirred. Sodium chloride is added until no more sodium chloride will dissolve and some remains undissolved.

A dry evaporating basin is weighed and some solution, without sodium chloride crystals, poured into the evaporating basin which is then weighed again. The solution is carefully evaporated to dryness by heating. After cooling the evaporating basin is weighed again.

Their results are summarised in the table below:

	Richard's results	Ann's results
Mass of evaporating basin	65.32 g	67.55g
Mass of evaporating basin + salt solution	125.32 g	137.55 g
Mass of evaporating basin + salt	75.32 g	87.55 g

(a) Calculate the solubility of sodium chloride from the results of Richard and Ann. Look up the solubility of sodium chloride on page 253. Which one of them got results closest to the value in the Data Section?

(b) Richard thought his result was inaccurate because he lost sodium chloride solid during evaporation when the contents of the evaporating basin were spitting. Explain how evaporation could be carried out to reduce spitting.

(c) Ann thought her sodium chloride was not completely dry when she made the final weighing. She repeated the experiment and obtained the following results:

Mass of evaporating basin
   = 67.55 g
Mass of evaporating basin + salt solution
   = 145.55 g
Mass of evaporating basin + salt
   = 88.55 g

She then reheated the evaporating basin for five minutes, allowed it to cool and then reweighed it. The mass was still 88.55g. What could she conclude from these results?

5. Look up the solubilities of potassium nitrate, copper(II) sulphate and sodium chloride at different temperatures in the Data Section on page 253. Plot these figures on a graph (on a piece of graph paper) and draw smooth curves to connect the points. Use these solubility curves to answer the following questions:

(a) Which of the three substances:
   i) has the smallest change of solubility with temperature?
   ii) is the most soluble at 5°C?
   iii) is the most soluble at 50°C?

(b) Find out from the graphs:
   i) the solubility of potassium nitrate at 30°C;
   ii) the temperature at which the solubility of copper(II) sulphate is 24 g per 100 g of water;
   iii) the maximum number of grams of copper(II) sulphate which will dissolve in 50 g of water at 70°C.

(c) A solution is made from 40 g of potassium nitrate dissolved in 100 g of water at 60°C. It is then cooled.
   i) At what temperature would this be a saturated solution?
   ii) If it were cooled to 20°C and no crystals appeared, what type of solution would it now be?
   iii) What would happen if another crystal of potassium nitrate was now added to the solution?

UNIT 16 Water pollution

16.1 Introduction

Over fifty million gallons of waste water enter rivers in Great Britain every day from sewage works, factories and farms. Great care has to be taken to ensure that unwanted impurities, called **pollutants** are not in the water.

At room temperature only about 30 cm^3 of oxygen will dissolve in one litre of water. This small amount of oxygen is all that is available to keep fish and all other river life alive. Anything which reduces the amount of dissolved oxygen in water will have an effect on the life of the river.

A temperature rise will reduce the amount of dissolved oxygen. If the temperature rises to about 40°C, the volume of dissolved oxygen in water is halved. Care has to be taken, therefore, not to pump large amounts of hot water into a river. Power stations return water to rivers but it is allowed to cool before it enters the river.

16.2 Pollution by nitrogen compounds

NEWS BRIEF NEWS BRIEF

High levels of nitrate in water may not afterall cause stomach cancer. A recent report has shown no evidence of more cancers in workers in the fertiliser industry, which uses large amounts of nitrates.

(See **nitrogen cycle**, page 131) A major reason for the reduction of dissolved oxygen in water is the addition of ammonia and ammonium compounds from sewage works, factories and farms. Bacteria in the water turn ammonia and ammonium compounds into nitrites and nitrates. This change uses up dissolved oxygen. Because nitrates encourage plant growth, green algae start to grow on the surface of the water. These algae prevent light getting into the water. When the algae die they decay and this again reduces the amount of dissolved oxygen. This process is sometimes called **eutrophication** and the result can be a completely dead river.

There is considerable concern at present about the high levels of nitrates in rivers and the effects that these high levels can have on health. These levels are four times larger than twenty years ago and are still increasing.

A fast-flowing river can dissolve oxygen from the air to replace any lost by pollution.

16.3 Pollution by metal compounds

More serious problems are caused when metal compounds are discharged into rivers. Compounds of lead, cadmium, mercury and iron, for example, can have awful effects on river life. They can cause death of all life in the river and make the river toxic. These metal compounds should be removed before the water is returned to the river.

16.4 Pollution by phosphates and detergents

Phosphates and detergents get into rivers from washing powders. Phosphates are added to washing powders to help give a whiter wash. Phosphates have a similar effect to nitrates in water encouraging growth of plants. Detergents now are usually biodegradable, i.e. they are broken down by bacteria in the water and do not build up.

ABOVE Dead fish in a polluted river – just one of the consequences of nitrogen compounds entering a river from sewage, industrial wastes or mis-use of fertilisers.

RIGHT A river polluted with foam from detergents. This is becoming less of a problem as detergents are now being made which can be broken down by bacteria.

NEWS BRIEF NEWS BRIEF NEWS BRIEF NEWS BRIEF NEWS BRIEF NEWS BRIEF NEWS BRIEF

In November 1986 there was a serious accident in Switzerland. Following a factory fire 30 tonnes of agricultural chemicals and mercury compounds were washed into the River Rhine. During the next 12 days they flowed up the Rhine to the North Sea. As they went they produced a number of problems. These included:

● Killing 34 varieties of fish and eel.
● The Rivers Waal and Ijssel had to be closed off to prevent dyke and land pollution.
● Alternative sources of drinking water had to be found in Germany.

After this accident a very close watch of the river was made. Many examples of pollution were found in the months that followed.
Mercury in a soluble form is toxic to man and other mammals, as well as green plants and fungi. It is also, like lead and cadmium, a cumulative poison.

Serious pollution problems have arisen in the past from the industrial use of mercury and mercury compounds such as methyl and ethyl mercurial salts. High concentrations of mercury from industrial sources have been found in fish, especially tuna. These have been linked to blindness, speech defects and the inability to co-ordinate movements. It also causes gastroenteritis and skin disorders.

1. What is a cumulative poison?

2. Explain how mercury in rivers could affect you, even if you live well away from the river.

QUESTIONS ON UNIT 16

Domain II: Handling information and solving problems

1. Below is a sketch map of a river. Water samples were taken at seven places along the river labelled A to G. These samples were analysed and the results are shown in the table opposite:

Sample	A	B	C	D	E	F	G
Temperature (°C)	6	7	6	6	10	7	6
pH	7	9	6	6	6	6	8
Dissolved oxygen (parts per million)	14	9	12	9	9	12	11
Free ammonia (parts per million)	0	10	2	7	6	2	3
Nitrates (parts per million)	0	0	4	7	8	5	9

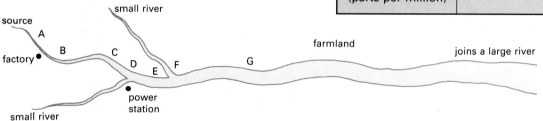

(a) Which sample A to G:
   i) is almost pure?
   ii) is at the highest temperature?
   iii) is exactly neutral?
   iv) contains the most free ammonia?
   v) contains the most nitrates?

(b) Explain the difference between the:
   i) pH of A and B;
   ii) dissolved oxygen levels between B and C;
   iii) the temperature between D and E;
   iv) nitrate levels between F and G.

2. Table **A** shows some small water creatures which can exist in water containing different amounts of pollution.

A river was examined at four places (W, X, Y and Z) and the only creatures present in the water are shown in Table **B**.

Arrange the four waters in order of pollution with the least polluted sample first.

Table **A**

Amount of pollution	Animals found		
Very high			
High			
Low			
Very low			

Table **B**

Sample W	X	Y	Z

3. The diagrams opposite show the concentrations of some metals in the mud in different estuaries around England and Wales. The levels are shown as a percentage (for iron) and in µg per gram (microgram per gram – a microgram is a millionth of a gram).

Using these diagrams and the map below, answer the following questions:

(a) Why is the information for iron recorded in different units?

(b) In which estuary:
   i) is the level of nickel highest?
   ii) is the level of copper highest?

(c) Explain why there are high levels of lead in Restronguet Creek and Fal Estuary.

(d) A factory in the Humber Estuary has been accused of depositing large amounts of heavy metals into the water. Is there any evidence that this is so from these figures?

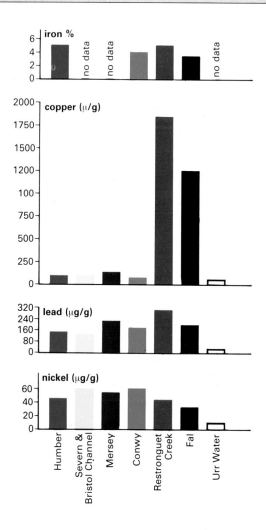

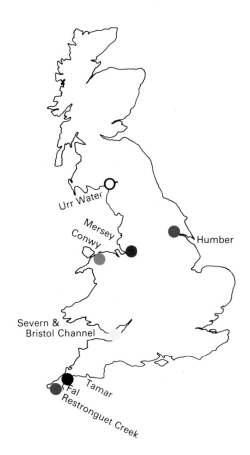

UNIT 17 Nitrogen, ammonia and nitric acid

17.1 Nitrogen

Although nitrogen makes up approximately four-fifths of the air, it is not as important in industry as oxygen. One reason for this is the unreactivity of nitrogen. Making ammonia (a compound of nitrogen and hydrogen, NH_3) is the most important industrial use of nitrogen.

17.2 Making ammonia by the Haber process

Ammonia is a very important fertiliser and is used to make other fertilisers. It is produced on a large scale in the Haber process. This process is named after the German chemist who developed it about 70 years ago.

Nitrogen and hydrogen are the two raw materials of the process. Nitrogen is made in large quantities from the fractional distillation of liquid air (Unit 12). Hydrogen used to be made from water but now it is usually made from natural gas.

The nitrogen and hydrogen are mixed together in the proportions 1 part nitrogen to 3 parts hydrogen. The mixture of gases is compressed to a very high pressure and passed over heated, finely divided iron which acts as a catalyst. (A catalyst is a substance which speeds up a reaction without being used up.) It does not produce more ammonia but enables the ammonia to be made more quickly, so increasing the capacity of the factory.

About 10% of the nitrogen and hydrogen combine together to form ammonia:

$$\text{nitrogen} + \text{hydrogen} \rightleftharpoons \text{ammonia}$$

The mixture of gases is cooled and the ammonia is liquefied and separated from the nitrogen and hydrogen. These gases are recycled.

The factory can be made to produce more ammonia if the pressure of the mixture of gases is increased. However, as the pressure is increased the risk of explosion increases and much larger sums of money are needed in plant construction.

Also, a larger amount of ammonia would be produced from a given amount of nitrogen and hydrogen if low temperatures were used, but the process would be very slow. A temperature of about 450°C is used.

The Haber process is summarised in Fig. 17.1 opposite.

A modern ammonia factory can produce about 7000 tonnes of ammonia each day. A factory is sited close to sources of energy (coal, gas or oil), water (river or sea), transport (road, rail or sea) and workers. In Great Britain there are ammonia plants at Billingham on the River Tees, at Immingham on the River Humber (page 122), at Ince Marsh on the River Mersey and at Avonmouth on the River Severn.

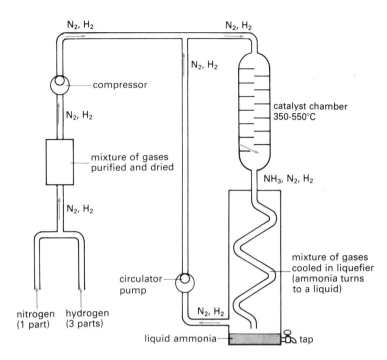

Fig. 17.1 The Haber process

17.3 Properties and uses of ammonia

Ammonia gas can be made easily in the laboratory by heating an ammonium compound with an alkali. For example ammonium chloride and sodium hydroxide:

ammonium chloride + sodium hydroxide → ammonia + sodium chloride + water

Ammonium chloride is a colourless gas with a very strong smell. It is the most soluble gas in water – in fact, 1 cm^3 of water will dissolve 1300 cm^3 of ammonia at room temperature. The apparatus in Fig. 17.2 can be used to prepare and collect some ammonia solution. The funnel is to prevent 'sucking-back' due to the high solubility of ammonia.

Ammonia gas is alkaline. It turns damp red litmus paper blue and damp Universal indicator paper purple.

An ammonia solution is alkaline and is sometimes called ammonium hydroxide. If ammonia solution is added to solutions of metal salts, insoluble metal hydroxides may be precipitated (Unit 30).

A solution of ammonia is used as a degreasing agent and is contained in household cleaners.

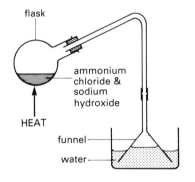

Fig. 17.2 Preparation of ammonium solution

17.4 Nitric acid

Nitric acid is one of the **mineral acids**. It has a formula HNO$_3$. It reacts with bases and alkalis to produce nitrates (Unit 11).

Much of the ammonia produced by the Haber process is immediately converted into nitric acid.

The two factories are often built side-by-side to avoid having to transport the dangerous material.

17.5 Converting ammonia into nitric acid in industry

The raw materials for this process are ammonia, air and water. A mixture of ammonia gas and air is passed over a heated platinum catalyst and the ammonia is oxidised to nitrogen monoxide. The gases are then cooled and nitrogen monoxide is converted into nitrogen dioxide. Finally, the nitrogen dioxide is dissolved in water in the presence of air to produce nitric acid. A small amount of nitrogen dioxide escapes from the chimney at the end of the process as a brown plume. This can cause the same air pollution problems as oxides of nitrogen from car exhausts.

The process is summarised in Fig. 17.3.

The main reactions taking place are summarised by the following word equations:

$$\text{ammonia} + \text{oxygen (from the air)} \rightarrow \text{nitrogen dioxide} + \text{steam}$$

$$\text{nitrogen dioxide} + \text{water} + \text{oxygen} \rightarrow \text{nitric acid}$$

The resulting acid solution contains about 65% nitric acid and 35% water. The acid can be concentrated further by fractional distillation (Unit 4).

Fig. 17.3 Manufacture of nitric acid

17.6 Uses of nitric acid

Fig. 17.4 summarises the main uses of nitric acid.

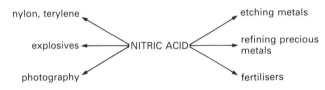

Fig. 17.4 Uses of nitric acid

A general view of a factory producing ammonium nitrate at Immingham on the river Humber. The main use of ammonium nitrate is for fertilisers.

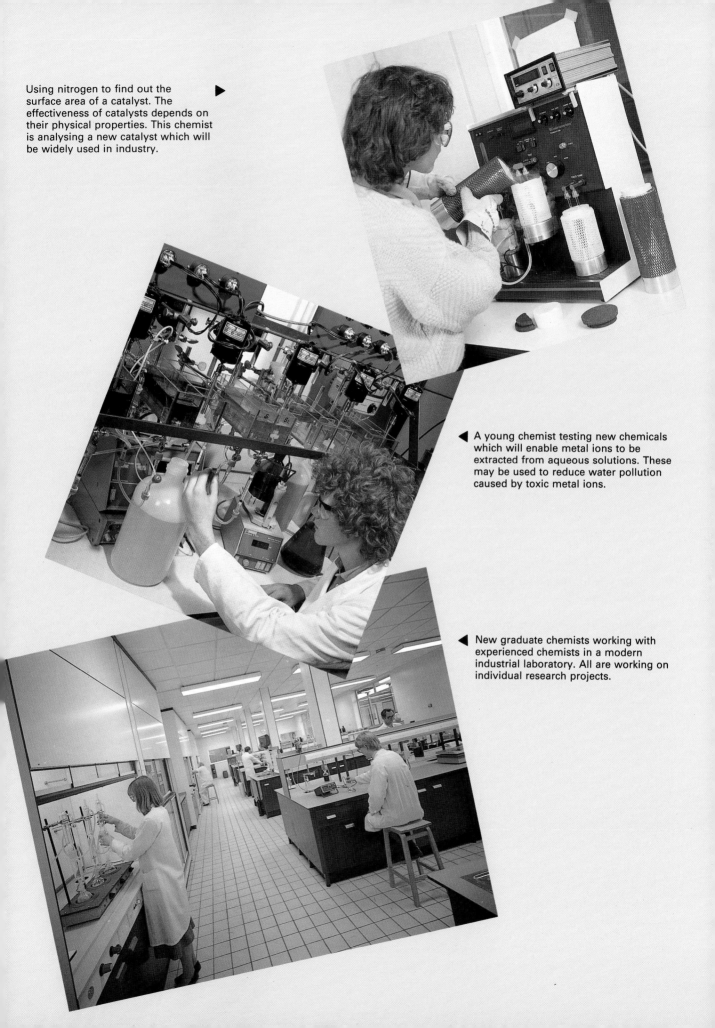

Using nitrogen to find out the surface area of a catalyst. The effectiveness of catalysts depends on their physical properties. This chemist is analysing a new catalyst which will be widely used in industry.

A young chemist testing new chemicals which will enable metal ions to be extracted from aqueous solutions. These may be used to reduce water pollution caused by toxic metal ions.

New graduate chemists working with experienced chemists in a modern industrial laboratory. All are working on individual research projects.

QUESTIONS ON UNIT 17

Domain I: Knowledge and understanding

1. Complete the flow diagram by identifying the substances A–G. Write word equations for the reactions labelled (i)–(v).

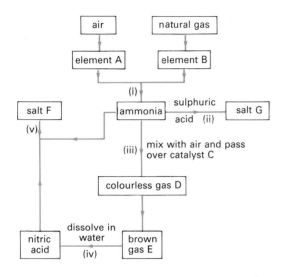

2. Complete the passage below by fitting in suitable words.

> Ammonia is produced in industry by the
> . . . . process using . . . . gas
> from the air and . . . . gas. The two
> gases are dried, mixed together and
> compressed. The mixture of gases is passed
> over a heated catalyst made of finely divided
> . . . .
>
> Some of the gases combine to produce
> ammonia, which is usually removed by
> . . . . The unreacted gases are
> then . . . .
>
> Much of the ammonia is then converted
> into . . . . acid. Ammonia gas is mixed
> with a larger volume of . . . . The mixture
> is then passed over a heated . . . .

continued . . . .

> gauze catalyst. The catalyst glows red hot
> because the reaction is . . . .
> The hot gases are then cooled in a
> . . . . exchanger and this energy can be
> re-used. At the lower temperature the brown
> gas . . . . is produced.
> When the gases are dissolved in . . . .
> the final acid is formed.

Domain II: Handling information and solving problems

3. The graph below shows the yield of ammonia produced at different temperatures and pressures. Each curve represents the change of yield with changing pressure at a constant temperature. Use the graph to help you answer the following questions:

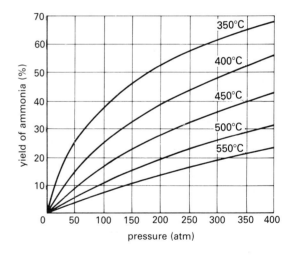

(a) A typical factory operates at 400°C and 200 atmospheres pressure. What is the yield of ammonia under these conditions?

(b) What is the effect on the yield of increasing the pressure of the reacting gases?

(c) Give one disadvantage of operating the factory with the reacting gases under a higher pressure.

(d) What is the effect on the yield of increasing the operating temperature?

(e) A manufacturer proposes increasing the temperature at which the process is carried out. Is there any advantage in doing this?

4. (a) 40 cm³ of dry ammonia (NH_3) was trapped in syringe A. The gas was passed from syringe A to syringe B several times, each time passing over heated iron wire. The 3-way tap was set so the gas could not enter syringe C. The gas was then collected in syringe B and 60 cm³ of gas remained when the apparatus had cooled to room temperature.

(b) The 3-way tap was then turned so that the gases in syringe B could pass over the heated copper(II) oxide into syringe C. The gas was passed backwards and forwards several times and finally transferred to syringe C. On cooling to room temperature, 20 cm³ of gas remained.

Decide whether each of the following statements about the second reaction are true or false:

i) Copper(II) oxide was reduced to copper.
ii) Copper(II) oxide removed nitrogen from the gas.
iii) Copper(II) oxide removed ammonia from the gas.
iv Copper(II) oxide removed hydrogen from the gas.
v) The gas remaining in syringe C was nitrogen.

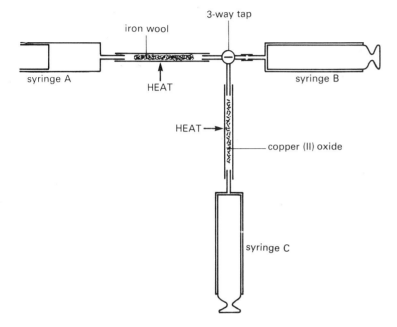

Decide whether each of the following statements about the above reaction is true or false:

i) Ammonia gas is decomposed when it is passed over heated iron wool.
ii) A mixture of nitrogen and hydrogen was collected in syringe B.
iii) The volume of gas collected in syringe B was greater than the volume of ammonia gas used.
iv) Iron wool was oxidised during the reaction.
v) The mass of the iron wool was unchanged at the end of the reaction.

NEWS BRIEF NEWS BRIEF NEWS BRIEF NEWS

More than a million Britons are drinking polluted tap water, according to a Government report produced in 1988. Levels of nitrate are above the limits laid down by the Common Market. These allow for 50 milligrams of nitrate per litre of water. People living in East Anglia, Lincolnshire, Nottinghamshire and Staffordshire receive water containing higher levels of nitrate than recommended. The full effects could take years to show up.

Recommendations are to be made to the farming community. These include using no artificial fertiliser between mid-September and mid-February, sowing autumn-sown crops rather than spring-sown ones and sowing crops in autumn as early as possible.

The Pollution Detectives

This study describes work actually carried out by fifth year pupils from Framwellgate Moor Comprehensive School, Durham. They spent an afternoon in the Chester-le-Street area of County Durham analysing the waters of the Lumley Park Burn and its tributaries. They then used their results to work out the origins of the various pollutants which they had identified.

REPORT

The afternoon began at site 1 (see map), a beautiful waterfall set in picturesque Durham woodlands. Everyone was, however, in for a nasty shock! As we approached the foot of the falls, the stink which reached our noses was truly appalling. Our on-the-spot analyses of the water soon gave us some explanation for the stench. We used meters and colour-cubes to get most of our results, but the amount of detergent could be estimated quite simply – just by shaking a sample of water and seeing how long the froth remained.

continued..............

The Lumley Park Burn and its tributaries. Sampling points: 1, Lumley Park Burn Waterfall; 2, Sewage Works effluent outlet; 3, Coke works 'toxic outflow'; 4, The Herrington Burn; 5 The Moors Burn.

The results of the Lumley Park Burn study (September 1984).

Measurement[1]	Unpolluted value[2]	Lumley Park Burn waterfall	Sewage effluent pipe	Coke works 'toxic outflow'	The Herrington Burn	The Moors Burn
Phosphate	<1	4	5	<1	1	1
Ammonium-N	<0.5	10	12.5	80	0.5	0.5
Nitrite-N	<0.2	0.6	0.2		<0.2	<0.2
Nitrate-N	<5	<5	<5	<5	<5	<5
Conductivity (μS cm^{-1})	100–500	1300	900	5000	2900	1400
pH	7–8.5	7.7	8.1	4.9	7.5	7.5
Dissolved oxygen (per cent)	80–100	90	62	48	80	74
Detergents (sec of froth)	0	30	30	5	10	15

1. Unless otherwise stated, units are mg l^{-3} (ppm).
2. The sign < indicates that the concentration is below the detection limit of the test.

We soon left the site, with its bobbing lumps of brown froth, behind as we headed back through the wood to the coach and off upstream to Lambton Coke Works. Here we were to spend the rest of the afternoon either tramping over dark coal-covered deserts or working alongside the sweet-smelling piles of sludge produced by Sedgeletch Sewage Works.

At sites 2 and 3, we tested the actual effluent being discharged into the Herrington Burn. Arriving at site 3, the 'toxic outflow' of the coke works led to gasps of revulsion all round. The stink matched that of the waterfall. Nevertheless, two brave souls were found who were willing to make the descent into the mire and collect samples. Revulsion soon turned to horror as the water first turned the nitrite test yellow instead of its more usual pink and then refused to give a measurable result for the ammonium-nitrogen test until it had been diluted by a factor of one hundred and twenty five!

So it was that, after further 'feats of bravery', we returned to school ready to process our results.

TOP   Lambton Coke works

MIDDLE The sewage outlet pipe, Lumley Park Burn

BOTTOM Students testing water for pollution at a sewage outlet pipe

ACTIVITIES ▼

The best way to work on the results is to begin by taking one 'pollutant' at a time and plotting its five values on a sketch map of the area. As in Case Study 2, histogram columns can be drawn, the height of the column representing the value of the result.

The Framwellgate pupils plotted their results on overhead projector transparency film (OHT). Each group of pupils tried to work out an explanation for the pattern of results for one particular 'pollutant' and, if appropriate, to identify its source. A spokesman from the group then used their OHT to present their findings to the rest of the class.

Here are some questions that you might like to think about:

1. What results tell you that the water coming over the waterfall is polluted?

2. Which water is the most acidic and which the most alkaline? Explain how the water at site 1 still has a pH within the normal unpolluted range.

3. How can the water at site 1 be so rich in oxygen?

4. What type of dissolved particles will lead to stream water having a high electrical conductivity?

5. What is the link between the phosphate results and the detergent results?

6. How is the ammonium concentration at the waterfall so much less than that at site 2 or site 3?

7. What might have made the nitrite test go the wrong colour at site 3?

8. In the light of the ammonium results, what do you think the nitrite concentration *really* was at site 3, the 'toxic outflow'?

9. What causes ammonium– and nitrite–nitrogen to be present in the sewage effluent?

10. The Moors Burn flows through farmland and was choked with large green algae – a sign that there is probably too much nitrate in the water. What must be the source of the nitrate? Why do our results not reveal this pollution?

UNIT 18 Feeding the world

18.1 Introduction

One in ten of the world's population is facing starvation. We are all aware of the famine in Africa, for example, from the disturbing pictures seen on television. But is it simply a question of the world not having enough food to feed everyone? In Fig. 18.1 you can see that growth of the world's population has soared in the last century.

Fig. 18.1 Growth of world population

As population increases there is pressure to use land for purposes other than growing food. 'Cash crops' such as coffee, cotton, sugar cane and rubber can be sold for much higher prices than grain, but are often grown in the countries where grain is needed most. Overall, the world produces enough grain to provide each person with 1 kg per day. However, most of this grain is produced in countries which do not need it. They can afford to use the grain to feed their animals to produce meat; 1 kg of meat requires 5 kg of grain.

In the poorer countries of the world, most of the land is owned by a few individuals and multinational companies who can choose what they grow on it. Smaller farmers in poorer countries need to find ways of producing more food on their own land, much of which is infertile or has been farmed so intensively that climatic problems such as drought and flooding have far-reaching effects.

The solution to this problem is very complicated. There are many social, political and economic issues involved. Scientists have made great strides in finding better ways of farming, such as the development of fertilisers and pesticides, machinery, irrigation and other technology, and genetically improved strains of crops. The challenge is to find ways of making such improvements accessible to those farmers is countries facing food shortages. Some of the ways scientists can help are listed opposite.

ACTIVITY

Imagine you are producing a TV documentary on Food Aid. Discuss the arguments for and against sending food to famine-struck areas of the world, and examine some long-term solutions to the problem. Find out about one country in the world which you could use to illustrate your documentary.

While women and children queue for food rations in Tigray, Ethiopia, there are 'mountains' of surplus food in other parts of the world.

- The development and supply of new fertilisers would enable greater quantities of food to be grown on the same area of land. Currently 85% of the world's fertilisers are used in Western Europe and North America, because they are too expensive for poorer farmers. Cheaper methods of producing fertilisers need to be found.

- New disease-resistant strains of plants and animals need to be bred which are more suited to the geographic and climatic conditions of the countries where food production is a problem.

- Better and cheaper pesticides would mean that less food is destroyed as it grows.

- Storage conditions need improving. Much of the good grown cannot be used because it is eaten by rats.

- New kinds of food could be developed. For example, cattle double their weight in 2-4 months, plants take 1-2 weeks, but yeast and bacteria take just 20 seconds. A shallow lake of protein-rich bacteria the size of Essex could supply enough protein to feed the whole world. Although we might not want to eat this, it could be used for high-protein animal feeds.

- Reclamation of land not used for agriculture, such as deserts and estuaries, and an education programme for farmers on how to prevent land wastage would increase the use of available land.

In this unit we will consider chemicals used as fertilisers to improve plant growth.

ABOVE   Improving the quality of plants. A scientist is injecting leaves of a plant with growth regulators.

ABOVE RIGHT   Aerial spraying of fields with pesticides in the United States. What are the advantages and disadvantages of aerial spraying?

RIGHT   Desert land is not good for growing food but is all that some people have. How can desert land be made more fertile?

18.2   Elements needed for healthy plant growth

In order to grow healthy plants various elements are needed from the soil. Nitrogen, phosphorus and potassium are needed in large quantities. Other elements such as magnesium, calcium and sulphur are needed in smaller quantities. Some elements such as boron, iron and copper are needed in tiny amounts. They are called **trace elements.**

As the soil is used from year to year, it is possible that it could become short (or **deficient**) of one or more of these elements. Fertilisers are required to replace essential elements.

18.3   Fertilisers

Nitrogen   Nitrogen is required in large amounts by plants. It is absorbed through the roots in the form of nitrate solutions. These nitrates are required to build up plant proteins in the plant. Fig. 18.2 shows the circulation of nitrogen and nitrogen compounds in nature. It is called the **nitrogen cycle.**

NITROGEN	Early Feb	Early Mar	Late Mar	Total N
kg/ha units/ac	0	0	0	0

NITROGEN	Early Feb	Early Mar	Late Mar	Total N	
kg/ha	50	200	0	250	Amm. Nit.
units/ac	40	160		200	

TOP LEFT A tractor being loaded with fertiliser.

CENTRE The fertilisers drops onto a revolving wheel which throws it out evenly in all directions.

ABOVE LEFT Fertilisers and pesticides for use in gardens.

TOP RIGHT Oil seed rape grown without the use of nitrogen fertilisers.

ABOVE RIGHT The same crop grown with regular application of ammonium nitrate. Notice the difference in growth of the two samples. What stops all farmers throughout the world achieving these results?

NEWS BRIEF NEWS BRIEF NEWS BRIEF NEWS BRIEF

In countries like India, fossil fuels are too expensive to import in large quantities. The basic fuel for ordinary people is firewood which is now in short supply. Dried cow dung is being used as a fuel but then it cannot be used as a natural fertiliser.

The Indian Government is encouraging the building of bio-gas units which are cheap and simple to build. They make methane gas from cow dung by the action of bacteria on carbohydrates in the dung. The waste from the unit still acts as a nitrogen fertiliser when put on the land.

The nitrogen cycle Nitrogen in the air is trapped in the soil by three methods:

1. Lightning causes nitrogen and oxygen to react together to form nitrogen monoxide. Nitrogen monoxide eventually forms nitrates in the soil.
2. Bacteria in root nodules of certain plants (called leguminous plants, e.g. beans, peas, clover) are able to absorb nitrogen directly from the air.
3. Certain bacteria in the soil can take nitrogen directly from the air.

The absorbing of nitrogen from the air directly in soil is called **fixing**.

Nitrogen also enters the soil from the decay of plants and animals and from animal faeces and urine. Bacteria convert proteins into ammonia and then, via nitrites, into nitrates.

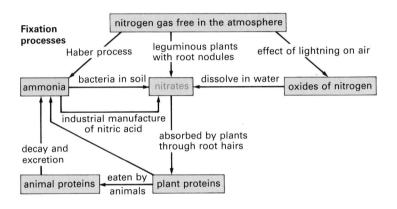

Fig. 18.2 The nitrogen cycle

Nitrogen fertilisers Because man interrupts the nitrogen cycle by picking crops and preventing crops from decaying, it is necessary to replace the nitrogen with fertilisers.

Nitrogen can be added to the soil using manure or dried blood. Where animals have been kept inside, their wastes can be spread onto fields. These natural forms of nitrogen can often improve the quality of the soil. There are natural deposits of nitrogen fertilisers such as sodium nitrate in desert areas of Chile.

Because there are not enough natural nitrogen compounds to add to soil, large amounts of artificial nitrogen fertilisers are used. These include ammonia, calcium nitrate, ammonium sulphate and urea.

Liquid ammonia is injected into the ground but this requires special equipment. It is more usual to use the nitrogen fertiliser in the form of solid pellets which can be distributed easily (see page 131).

If a fertiliser is very soluble in water it can be washed out of the soil easily. This can cause water pollution problems (Unit 16). A soluble fertiliser would, however, give a rapid result. Ammonium nitrate is such a a fertiliser. It is suitable for use on grassland in spring to give a rapid boost to grass before turning out cattle. Its effect is quick but relatively short-lived.

Urea is less soluble in cold water. It reacts slowly with cold water to form ammonia and can be used for a slow-acting fertiliser whose effects will be there for months.

Making nitrogen fertilisers is a very large-scale business. Ammonium nitrate, NH_4NO_3 is the most common nitrogen fertiliser used in Great Britain. Fig. 18.3 summarises the process used to make ammonium nitrate from ammonia and nitric acid.

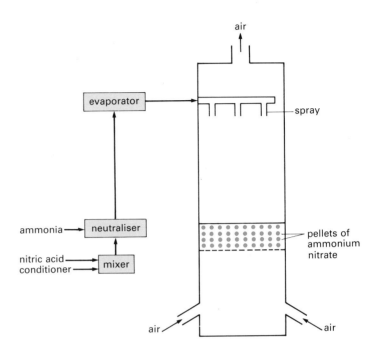

Fig. 18.3 Ammonium nitrate production

In the final stage, the solution of ammonium nitrate is evaporated. Solid ammonium nitrate is melted and sprayed down a tall tower. As the droplets fall they are met by a stream of cold upward-flowing air. The fertiliser solidifies and small, hard pellets called **prills** are formed. These are easy to store and spread on fields.

Phosphorus fertilisers

Plants needs phosphorus from the soil to produce a good root system. This is necessary before a healthy plant can grow.

Phosphorus can be put into the soil by slag from iron and steel making (Unit 9) or bone meal. Natural deposits of calcium phosphate, $Ca_3(PO_4)_2$, are not very suitable because they are insoluble. However, if calcium phosphate is treated with concentrated sulphuric acid, calcium superphosphate is formed. Calcium superphosphate contains soluble phosphates.

Potassium fertilisers

Plants need potassium for forming flowers and seeds. Potassium can be added to the soil using wood ash or chemicals such as potassium sulphate.

Mixed fertilisers

Ready-mixed fertilisers are sometimes called **NPK** fertilisers because they supply nitrogen, phosphorus and potassium.

When fertilisers are used they may change the pH of the soil. Ammonium sulphate, for example, makes the soil more acid. Also, soils tend to become more acidic as soluble alkalis are washed out of the soil. The pH of acidic soil can be corrected by using lime.

UNIT 19 Rates of reaction and reversible reactions

19.1 Rate of reaction

Reactions take place at very different speeds. An explosion is a very fast reaction which is over in the tiniest fraction of a second. For example, when a lighted splint is put into a mixture of hydrogen and oxygen, a squeaky pop is heard and the reaction is over.

The rusting of iron is a slower reaction. It is possible to change the speed at which this reaction takes place (Unit 14). Carbon dioxide, air pollution and salt will speed up rusting. Painting or galvanising will slow down rusting. We are going to look at changes we can make to speed up or slow down reactions in general.

19.2 Factors affecting rate of reaction

If a chemical reaction takes a long time then it is a slow reaction. If it is over very quickly it is a fast reaction.

There are various ways of speeding up a chemical reaction. These include:

1. *Increasing the surface area.* Small lumps have a much larger surface area than a single lump of equal mass. Large lumps react slower than powders. The differences can be quite dramatic. Mixtures of coal dust and air are explosive but coal and air do not spontaneously react.

2. *Increasing the concentration of reacting substances.* This increases the rate of reaction. Often doubling the concentration of one of the reacting substances will double the rate of reaction. In reactions involving gases, the concentration can be increased by increasing the pressure. This moves the particles closer together.

3. *Increasing the temperature.* The rate of reaction approximately doubles with a 10°C temperature rise.

4. *Using a catalyst.* A **catalyst** is a substance which alters the rate of reaction without being used up. A catalyst is usually used to speed up a reaction. Resins used to repair minor damage to car bodies are hardened by adding a catalyst. Catalysts which slow down reactions are called **negative catalysts** or **inhibitors.** Unstable chemicals such as hydrogen peroxide can be stabilised by adding an inhibitor.

19.3 Simple rate of reaction experiments

Experiment 1   *The effect of surface area on the rate of reaction between marble chips and dilute hydrochloric acid.*

calcium carbonate + hydrochloric acid → calcium chloride + water + carbon dioxide

Demolition of a tower block. An explosion is a very rapid chemical reaction.

In two separate experiments (a) and (b), equal masses of (a) marble chips and (b) powdered calcium carbonate are reacted with equal volumes of dilute hydrochloric acid (of the same concentration and at the same temperature). It is important to keep all of the possible variables the same except for the one you are considering – surface area in this case.

The apparatus used in Fig. 19.1 could be used to measure the volume of carbon dioxide gas produced at the end of each half-minute. Note that the reactants are put in a small test tube to prevent them coming into contact with the acid before the start of the experiment. At time 0, the apparatus should be shaken gently to knock the small test tube over.

The graph in Fig. 19.2 shows results of the experiments (a) and (b).

At the start of both experiments the volume reading on both syringes was 0 cm³. At the end of both experiments the volume of gas collected was 40 cm³. However, in experiment (a), with large lumps, the gas is produced more slowly. The graph in experiment (a) is less steep. In experiment (b),

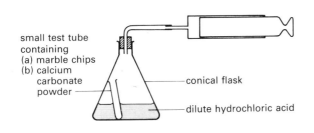

small test tube containing
(a) marble chips
(b) calcium carbonate powder

conical flask

dilute hydrochloric acid

Fig. 19.1

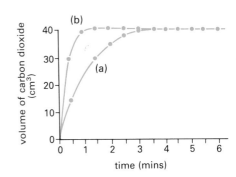

Fig. 19.2

with powder, the gas is produced quickly and the graph is steep. In both cases the graph is eventually flat and then the reactions have stopped.

An alternative way of doing the same experiment is shown in Fig. 19.3. This time the flask and contents are weighed at half-minute intervals. The mass decreases because the carbon dioxide gas escapes into the atmosphere. The loss of mass is the same as the mass of carbon dioxide produced. The piece of cotton wool in the neck of the flask is not to stop the carbon dioxide escaping but to prevent the escape of acid spray.

The graph obtained, if loss of mass of flask and contents is plotted against time, is the same shape as before.

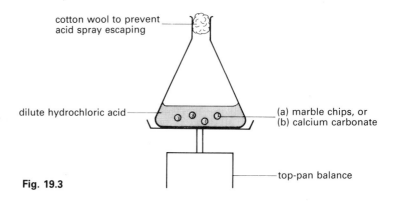

cotton wool to prevent acid spray escaping

dilute hydrochloric acid

(a) marble chips, or
(b) calcium carbonate

top-pan balance

Fig. 19.3

Experiment 2   *The effect of concentration on the rate of reaction between sodium thiosulphate solution and dilute hydrochloric acid.*

sodium thiosulphate + hydrochloric acid → sodium chloride + water + sulphur dioxide + sulphur

When colourless solutions of sodium thiosulphate and hydrochloric acid are mixed together, the solution obtained is initially colourless. After some time. The reaction is not complete but has reached a stage where fair comparisons can be made when the experiment is done again.

The experiment is repeated with solutions of sodium thiosulphate of different concentration. Everything else is kept the same. The time for the cross to disappear in each case is found.

If the results of these experiments are plotted on a graph, it will be seen that more concentrated solutions produce steeper curves. A steeper curve means a faster reaction.

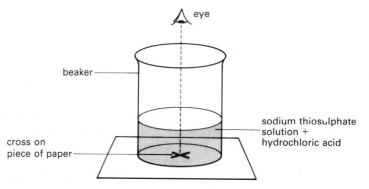

eye

beaker

sodium thiosulphate solution + hydrochloric acid

cross on piece of paper

Fig. 19.4

Experiment 3   *The effect of temperature on the rate of reaction.*

Experiment 2 can also be used to show the effect of temperature on the rate of reaction. This time the same experiment is carried out with the same volume of the same concentration sodium thiosulphate solution but at different temperatures. If the results are plotted on a graph, it will be seen that higher temperatures produce steeper curves (i.e. faster reactions).

Experiment 4   *The effect of a catalyst on the rate of reaction.*

hydrogen peroxide $\rightarrow$ water $+$ oxygen

Fig. 19.5 shows apparatus suitable for demonstrating the effect of a catalyst on the decomposition of hydrogen peroxide solution. The volume of gas collected was measured every half-minute.

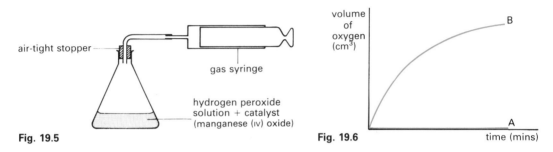

Fig. 19.5

Fig. 19.6

In the first experiment, 25 cm^3 of hydrogen peroxide was put into the flask with no catalyst. The results are labelled A in Fig. 19.6. This experiment is a **control**. Notice that no gas was produced during the experiment. (The gas would have been produced if it had been left longer).

The experiment was repeated with one spatula measure of manganese(IV) oxide added. This is labelled B in Fig. 19.6. This time the reaction is much faster.

If at the end of the experiment the manganese(IV) oxide was removed by filtering, then washed and dried, the mass remaining should be the same as the original mass.

19.4 Industrial applications of rate of reaction

The rate of souring of milk or spoiling of food is reduced by cooling. A refrigerator or deep freeze cools the food and the chemical reactions which lead to spoiling are drastically slowed down.

Many industrial processes (e.g. the Haber process and the Contact process) use a catalyst to speed up reactions. In both cases, increasing temperature is not possible as it reduces the yield. Using a catalyst is a way of speeding up reactions without altering temperature.

Inhibitors are widely used to slow down reactions. Inhibitors are added to rubber during manufacture to prevent it from cracking.

In some modern coal-fired industrial boilers powdered coal, which has a larger surface area than lumps of coal, is blown into the boiler. It burns faster than solid lumps of coal.

Flour dust, because of its very large surface area, can explode when mixed with air. Good ventilation is needed to ensure there is no build-up of flour dust.

Catalysts are used in industry to speed up chemical reactions. These complex catalysts are used to polymerise alkenes to produce a wide range of plastics.

19.5 Reversible reactions

Some reactions can be made to occur in the reverse direction, that is, products can be changed back into the reactants. Reactions which do this are called **reversible reactions.**

An example is heating blue copper(II) sulphate crystals to produce white anhydrous copper(II) sulphate and water. If water is added to anhydrous copper(II) sulphate, blue copper(II) sulphate is formed. This can be summarised as follows:

heat + copper(II) sulphate crystals ⇌ anhydrous copper(II) sulphate + water

The sign ⇌ is used to show a reversible reaction. If a reaction is reversible, it is usually impossible to turn all of the reactants into the products.

19.6 Explaining changes in rate

In Unit 3 it was explained that matter is made of tiny particles. The particles in solids, liquids and gases are in a state of continuous motion. Reaction takes place when particles of reacting substances collide.

Consider a reaction between two gases. We can increase the number of collisions between particles, and hence the rate of reaction, by:

1. increasing the temperature. This speeds up the particles and results in more collisions;

2. increasing the concentration or increasing the pressure. These both make the particles move closer together and again produce more collisions.

QUESTIONS ON UNIT 19

Domain I: Knowledge and understanding

1. List five ways of speeding up a chemical reaction.

2. Write word equations for three reversible reactions.

3. What difficulty is caused when the chemical reaction used in industry to make a chemical is reversible?

Domain II: Handling information and solving problems

4. An experiment was carried out to find which of two metal oxides (A or B) was the better catalyst for the decomposition of an aqueous solution of hydrogen peroxide, H_2O_2.

   10 cm^3 of hydrogen peroxide was measured into a conical flask and 40 cm^3 of distilled water added. After 5 minutes no oxygen gas had been produced. 0.5 g of metal oxide A was added to the hydrogen peroxide solution in the flask. The volume of oxygen, O_2, produced was measured at intervals and the results are shown in the table below:

Time in minutes	0	1	2	4	6	8	10	12	14
Volume of gas (cm^3)	0	21	32	45	52	57	59	60	60

   (a) Draw a labelled diagram of apparatus suitable for carrying out this experiment.

   (b) What piece of apparatus would be suitable for measuring out 40 cm^3 of water?

   (c) Write a balanced equation for the decomposition of hydrogen peroxide, H_2O_2.

   (d) Plot a graph of the volume of gas collected against time.

   (e) The experiment was repeated with oxide B. Explain clearly what should be done to complete the experiment. How could you make sure that the results would give a fair comparison with those using oxide A?

   (f) How would your graph help you to decide which metal oxide is the better catalyst?

   (g) i) What was the maximum volume of oxygen obtained in the experiment?

   ii) The concentration of a hydrogen peroxide solution is sometimes given in terms of its **volume strength**. A 10 volume solution produces 10 cm^3 of oxygen when 1 cm^3 of the solution is decomposed. What is the volume strength of the original hydrogen peroxide in this experiment?

   (h) Suggest reasons why:
   i) an inhibitor is added to hydrogen peroxide after manufacture;
   ii) hydrogen peroxide solution should be stored in a dark glass bottle;
   iii) hydrogen peroxide should NOT be stored in a glass bottle with a tight-fitting screw cap.

   (LEAG Joint Chemistry Syll.B. 1987 Paper 3)

5. Strips of magnesium ribbon of the same width but different lengths were cut. Each strip was added to excess dilute hydrochloric acid at 20°C and the mixture was shaken. The rate at which hydrogen was given off was measured. The graph shown below was plotted.

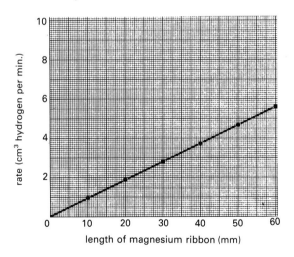

   (a) What conclusion about the rate of reaction can you draw from the graph?

   (b) On the same axes, draw a graph to show the results you would expect to obtain from an identical experiment at 50°C. Label this graph X.

   (c) On the same axes, draw a graph to show the results you would expect to obtain with all the conditions the same as in (b) except a wider magnesium ribbon was used. Label this graph Y.

6. Nine experiments were carried out to find the rates of reaction between magnesium and hydrochloric acid.

In each experiment the acid was placed in a flask and its temperature taken. A weighed amount of magnesium was added. The mixture was stirred and the time taken for the magnesium to disappear. The results are shown in the table below:

(a) Which of the results could be used to plot a graph of concentration of acid against time?

(b) Choose the fastest reaction from A, F, H or J and suggest a reason why it would be the fastest of the four.

(c) How does the rate of reaction in B compare with that in A and C? Suggest a reason for the difference.

Experiment	Concentration of acid (moles per dm^3)	Volume of of acid (cm^3)	Temperature (°C) Before	Temperature (°C) After	Mass of magnesium (g)	Form of magnesium	Time (secs)
A	0.5	40	21	31	0.1	ribbon	500
B	0.6	40	21	32	0.1	powder	50
C	0.7	40	21	32	0.1	ribbon	250
D	0.8	40	21	33	0.1	ribbon	160
E	0.9	40	21	39	0.2	ribbon	230
F	1.0	40	21	33	0.1	ribbon	100
G	1.0	40	35	44	0.1	ribbon	50
H	1.1	40	21	33	0.1	ribbon	75
J	1.5	40	21	31	0.1	ribbon	30

A research scientist using an electron microscope to examine a paint film, whilst x-ray analysis provides the chemical composition of the paint sample.

UNIT 20 Electrolysis

20.1 Conductors and insulators

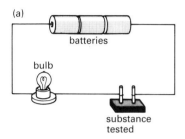

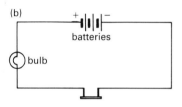

Fig. 20.1 Apparatus for testing conductivity

Substances which allow electricity to pass through them are called **conductors**. Common conductors include all metals and carbon in the form of graphite. Substances which do not allow electricity to pass through them are called **non-conductors** or **insulators**. There are a few substances which conduct electricity only very slightly under certain conditions. These substances include silicon and are called **semi-conductors**. They are used in transistors.

When electricity flows through a conductor, electrons move to carry the current. These electrons are said to be **mobile**. When electricity passes through a conductor it does not usually bring about any chemical change.

Fig. 20.1 shows apparatus that can be used to show whether a solid is a conductor or an insulator. In (a) the circuit is shown as we would see it. We need a supply of electricity (a battery or a transformer), a bulb (to show when electricity is passing through the circuit) and some wires. It is more usual to draw a circuit diagram as in (b).

If the solid tested is a conductor, a current will flow through the wires and the bulb will light up. If the solid is an insulator the bulb will not light up.

20.2 Electrolytes and non-electrolytes

Solid sodium chloride is made up of ions closely packed and held tightly in a lattice (Unit 7). Solid sodium chloride does not conduct electricity. The ions are not free to move and there are no free electrons.

The sodium chloride lattice can be broken down by either:
1. melting the sodium chloride; or
2. dissolving the sodium chloride in water and forming a sodium chloride solution.

Both molten sodium chloride and sodium chloride solution conduct electricity. When electricity is conducted through an electrolyte a chemical change takes place and the electrolyte is split up. This splitting up of an electrolyte is called **electrolysis.** Electrolysis is an extremely important industrial process.

Substances which conduct electricity when molten or in solution but not when solid are called electrolytes. Electrolytes include:

metal oxides
metal hydroxides
metal salts
acids

Substances which do not conduct electricity under any circumstances are called **non-electrolytes**.

20.3   Electrolysis of molten lead(ɪɪ) bromide

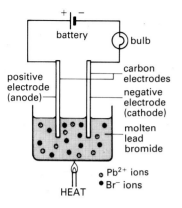

Fig. 20.2 Electrolysis of lead (ɪɪ) bromide

Lead(ɪɪ) bromide, $PbBr_2$ is an electrolyte. It is frequently used to demonstrate electrolysis of molten electrolytes. This is probably because most electrolytes have very high melting points and are therefore difficult to melt. Lead(ɪɪ) bromide melts at 370°C which is less than other electrolytes.

The apparatus in Fig. 20.2 is used. Rods of conducting material called **electrodes** are used to make contact between the circuit and the molten lead(ɪɪ) bromide. The electrodes are usually made of graphite and they must be good conductors.

The electrode which is attached to the wire from the positive terminal of the battery or transformer is called the positive electrode or **anode**. The electrode which is attached to the wire from the negative terminal is called the negative electrode or **cathode**. The electrodes dip into the lead(ɪɪ) bromide but they must not touch.

The bulb does not light while the lead(ɪɪ) bromide is solid. When the lead(ɪɪ) bromide has melted the bulb starts to glow and remains alight while the lead(ɪɪ) bromide remains molten.

During this stage of the experiment the lead(ɪɪ) bromide is being split up into lead and bromine. Electrolysis is taking place.

Lead is formed at the cathode and bromine is formed at the anode.

The electrolysis can be summarised by:

$$\text{lead(ɪɪ) bromide} \rightarrow \text{lead} + \text{bromine}$$

Lead(ɪɪ) bromide is composed of a regular arrangement of Pb^{2+} and Br^- ions. On melting, the lattice breaks down and the ions are now free to move.

The positive ions (Pb^{2+}) are called **cations** and are attracted towards the negative electrode (cathode).

The negative ions (Br^-) are called **anions** and are attracted towards the positive electrode (anode).

The electricity is carried through the molten lead(ɪɪ) bromide by the movement of charged ions. The changes which take place at the electrodes involve **discharging** of ions.

At the cathode the positive ions are discharged. A Pb^{2+} ion has two electrons less than a lead atom. The cathode is negatively charged because it has a surplus of electrons. The change which takes place when the lead ions are discharged is:

$$Pb^{2+}(l) + 2\,e^- \text{ (from the cathode)} \rightarrow Pb(l)$$

At the anode the negative ions are discharged. A Br^- ion has one more electron than a bromine atom. The anode is positively charged because it has a shortage of electrons. The change which takes place when the bromide ions are discharged is:

$$2Br^-(l) \rightarrow Br_2(g) + 2\,e^- \text{ (to the anode)}$$

The electrons flow through the wire from anode to cathode and this makes the electric current.

Usually, a metal is formed at the cathode and a non-metal is formed at the anode during the electrolysis of any molten (or fused) compound.

Electrical cable. Within the white plastic covering are three metal wires (conductors) each in plastic casings (insulators). The plastic prevents electric current passing from the wires to the outside of the cable.

20.4 Electrolysis of aqueous solutions

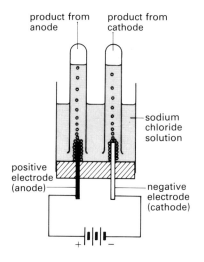

product from anode   product from cathode

sodium chloride solution

positive electrode (anode)

negative electrode (cathode)

Fig. 20.3 Electrolysis of sodium chloride

Electrolysis of aqueous solutions can produce different products from the electrolysis of molten substances.

If we consider an aqueous solution of sodium chloride, there are four ions in the solution:

Ions from water: H^+ and OH^-
Ions from sodium chloride: Na^+ and Cl^-

(Any aqueous solution will contain H^+ and OH^- ions from the splitting up of a few water molecules).

The apparatus in Fig. 20.3 can be used for the electrolysis of a concentrated solution of sodium chloride. The gaseous products of discharging ions at the anode and cathode are collected in the two test tubes.

In the test tube above the cathode, hydrogen gas is collected. This is formed when hydrogen ions (H^+) are discharged at the cathode. The sodium ions are not discharged.

In the test tube above the anode, chlorine gas is collected. This is formed when chloride ions (Cl^-) are discharged at the anode.

It is usual when carrying out the electrolysis of aqueous solutions to find that only one of the positive and one of the negative ions are discharged. The following general rules may be useful when considering electrolysis of aqueous solutions:

1. Hydrogen is frequently produced in electrolysis and always at the cathode.
2. Reactive metals such as sodium and potassium are never produced during electrolysis.
3. Unreactive metals such as copper may be produced. If so, they are produced at the cathode.
4. Non-metals, apart from hydrogen, are produced at the anode. Common products at the anode include oxygen and chlorine.

BELOW LEFT Electrolysis of dilute sulphuric acid using a Hoffman voltameter with platinum electrodes. The products are hydrogen and oxygen. What do you notice about the volumes of the two gases Tekehn has collected?

BELOW RIGHT Small scale electrolysis of copper(II) sulphate solution using carbon electrodes.

FAR RIGHT The body of a car coming out of an electroplating bath (see page 144).

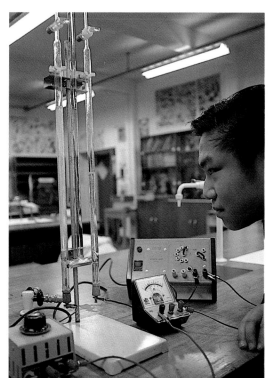

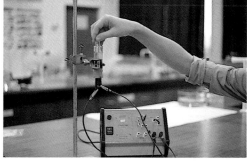

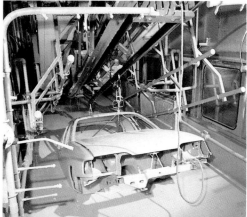

20.5   Coating a metal object with copper

The apparatus in Fig. 20.4 can be used to coat a metal object with a thin layer of copper. The metal object is made the cathode and a piece of copper is made the anode. The electrolyte is an aqueous solution of copper(II) sulphate.

The solution contains H^+, OH^-, Cu^{2+} and SO_4^{2+} ions. The copper anode dissolves during the electrolysis.

At the cathode, copper is deposited from the discharge of copper ions. This copper forms the copper coating on the metal object.

This is the basis of the process of electroplating.

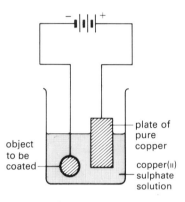

object to be coated

plate of pure copper

copper(II) sulphate solution

Fig. 20.4   Copper-coating an object

20.6   Applications of electrolysis

There are many examples of electroplating where a metal is coated with a thin layer of another metal. These include:

1. Silver-plating cutlery, trays, etc. to give a good decorative finish.

2. Chromium-plating handlebars, etc. Again, we get a good finish but electroplating also prevents corrosion. A steel object is first nickel-plated to prevent corrosion and then chromium-plated to improve the appearance. The metal coating is extremely thin but even over the whole surface.

3. Electroplating the bodywork of cars.

Electrolysis can also be used to extract reactive metals from their ores (Unit 9). It is used in the recovery and purification of tin from scrap tin cans. It can also be used to produce a whole range of important chemicals. Electrolysis of sodium chloride solution (Unit 26) industrially can produce sodium hydroxide, hydrogen, chlorine and household bleaches.

NEWS BRIEF NEWS BRIEF

A plastic devised at the University of St Andrews in Scotland can conduct electricity. The plastic looks black and shiny like a metal. It is made up of long chains of carbon atoms. Because of the way the atoms are bonded together, electrons can scuttle from one end of the chain to the other in the presence of certain additives.

QUESTIONS ON UNIT 20

Domain I: Knowledge and understanding

1. lead, sodium, chloride, sulphur, copper, plastic, carbon, wood, magnesium, copper(II) chloride, calcium oxide, sodium hydroxide.

   From the above list select:

   (a) three substances which do not conduct electricity under any conditions;
   (b) four substances which conduct electricity when solid;
   (c) one non-metal which conducts electricity;
   (d) four substances which are electrolytes;
   (e) two substances which produce chlorine during electroylsis.

2. The apparatus below is suitable for the electrolysis of dilute sulphuric acid. The products of the electrolysis are collected in the small test tubes.

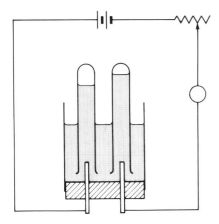

   (a) Label the battery, the variable resistance, the ammeter, the anode, the cathode, the electrolyte.
   (b) What is the reason for using:
     i) the variable resistance?
     ii) the ammeter?
   (c) Describe clearly what you would see during the experiment.
   (d) List methods which could be used to speed up the electrolysis.

3. Complete the following table showing the products of electrolysis of some aqueous solutions using inert electrodes.

Solution	Product at anode (positive electrode)	Product at cathode (negative electrode)
copper(II) sulphate	oxygen	copper
sodium sulphate		
sodium chloride	chlorine	
hydrochloric acid		
sulphuric acid		hydrogen

Domain II: Handling information and solving problems

4. You are asked to set up an experiment to coat a brass key with nickel by electrolysis.

   (a) Draw a diagram of the apparatus you would use.
   (b) Outline the steps you would carry out in order to nickel plate the key.
   (c) The nickel coating does not stick well to the key but flakes off. Can you suggest how this could be avoided?

5. Electrolysis of molten sodium hydride, NaH, produces hydrogen at the anode and sodium at the cathode. How can you explain these results?

NEWS BRIEF NEWS BRIEF NEWS BRIEF NEWS

Superconductors are being developed which conduct electricity much better than ordinary conductors (i.e. with zero resistance). However, these superconductors operate only at very low temperatures. Research is going on rapidly to find super-conductors which will work closer to room temperature. New chips containing a film of the metal thallium can be used ás superconductors at temperatures of −176°C.

UNIT 21 Carbon and fuels

21.1 Different forms of carbon

Carbon is a most important element and without it life would be impossible. There are two pure crystalline forms of carbon, called diamond and graphite.

The existence of these two forms of the same element in the same physical state is called **allotropy**. The different forms, diamond and graphite, are called **allotropes**.

Table 21.1 compares the properties of diamond and graphite.

Table 21.1 Comparison of diamond and graphite

	Diamond	Graphite
Appearance	Transparent crystals, can be colourless or coloured	Black shiny solid, slippery to the touch
Hardness	Very hard indeed	Very soft
Density in g per cm³	3.5	2.2
Volume of 12 g of carbon cm³	3.4	5.4
Electrical conductivity	Non-conductor	Conductor of electricity, electrons can move through the structure
Burning in oxygen	Burns with difficulty when heated to a high temperature. Carbon dioxide produced and no residue	Burns readily to produce carbon dioxide. No residue
	Equal masses of diamond and graphite on complete combustion produce equal masses (and volumes) of carbon dioxide	

Samples of diamond, graphite and charcoal. Each is made of carbon.

diamond structure

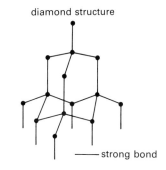

——— strong bond

graphite structure

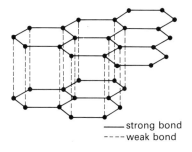

——— strong bond
---- weak bond

Fig. 21.1 The two allotropes of carbon

The properties of the two allotropes of carbon can be understood by comparing the arrangement of carbon atoms. Fig. 21.1 shows the arrangement of carbon atoms in diamond and graphite.

In diamond all of the carbon atoms are strongly bound together. All bonds are covalent bonds. The resulting three-dimensional giant structure is extremely strong. Melting or cutting diamond would be extremely difficult because the strong bonds would have to be broken.

In graphite the carbon atoms form giant molecules in flat layers. The bonds within each layer are strong and covalent. They are very difficult to break. However, the forces between the layers themselves are very weak and it is easy for layers to slide over one another.

Coal, charcoal and soot are impure forms of carbon. Carbon occurs naturally in a large number of compounds – petroleum, natural gas and carbonate rocks, e.g. calcium carbonate and magnesium carbonate. Carbon is also the essential element in all living organisms.

Carbon burns in excess air or oxygen to form carbon dioxide. In a limited supply of air or oxygen, it burns to produce carbon monoxide:

$$\text{carbon} + \text{oxygen} \rightarrow \text{carbon dioxide}$$

$$\text{carbon} + \text{oxygen} \rightarrow \text{carbon monoxide}$$

Carbon is a good reducing agent. If a mixture of lead(II) oxide and carbon is heated, little beads of metallic lead are formed:

$$\text{lead(II) oxide} + \text{carbon} \rightarrow \text{lead} + \text{carbon monoxide}$$

Other metals low in the reactivity series can be obtained similarly by reduction with carbon.

21.2 Fossil fuels

BELOW LEFT   Coal being mined deep underground. Some coal is mined in open cast mines. What are the advantages and disadvantages of the open-cast and underground mining?

BELOW RIGHT   A tabular iceberg. A vast area of the Earth's surface is covered in ice. What will happen if there is a rise in global temperature, as predicted?

Coal, petroleum and natural gas are all **fossil fuels.** Coal was produced by the action of heat and pressure on trees and plants over millions of years. Petroleum and natural gas were produced by the action of heat and pressure on tiny sea creatures over millions of years. Because the coal, petroleum and natural gas took millions of years to be produced, and we are using them up at a rapid rate, we will run out of them at some time in the future. In the case of petroleum, we have perhaps less than fifty years at the present rate of use. It is important to use these fuels carefully and to consider alternative sources of energy for use in the future (see Case Study 8).

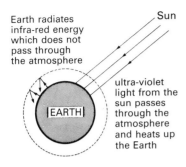

Earth radiates infra-red energy which does not pass through the atmosphere

Sun

ultra-violet light from the sun passes through the atmosphere and heats up the Earth

EARTH

Fig. 21.2   The 'greenhouse' effect

When fossil fuels burn in excess air or oxygen they produce carbon dioxide. There has been concern about the burning of fuels producing more carbon dioxide and the 'greenhouse effect', as shown in Fig. 21.2. (See also Case Study 5, page 98.) Solar energy from the sun passes through the carbon dioxide in the Earth's atmosphere. The heated Earth gives out radiation which is of shorter wavelength and does not pass through the carbon dioxide in the atmosphere. The result is that the temperature of the Earth rises. the changing climate has far-reaching environmental effects.

When fossil fuels burn in a limited supply of air or oxygen, the poisonous gas carbon monoxide is produced. This is why it is necessary to have adequate ventilation in a room with a coal fire or a gas fire.

21.3   Alternatives to fossil fuels

In Brazil tremendous efforts have been made to produce ethanol from sugar on a large scale. We usually prepare ethanol for industry from petroleum. The advantage of using sugar as the starting material is that it can be replaced easily. Every year fresh sugar cane grows trapping solar energy and converting it into chemical energy. Brazil was encouraged into this programme because the world price of sugar was low. Many cars in Brazil run on ethanol or ethanol-enriched fuel. This produces much less pollution than fuel derived from petroleum.

Nuclear power is seen as an alternative source of electrical energy for the future. However, accidents such as Chernobyl may encourage people away from building further nuclear power stations. There are vast amounts of radioactive material such as uranium but disposal of radioactive waste is a problem.

Hydroelectric power is now a significant source of energy in places such as the Highlands of Scotland and North Wales. Wind power and wave power are possible sources of electricity but research is still needed to make them economic propositions.

Solar power is another possibility – solar energy converted into electrical energy. You may have seen solar-powered calculators or even solar-powered cars.

NEWS BRIEF NEWS BRIEF

The first step in reversing the 'greenhouse' effect is to reduce the amount of fossil fuel used. Two additional ideas have been put forward.

White-washing the rooves of all the buildings in the world and floating white polystyrene chips on the oceans would reflect more of the Sun's rays back into space.

The development of vast slicks of CO_2-absorbing algae in the oceans and a programme of forest replantation would reduce carbon dioxide in the atmosphere.

'The atoms have destroyed us' – this West German market stall-holder is protesting about the contamination of vegetables by nuclear fall-out from the disaster at the Chernobyl nuclear plant in 1986.

DIE ATOME HABEN UNS KAPUTT GEMACHT

21.4 The carbon cycle

Photosynthesis produces oxygen to replace the oxygen used up by respiration (Unit 12).

Fig. 21.3, the carbon cycle, shows how carbon compounds are related.

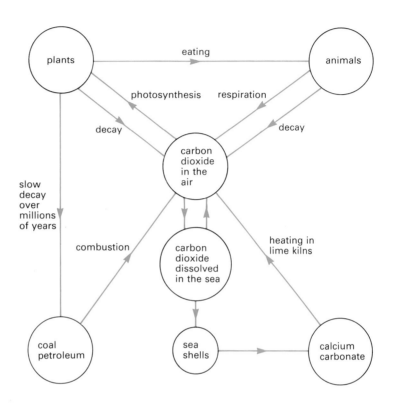

Fig. 21.3 The carbon cycle

21.5 Fractional distillation of petroleum

Petroleum is useless in the form in which it comes out of the ground. In fact, in Texas they used to burn it when it escaped onto the surface of the earth to get rid of it!

Petroleum comes from a number of countries. Important sources are the Middle East, Alaska, Texas, Nigeria and, of course, the North Sea. The petroleum from the North Sea is of extremely high quality and is usually sold to buy lower quality petroleum from the Middle East. This is more suited to our refineries.

In a refinery, fractional distillation of petroleum separates petroleum into different fractions or parts. Each fraction consists of compounds boiling within a certain temperature range. These fractions are not pure compounds. Each fraction has a different use.

Fig. 21.4 (page 152) shows a fractional distillation column. Petroleum vapour enters at the bottom. As the vapour rises up the column the different fractions condense. The lower the boiling point the higher up the column the fraction reaches before it condenses. You will see that the

SITING A COAL-FIRED POWER STATION

About twenty years ago it was proposed that a new power station be built at Radcliffe near Nottingham using coal from the nearby Nottinghamshire coal-field.

The working of a coal-fired power station is summarised in the diagram below. The plan caused considerable opposition but was finally approved and the power station is now built and operating successfully (see facing page).

The map opposite shows the area around the proposed power station.

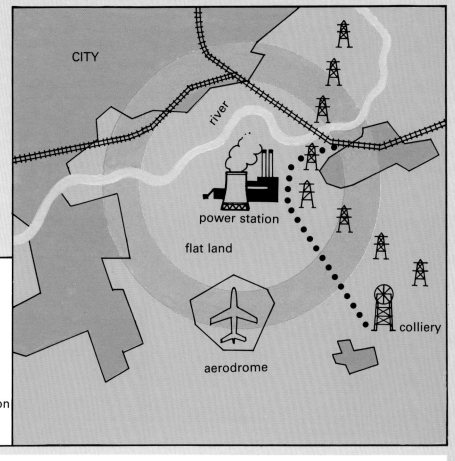

Key

- built-up area
- transmission lines
- railways
- • • • railways being built
- zone of greatest pollution from 200 m chimney

0   1 km

CITY

river

power station

flat land

aerodrome

colliery

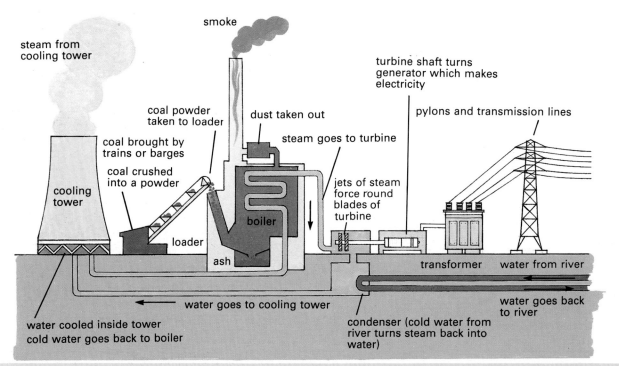

steam from cooling tower

smoke

coal powder taken to loader

dust taken out

turbine shaft turns generator which makes electricity

coal brought by trains or barges

steam goes to turbine

pylons and transmission lines

coal crushed into a powder

cooling tower

jets of steam force round blades of turbine

boiler

loader

ash

transformer

water from river

water goes to cooling tower

water cooled inside tower cold water goes back to boiler

condenser (cold water from river turns steam back into water)

water goes back to river

Radcliffe power station.

ACTIVITIES ▼

1. Above is a photograph of the Radcliffe power station. Draw a sketch of the power station and add one of the following labels for each of the dots:

   river for cooling water   coal store
   chimney   main building with
   cooling tower   boilers and
   electricity pylons   generators
   railway

2. Imagine you are an employee of the Central Electricity Generating Board. Write a report which summarises completely the reasons for choosing this particular site.

3. Imagine you are the Secretary of the Radcliffe Residents' Committee and you have been asked to write a letter to the CEGB explaining why this is not a suitable site for a coal-fired power station.

4. Alternatively, you could divide into pairs. One person writes a report in support of the power station and one against it. You then discuss the two reports and come to an agreement and write one report summarising the advantages and the disadvantages.

5. There has been considerable discussion about acid rain caused by sulphur dioxide and oxides of nitrogen from coal-fired power stations. The emissions can be reduced by fitting a flue gas desulphurisation plant. Fitting this equipment could cost £160 million pounds per power station and the running costs would be £35 million per year. Briefly summarise the advantages and disadvantages of the building of a desulphurisation plant into a new power station.

NEWS BRIEF NEWS BRIEF NEWS BRIEF

Pollutant gases from coal-fired power stations are being treated with ammonia in an effort to reduce acid rain.

The new method involves the neutralising of sulphur dioxide in flue gases with ammonia, to form ammonium sulphate, followed by the oxidation of nitrogen monoxide by ozone, to form nitrogen dioxide. The flue gases are then further treated with ammonia, and ammonium nitrate is formed.

The high costs of this process are off-set by the value of ammonium sulphate and ammonium nitrate as fertilisers.

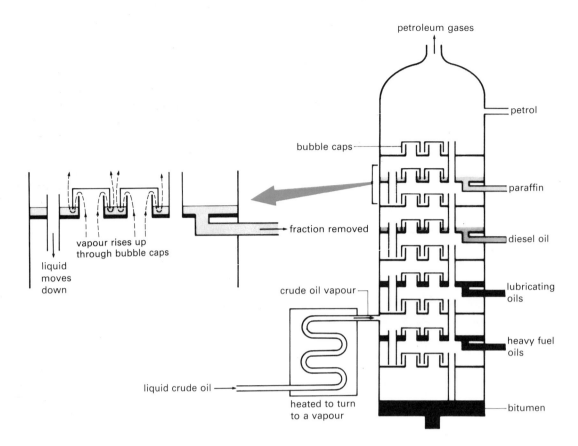

Fig. 21.4   Fractional distillation of petroleum

Fig. 21.5   Oil refineries in the United Kingdom

NEWS BRIEF NEWS BRIEF

An explosion on the
Piper Alpha oil rig in
the North Sea in July
1988 killed 166 people
and cut Britain's oil and
gas production by 12%.
This accident highlights
the dangers associated
with obtaining oil and
gas.

different fractions from the column include petrol, kerosene, diesel oil, fuel oil, lubricating oil and bitumen. Gases which pass through the column can be used for heating the petroleum or sold as 'liquified petroleum gases, LPG'.

All of the products of a refinery are used. Ones not used as fuels are used as starting materials for chemical factories (Unit 24). An oil refinery is usually built near the coast because the oil is imported. Fig. 21.5 shows where oil refineries are sited in the UK. A site on a deep estuary is best so that large tankers can dock. The site should be on land away from housing because of the risk of explosion and fire with flammable materials. A large site is necessary and land away from built-up areas is cheaper. Workers must live fairly near and a good communication network (road, rail, sea) is essential.

Exothermic and endothermic reactions

In many chemical reactions there is an energy change. For example, when dilute hydrochloric acid and sodium hydroxide solutions are mixed, the temperature of the solution rises. We would perhaps notice these small temperature changes if we stirred the solutions with a thermometer rather than a glass rod. A reaction where energy is given out is called an **exothermic reaction**. The diagram below shows the energy change during such a reaction. The amount of energy given out is called $\triangle H$.

When sodium carbonate solution and calcium nitrate solution are mixed a precipitate of calcium carbonate is formed:

sodium carbonate + calcium nitrate → calcium carbonate + sodium nitrate

This time there is small drop in temperature when mixing takes place. This is called an **endothermic reaction** and can be represented by the energy level diagram below:

There are many examples of exothermic reactions. For example, the combustion of fuels are exothermic reactions. There are few endothermic reactions – so few, in fact, it led chemists at one time to state that only exothermic reactions could take place!

NEWS BRIEF NEWS BRIEF NEWS BRIEF NEWS BRIEF NEWS

Canada is planning to build a 1000 megawatt tidal power station at the Bay of Fundy, Nova Scotia.
 Building such a plant, however, causes environmental problems. Sea levels would change and migrating fish could die.

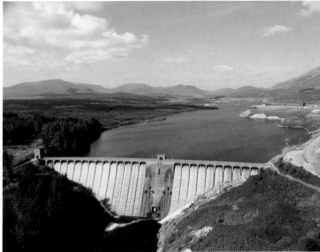

TOP LEFT   Sellafield nuclear plant in Cumbria. On the left are the cooling towers of the Calder Hall nuclear reactors. The two cube-shaped buildings at the right of the cooling towers house the original Windscale reactors which were closed after a major fire in 1957. The metallic dome houses a prototype advanced gas-cooled reactor (now disused). The nuclear fuel reprocessing plant is to the right of this.

TOP RIGHT   Fort William hydroelectric power station, Scotland. The fall of water from the lake behind through a generator produces electricity.

LEFT   A production platform in the North Sea. Drilling, oil and gas production, metering, storage and pumping take place on this platform. What advantages and disadvantages are associated with obtaining oil from under the sea bed?

ABOVE   The Pernis oil refinery near Rotterdam in the Netherlands. On the same site is a leading producer of chemicals made from petroleum. What makes Rotterdam a suitable site for oil refining and associated industries?

QUESTIONS ON UNIT 21

1. isotopes, allotropes, isomers, slide, regular, irregular, random, carbon, covalent, ionic, electrons, ions, atoms, layer

   Use the words above to fill in the spaces below:

   Both diamond and graphite are forms of the element . . . . Different forms of the same element are called . . . .

   Diamond and graphite are made up from a . . . . arrangement of . . . . atoms.

   In the case of diamond the atoms are held together by strong . . . . bonds in a three-dimensional arrangement. It is very difficult to break these bonds and the diamond is therefore very hard.

   Graphite is a . . . . structure. The atoms in each layer are held together by strong . . . . bonds. The forces between the layers, however, are weak and the layers are able to . . . . over one another. Graphite conducts electricity because it contains free . . . .

2. peat, paraffin, petrol, ethanol, coal, coke, methane, LPG (liquefied petroleum gas)

   (a) From the list above, name:
      i) three solid fuels
      ii) four liquid fuels
      iii) a gaseous fuel.

   (b) Which fuel in the above list is not a fossil fuel?

   (c) What are the products of burning methane gas in:
      i) a plentiful supply of air or oxygen?
      ii) a limited supply of oxygen?

3. Petroleum is a complex mixture of hydrocarbons. Refining petroleum produces a number of useful fractions. Each fraction (labelled W, X, Y and Z on the diagram below) is made up from hydrocarbons boiling within a certain range of temperature.

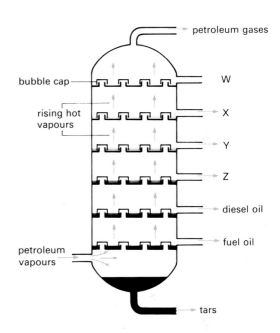

(a) Why do the fractions come out of the column at different levels?

(b) Which of the fractions W, X, Y or Z:
   i) boils at the lowest temperature?
   ii) is composed of the largest molecules?
   iii) is the most flammable?

(c) What are the petroleum gases used for?

(d) Give two reasons why oil refineries are often built on the coast and away from houses.

(e) What are motorists asked NOT to do when they put petrol in cars?

Domain II: Handling information and solving problems

4. Part of the carbon cycle is shown on the right. Use this diagram to help you answer the following questions:

   (a) What two processes in the diagram are energy-producing processes?
   (b) Name the substance which reacts with carbon dioxide during photosynthesis to produce carbohydrates.
   (c) What type of energy is used in photosynthesis?

   (d) Why are fossil fuels being used up in the earth so quickly? Are there any side-effects produced by the rapid use of fossil fuels?
   (e) What are the problems caused by the destruction of rain-forests in South America?

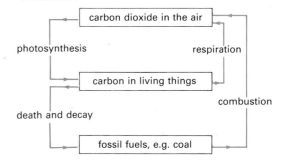

5. The graph below shows the percentage of petroleum which boils off at different temperatures.

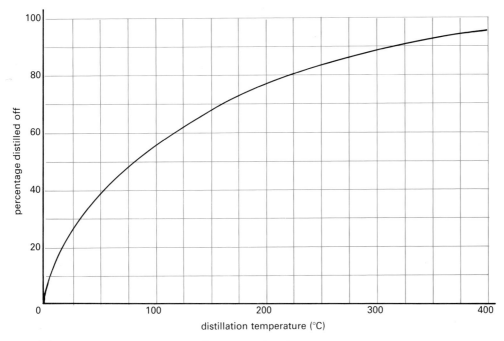

   (a) Use this graph to complete the table:

Boiling point in °C	below 70	70–120	120–170	170–220	220–270	270–320	above 320
Percentage of petroleum which boils off							

   (b) Draw a pie diagram to represent these results.
   (c) For this petroleum sample, which temperature range produces the most product?

   (d) Petroleum from the North Sea contains a larger proportion of lower boiling point hydrocarbons. Why does it sell at a higher price than petroleum from the Middle East?

UNIT 22 Hydrocarbons

22.1 Introduction

Hydrocarbons are compounds of carbon and hydrogen only. A compound of carbon and hydrogen containing another element, perhaps oxygen or nitrogen, cannot be a hydrocarbon.

There are different families of hydrocarbons. A family of compounds with the same general formula and similar properties is called an **homologous series.** One important homologous series is the **alkanes.**

22.2 Alkanes

Alkanes are hydrocarbons with a general formula C_nH_{2n+2}. The simplest members of the alkanes are given in Table 22.1, on page 160, along with their formulae, structure and melting and boiling points. Other members of the alkane family include butane and octane.

Alkanes:

1. all have names ending in –ane;
2. all fit the general formula C_nH_{2n+2} (e.g. when n = 2, the formula is C_2H_6);
3. all have covalent bonds linking the atoms together and all of the bonds are single bonds. Compounds containing only single bonds are said to be **saturated;**
4. show a gradual change in melting and boiling point. The simplest members of the family are gases but the melting and boiling points increase as the molecules get larger. Some of the alkanes, e.g. octane, are liquids and some of the higher alkanes are solids.

Alkanes are generally unreactive. The only reactions they readily undergo are combustion reactions and, because these reactions are exothermic, alkanes make good fuels.

Combustion of alkanes in excess air or oxygen produces carbon dioxide and water.

Combustion in limited amounts of oxygen produces carbon monoxide and water.

Fractional distillation of petroleum produces relatively small amounts of petrol and kerosene and larger amounts of high boiling point products which are more difficult to sell. The process of **catalytic cracking** breaks down long chain alkanes into shorter molecules including alkenes.

Where Will the Watts Come From?

Britain is in danger of having insufficient capacity to meet electricity demand at the start of the twenty-first century. This shortfall, reckoned to be 8 000 000 kilowatts, could be met by building additional power stations. These could be coal-fired power stations using home-produced or imported coal. Alternatively, they could be oil- or gas-fired, or nuclear power stations.

A more radical approach, proposed by environmentalists, encourages a greater effort to save electricity and a positive use of renewable or natural energy sources.

Solar power

More energy arrives at the Earth's surface in an hour than is consumed by the World in a whole year. Even in Britain, lying in the Northern Hemisphere with its cold winters and the sun frequently obscured by heavy cloud, the total of solar energy received each year is around 80 times our present total primary energy demand.

Solar power can be turned directly into electricity in solar cells. These are frequently used in calculators and watches. In 1983, for example, 60 million solar-powered calculators were sold worldwide. Solar electricity will be important in developing countries for water pumping and household electricity, although solar cells still remain very expensive. In Britain, a small 30 kW scheme, producing enough electricity for the equivalent of 30 single bar electric heaters, has recently been built at Marchwood near Southampton.

A more revolutionary method involves locating the solar cells in orbit around the Earth. They can be more effective there. The electricity is then converted into microwave energy which is then transmitted back to a ground station where it is converted into electricity.

Another method involves enormous heat- and radiation-collecting spheres or mirrors, activated by computers to face the Sun as it moves around the Earth (see below).

Harnessing solar energy in space

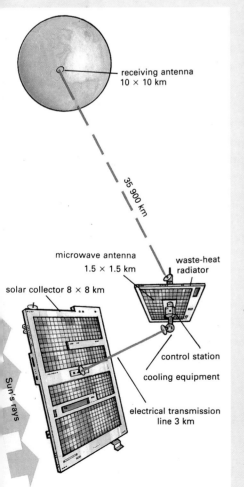

receiving antenna
10 × 10 km

35 900 km

microwave antenna
1.5 × 1.5 km

waste-heat radiator

solar collector 8 × 8 km

control station

cooling equipment

electrical transmission line 3 km

Sun's rays

ABOVE A solar power station in the Mojave Desert in the USA

BELOW Trapping sunlight with mirrors

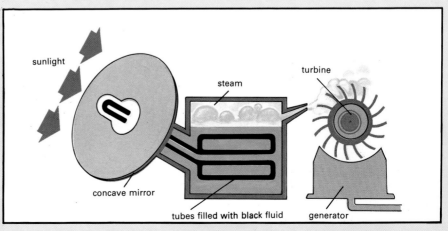

sunlight

steam

turbine

concave mirror

tubes filled with black fluid

generator

Wind and hydroelectric power

In Britain, 2% of our electricity comes from water power, mainly in Scotland. There is scope to double the amount of electricity made this way.

Wind energy is starting to be used on a grand scale in many countries. California aims to get 10% of its electricity from large 'wind farms' by the end of the century. In Britain, we have 300 kW wind generators operating in the Orkneys, Wales and Devon. Machines capable of producing 3000 kW are being developed. Britain has an ideal climate for wind power, which could generate at least 20% of our electricity. This would mainly come from off-shore 'wind-farms' which would cause less trouble to the environment.

Tidal power

In the estuary of the River Rance in France, there is a power station which generates electricity using tidal power. The working of this power station is shown on the right. A similar dam could be built across the Severn Estuary and other estuaries in Great Britain. This could produce up to 20% of our electricity needs. The major concern with this kind of dam, however, is the effect on wildlife habitats.

Wave power

The movement of ocean waves could be harnessed to produce power. Experiments have been carried out using large rafts which float up and down with the waves. This rocking movement can be converted into electricity which can be brought ashore by cable. The large waves in the Atlantic Ocean could be used for this.

Geothermal power

This is not a renewable source of energy. It relies upon the fact that the rocks beneath the Earth's surface are much hotter than the surface rocks. Countries as far apart as France, Hungary, Japan and New Zealand rely on geothermal energy for heating. There are hot springs in Britain at Bath and near Bristol. The water below ground can reach 80°C but by the time it reaches the surface it is at about 46°C. This could be used as preheated water in electricity generation and so reduce the amount of fuel required.

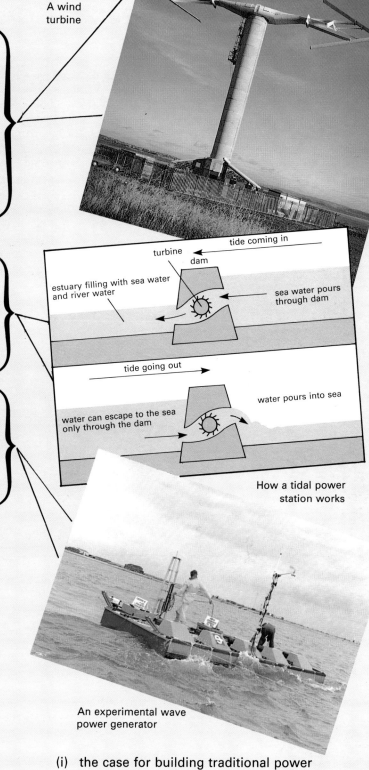

A wind turbine

How a tidal power station works

An experimental wave power generator

ACTIVITIES ▼

1. Using diagrams, explain how electricity is generated from tidal power.

2. Using the information on page 255 of the Data Section, write a paragraph on the changing pattern of energy sources in the United Kingdom between 1950 and 1985.

   Give, with social, economic and environmental reasons, an account of what you think will be the sources of energy in the year 2000.

3. Write a report of approximately 400 words summarising *either*:

(i) the case for building traditional power stations to meet the increasing demand. These power stations could be coal-fired, oil- or gas-fired or nuclear-powered. In your report, suggest the fuels which should be used and the best locations of these power stations.

or:

(ii) the case for investing money in the development of alternative energy supplies. As money for research is limited, which of the alternative energy sources should be developed?

Table 22.1 Simplest members of the alkane family

Alkane	Formula	Structure	Melting point in °C	Boiling point in °C	Mass of 1 mole in g	State at room temperature and pressure
Methane	CH_4	H | H–C–H | H	−182	−161	16	Gas
Ethane	C_2H_6	H H | | H–C–C–H | | H H	−183	−89	30	Gas
Propane	C_3H_8	H H H | | | H–C–C–C–H | | | H H H	−188	−42	44	Gas
Butane	C_4H_{10}	H H H H | | | | H–C–C–C–C–H | | | | H H H H	−138	0	58	Gas
Pentane	C_5H_{12}	H H H H H | | | | | H–C–C–C–C–C–H | | | | | H H H H H	−130	36	72	Liquid
Hexane	C_6H_{14}	H H H H H H | | | | | | H–C–C–C–C–C–C–H | | | | | | H H H H H H	−95	68	86	Liquid

The next members of the alkane family are heptane (C_7H_{16}), octane (C_8H_{18}), nonane (C_9H_{20}) and decane ($C_{10}H_{22}$).

22.3 Catalytic cracking

The vapour of high boiling point alkanes is passed over a heated catalyst. The large molecules are broken down into smaller molecules including alkenes.

Fig. 22.1 shows apparatus which can be used in the laboratory to break down liquid paraffin vapour into ethene. The vapour is passed over heated broken china. This breaking down process is called **cracking.**

In industry the process is more sophisticated and it is possible to break down long-chain molecules into short molecules and then reform them into larger, more saleable molecules. By these methods the oil companies are able to produce petrol from high boiling point alkanes. The details of these processes are 'trade-secrets'!

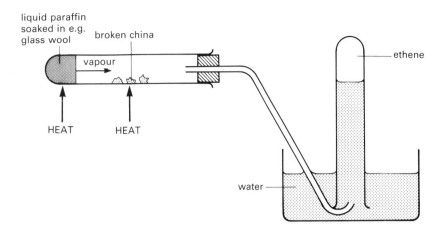

Fig. 22.1 Cracking of liquid paraffin vapour

22.4 Ethene and propene

Ethene and propene are members of the homologous series called alkenes. Information about these is given in Table 22.2.

Table 22.2 Comparison of ethene and propene

Alkane	Formula	Structure	Melting point in °C	Boiling point in °C	Mass of 1 mole in g	State at room temperature and pressure
Ethene	C_2H_4		−169	−104	28	Gas
Propene	C_3H_6		−185	−48	42	Gas

They fit a general formula C_nH_{2n}. They are **unsaturated** as they each contain one double covalent bond between two carbon atoms. Apart from combustion, which they undergo in a similar way to alkanes, they undergo important **addition reactions.**

The addition reaction with bromine solution is used to distinguish an alkene from an alkane. A solution of bromine in a solvent such as **hexane** is red in colour. When it is added to an alkene the bromine colour disappears until the solution is colourless.

ethene + bromine → dibromoethane

During the reaction the double bond becomes a single bond and a bromine atom joins onto each carbon atom. The product is saturated and related to ethane.

No similar reaction takes place with a bromine solution and an alkane. The solution stays red.

22.5 Other hydrocarbons

Apart from alkanes and alkenes, there are other homologous series of hydrocarbons and other individual hydrocarbons of importance.

Ethyne, C_2H_2, is the simplest member of the alkyne family. It is sometimes called acetylene, which is its old-fashioned name. Ethyne mixed with oxygen burns at a high temperature (about 3000°C) and this flame is used for cutting and welding metals.

Benzene, C_6H_6, is a hydrocarbon solvent which used to be widely used but is not so now because it has been shown that it causes cancer. Unlike other hydrocarbons mentioned, it consists of a ring of carbon atoms rather than a chain.

ABOVE A blow torch fuelled by butane gas in a small cylinder, used for removing paint.

RIGHT A mixture of ethyne and oxygen (oxyacetylene) being used in industry to cut and weld steel. Its flame is hot enough to melt metals and it burns without leaving oxides in the weld area. Users have to wear goggles and gloves to protect themselves from the shower of sparks.

UNIT 23 Polymers and plastics

23.1 Addition polymerisation

Alkenes can be converted into long chain molecules called **polymers.** People frequently call polymers by the name **plastics.** A polymer is produced when a series of addition reactions takes place, and so we call it addition polymerisation. The starting materials come from cracking petroleum and these small molecules are called **monomers.** They contain a double bond between two carbon atoms and the polymer does not contain a double bond.

Table 23.1 contains information about the formation and uses of four polymers.

The actual formation of polymers is easy. Usually the monomer is heated with a suitable catalyst and the polymer forms.

Addition polymerisation is actually the opposite of cracking.

Table 23.1

Monomer	State of monomer at room temperature and pressure	Polymer	Uses
Ethene	Gas	Poly(ethene)	Sheeting food containers (called polythene)
Vinyl chloride (chloroethene)	Liquid	Poly(vinyl chloride) (PVC)	Waste pipes, electrical wire – insulation
Styrene (phenylethene)	Liquid	Poly(styrene)	Flowerpots. ceiling tiles (called polystyrene)
Methyl methacrylate (methyl 2-methylpropenoate)	Liquid	Perspex	Plastic windshields for motor cycles – visors

23.2 Advantages and disadvantages of polymers

Since the Second World War (1945) there has been a tremendous growth in the use of polymers. A car dashboard now is usually a one-piece plastic moulding, e.g. poly(styrene).

One of the great advantages of polymers is the ease with which they can be moulded. All addition polymers are **thermoplastic.** That means they melt on heating without decomposing. All sorts of methods of moulding can be used. Polymers also have low density, they are very unreactive to chemicals and, for that reason, they do not corrode. They are easy to make but their price is directly related to the costs of petroleum.

The disadvantage of polymers comes really from their unreactivity. They do not rot away quickly like other materials. They are said to be non-biodegradable. Plastic packaging can be seen washed up on our beaches and blowing around the countryside. The problem will get worse. In Japan they are trying to develop biodegradable polymers.

Polymers can be separated from household refuse but it is impossible at present to separate poly(ethene) from poly(styrene), etc. This makes recycling polymers difficult. The mixed polymers obtained from household refuse can be melted down to make insulating blocks for houses. Polymers can be destroyed by burning but often poisonous gases can be produced. Also this is a terrible waste of a scarce resource.

Polymers used in some foam-filled settees are highly dangerous as they can easily catch on fire, giving off poisonous fumes.

23.3 Thermosetting plastics

Some plastics do not easily melt on heating. They are said to be **thermosetting**. Instead of melting they decompose. Bakelite (a plastic but not an addition polymer) is used to make electric plug sockets and switches. These items cannot be melted. Often, when there is an electrical fault and a plug is overheating, a fishy smell can be detected. This is the plastic decomposing.

The first plastic

The first plastic to be developed was Celluloid. In the 1860s there was a threat of the shortage of elephants. Large numbers were being shot to provide ivory. Billiard ball manufacturers were concerned because they made the balls from elephants' tusks. They offered a prize of $10 000 to anyone who could make a substitute for ivory.

John Hyatt set about finding such a substitute. He produced a billiard ball coated with Celluloid made of cellulose from trees. The Celluloid was very flammable and occasionally the violent impact of two balls would produce a mild explosion. A billiard hall owner in Colorado complained that, although this did not concern him too much, when it happened every man in his hall drew his gun!

John Hyatt was awarded the prize and this was the start of the plastics industry.

The interior of a modern car relies heavily on polymers. Study *either* this picture *or* the interior of a modern car and list as many items made from polymers as you can. What are the advantages of using polymers rather than wood, metal, natural fabric or leather?

NEWS BRIEF NEWS BRIEF NEWS BRIEF NEWS BRIEF NEWS BRIEF NEWS BRIEF NEWS BRIEF

Since 1989 in Florence in Italy the use of non-biodegradable polymers for non-durable goods such as food wrappings has been made illegal.

Photo- or biodegradable plastics have been known for years but the mass market has been hampered by drawbacks such as cost and material problems. Plastics that rot away to fast may rot away on the supermarket shelves. Additives in the plastic may affect the food.

A small chemical firm in Switzerland has developed a new plastic product which does not rot away until it is sprayed with water containing a certain dissolved chemical. BMW are interested in coating their cars with it.

UNIT 24 Ethanol and ethanoic acid

24.1 Ethanol

Ethanol is an important carbon compound and, as its name suggests, it is closely related to ethane. It is the 'active ingredient' in alcoholic drinks and some people call ethanol 'alcohol'.

It is a neutral, colourless liquid with a formula C_2H_6O. This is better written as C_2H_5OH as this shows the OH group. The structure of ethanol is:

$$
\begin{array}{ccc}
& \text{H} & \text{H} \\
& | & | \\
\text{H}- & \text{C} - \text{C}- & \text{OH} \\
& | & | \\
& \text{H} & \text{H}
\end{array}
$$

Ethanol in some ways resembles water. However, being a carbon compound it burns easily producing carbon dioxide (or carbon monoxide in limited air) and water.

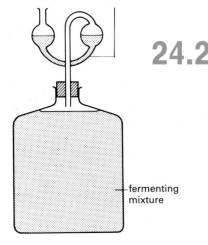

fermentation lock allowing the escape of carbon dioxide

fermenting mixture

Fig. 24.1 Apparatus for fermentation

24.2 Producing ethanol by fermentation

Ethanol can be prepared by the action of biological catalysts called enzymes on either a solution of sugar or starch.

If a glucose solution is mixed with yeast and the mixture kept at a temperature between about 25°C and 30°C, the mixture starts to froth as carbon dioxide is produced. The mixture is fermenting.

$$\text{glucose} \rightarrow \text{ethanol} + \text{carbon dioxide}$$

The apparatus in Fig. 24.1 is suitable for fermentation as it lets the carbon dioxide out but does not let the air in.

Fermentation of sugars produces only a dilute solution of ethanol – up to about 20% ethanol. At this point the enzymes are poisoned by the ethanol.

24.3 Importance of fermentation

Beers contain 3–4% ethanol. They are brewed and this involves the fermentation of malt from barley using yeast. Hops are added to give flavour.

Wine is made by fermenting a large range of fruits, vegetables, etc. Most wine that we buy is made by fementing grape juice. The starches and sugars are broken down and converted to ethanol by fermentation. Wines contain up to about 12% ethanol. Fortified wines such as port and sherry are made by adding spirits to wine to increase the percentage of ethanol. Other additives are added to wine and you will remember the scare when

TOP LEFT Grapes being tipped into a pressing machine prior to fermentation.

TOP RIGHT A food technologist testing a newly developed emulsifier for the breadmaking industry.

ABOVE LEFT AND RIGHT A reconstruction of an accident caused by a driver who has been drinking. Alcohol affects judgement and reaction time. The driver involved in the accident is being breathalysed at the scene of the accident to see if he has consumed more than the legal limit of alcohol. Should drivers be allowed to drink *any* alcohol?

large amounts of ethylene glycol (car antifreeze) was found in some wines. Other alcohols, e.g. methanol, are also highly poisonous.

Spirits such as whisky, gin and brandy cannot be made by fermentation alone. They contain about 35% ethanol, more than can be obtained by fermentation. The ethanol concentration can be increased by **fractional distillation** (Unit 4). When an aqueous solution of ethanol is heated, the first fraction is much richer in ethanol because ethanol has a lower boiling point than water. Even so, it is impossible to produce pure ethanol just by distillation. Spirits are produced by fractional distillation of ethanol solutions. It is illegal to carry out fractional distillation of ethanol at home as it is avoiding duty payments to the Government.

In breadmaking, the flour, fat, salt, water and yeast are made into a dough. This is then left to rise in a warm place. Fermentation takes place and bubbles of carbon dioxide are formed which make the dough rise. This makes the bread lighter and gives it its texture.

24.4 Souring of wine

It is important that fermentation takes place out of contact with air, and that wine is kept tightly corked. Bacteria and oxygen in the air oxidise wine to ethanoic acid. The wine turns sour because acids, of course, have a sour taste. This was the original way of making vinegar.

Ethanoic acid was previously called acetic acid and has a formula CH_3COOH. It reacts with alkalis and bases to produce salts called ethanoates (or acetates).

24.5 Industrial manufacture of ethanol from ethene

Ethene is produced by the catalytic cracking of high boiling point fractions from fractional distillation of petroleum. Apart from making poly(ethene), much of the ethene is used to make industrial chemicals including ethanol.

To make ethanol from ethene a two-stage process is used. Ethene is dissolved in concentrated sulphuric acid to form ethyl hydrogensulphate. This is then diluted with water to produce ethanol.

24.6 Uses of ethanol

Ethanol is an extremely good solvent. Usually we use industrial methylated spirits, IMS, which is nearly pure ethanol with a little methanol added to it. IMS will remove ballpoint pen ink or grass stains from material. For household use (and so that it is not confused with other liquids) a purple dye is added and the liquid is called 'methylated spirits'.

Apart from acting as a solvent, ethanol is also a good fuel. It was mentioned earlier about the use of ethanol as a fuel for motor cars in Brazil (page 148). Either the engine can be adjusted to run on pure ethanol or ethanol is added to petrol. In either case, good results have been obtained – good, clean burning and reduced levels of pollution.

Ethanol is, of course, consumed in large quantities in alcoholic drinks. Much of the ethanol is consumed for 'social drinking' but there are serious side-effects. Drinking ethanol can be addictive, can produce after-effects which might be expressed as a 'hangover' and can produce serious health problems especially to liver and kidneys. Drinking ethanol can affect judgement and increase the time necessary to react in an emergency. The amount of ethanol permitted in the blood of car drivers is limited by law.

NEWS BRIEF NEWS BRIEF NEWS BRIEF NEWS BRIEF NEWS

Scientists in the United States have shown that algae could provide an economic source of carbon compounds when petroleum runs out.

Certain algae produce large amounts of lipids (molecules made up of chains of carbon atoms). The algae grow rapidly in big tanks using up large amounts of carbon dioxide. The tanks need to be positioned in good sunlight.

When the lipids are harvested and treated with hydrochloric acid and methanol, diesel oil is produced. Catalytic reduction can be used to produce petrol.

QUESTIONS ON UNITS 22, 23 and 24

(Note, one set of questions for three very inter-related units)

Domain I: Knowledge and understanding

1. Write down the name and formula of:

   (a) the simplest alkane
   (b) the simplest alkene
   (c) the simplest alkyne
   (d) the alkene containing three carbon atoms
   (e) the chief constituent of petrol
   (f) the alkane containing four carbon atoms

2. Ethane is a **saturated hydrocarbon**. Ethene is an **unsaturated hydrocarbon**. It is produced by **cracking** high boiling point hydrocarbon fractions. Ethene can be converted into the **addition polymer** called poly(ethene).

   Explain the **bold** words in the sentences above.

3. The flow diagram below shows some common carbon compounds and how they are related. Identify A–F in the diagram:

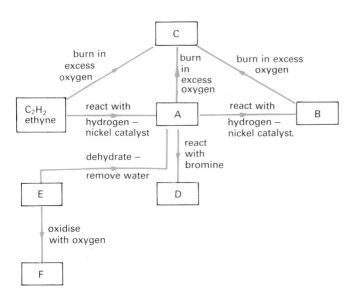

4. (a) State two uses of ethanol.
   (b) What are the problems caused by the abuse of ethanol?

5. (a) Write down the formula of ethanol and draw its molecular structure.
   (b) Ethanol is produced by fermentation of sugar solutions.
      i) Name the other product of this fermentation.
      ii) Give two other conditions which are necessary before this fermentation will take place.
      iii) How can the dilute solution of ethanol produced by fermentation be concentrated?

Domain II: Handling information and solving problems

6. The information in the Data Section on page 252 should be used to answer the following questions:

   (a) Name an alkane which is solid at room temperature.
   (b) What would you expect the melting point and boiling point of octane, C_8H_{18} to be?
   (c) Draw out the structural formulae of methanol and propene.
   (d) Butane can exist in two possible structures. These are:

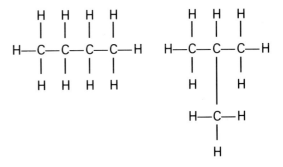

   These different forms are called isomers. Draw out the three isomers of pentane.

Biotechnology is the use of biological processes to produce useful substances. Although there have been considerable developments in biotechnology in recent years, it is not new. Wine-making, beer-brewing, the baking of bread and cheese-making all depend upon fermentation processes brought about by yeasts, other fungi and bacteria, or enzymes from these organisms.

Biotechnology:

1. can produce high-protein animal feed quickly and cheaply. Microbes, like miniature factories, can live on low-grade hydrocarbon wastes and produce protein, which can be extracted, dried and compressed to produce animal food. A shallow lake the size of Essex could provide sufficient protein to meet the whole world's needs;

2. can produce chemicals cheaply, such as penicillin, citric acid and lactic acid;

3. can help to destroy unwanted waste in sewage;

4. can extract metal compounds from low grade ores. Spoil heaps of residues from copper mines can be sprayed with acidified water. This promotes the growth of *Thiobacillus* which can use the sulphur in the ore to produce sulphuric acid. The acid then dissolves out the copper as copper(II) sulphate solution.

Application of biotechnology to brewing

Most brewers use a strain of brewer's yeast *Saccharomyces cerevisiae*. There are over 300 strains of this type of yeast. The sort of yeast that brewers use is crucial, because the micro-organisms do more than produce ethanol. The characteristic taste of a drink depends on its 'flavour profile', which comes from the cocktail of organic chemicals made by yeasts as they grow. All yeasts produce ethanol using the same route. But different strains vary in the by-products which they produce, including esters and ketones.

Brewers, despite advances in technology, still produce beer in batches rather than in a continuous process. This is because the product must always have the same flavour and it is easier to secure this in batches rather than risk the small differences which could creep in during a continuous process, owing to contamination by unwanted micro-organisms. This is a particular problem in brewing because absolutely antiseptic conditions *cannot* be used as the yeast would not thrive.

Yeasts produce ethanol from starch stored in barley malt. Yeasts cannot themselves perform the first step in the breakdown of starch. Fortunately, a germinating barley seed can. It produces an enzyme called amylase which splits up starch. Hence brewers soak malt, so that it germinates and allows the amylase to break down the starch to sugar units, which the yeast can then use. Brewers then boil the mixture to stop further action by the enzymes. They filter it to produce the 'wort' and add hops to provide resins that add to the flavour and act as preservatives. The hopped wort is then ready for fermentation. Brewers then add the desired yeast.

Fermentation takes place in a cylindrical or cone-shaped vessel. Different strains of yeast grow best at different places in the vessel. Lagers, for example, are made from a bottom-fermenting yeast, whereas most ales come from a yeast growing on the surface. During fermentation yeasts produce bubbles of carbon dioxide, which mix the beer and help to keep the conditions inside the vessel uniform. Once fermentation is complete, brewers filter the beer to remove the spent yeast and other impurities. They may recycle the yeast or use it as a food product.

Is there room for improvement in brewing beer? One improvement would be if a strain of yeast could be developed which would break down the starch without need for amylase. Biologists can mutate existing strains, select desirable ones and cross these strains with others to introduce desirable features.

Brewers are also attempting to develop yeasts which are more tolerant to ethanol. Traditional fermenting techniques produce an ethanol concentration of about 6.5%. Then the yeast dies. Economically, the more ethanol a brewer can obtain from a fermentation the better. The ethanol, when diluted, will give a larger volume of the final beer. The sensitivity of the yeast to ethanol means that manufacturers spend a lot of money removing ethanol from the vessel before it kills too many yeast cells. Distillation and solvent-extraction are two methods of doing this but they are expensive. Any increase in tolerance of yeast to ethanol would, therefore, save money.

ABOVE A goshawk poisoned by DDT.

ABOVE The froth on the top of the fermentation tank is caused by carbon dioxide produced during fermentation. In the modern breweries the fermentation is carried out in sealed tanks and it is not possible to see the fermentation products.

BELOW The end result of the brewing process.

Applications of biotechnology to waste disposal

Chemicals such as DDT, dioxins and polychlorinated biphenyls (PCBs) are extremely toxic man-made chemicals which have caused, and are causing, considerable environmental problems. The problem with these chemicals comes from the fact that they remain in the soil and do not break down. Biotechnology can come to the rescue and break them down.

An American scientist, Ananda Chakrabarty, has developed a strain of soil bacteria which will treat hydrocarbon wastes. Hydrocarbons are hydrophobic — they repel water — and bacteria live in water or in the film of water around soil particles. Normally a bacterium cannot get near enough to a hydrocarbon particle to take it in and digest it. Chakrabarty's strain of bacteria has a mutant gene that codes for an emulsifying agent which enables the solution of bacteria and the oil to mix. Trials have been successful and hydrocarbon wastes can be broken down. Now this approach has to be developed to produce micro-organisms which will break down the stable organic compounds containing chlorine.

Chakrabarty has already produced bacteria which will reduce the levels of these chlorinated compounds in soil from 1000 p.p.m. to 7 p.p.m. in a week. The soil remaining will now allow seeds to germinate.

Disposal of PCBs otherwise required very careful burning. The burning has to be carried out in special industrial incinerators at high temperatures otherwise there may be health problems to people and animals in the surrounding area.

NEWS BRIEF NEWS BRIEF

Mouldy bread may help to reduce acid rain. Scientists at North Staffordshire Polytechnic, Stoke-on-Trent, discovered a method of taking inorganic sulphur compounds out of coal using *Thiobacillus ferroxidous*, a bacterium found in mouldy bread.

ACTIVITIES ▼

1. Keep a diary of newspaper cuttings and other information on the applications of biotechnology. When you start to look you will find many examples.

2. Find out what you can about:

    (a) the tragic accident at Seveso in Northern Italy in 1976;

    (b) the use of Agent Orange (2,4,5-trichlorophenoxyacetic acid) in the Vietnam War;

    (c) the problems caused in the environment by pesticides such as DDT (dichloro-diphenyl-trichloroethane).

UNIT 25 Chalk, limestone and marble

25.1 Introduction

Chalk, limestone and marble are three forms of the same chemical compound – calcium carbonate. It has been estimated that there are about 60 000 000 000 000 000 tonnes of these minerals in the rocks of the Earth. Large amounts of these minerals are used by the chemical industry. Unfortunately, much of the limestone needed for industry has to be quarried in areas of natural beauty. This can cause problems (see Case Study 10).

25.2 How were these minerals formed?

Millions of years ago the seas were filled with sea creatures with shells. When the animals died the shells fell to the sea bed and built up a deposit up to 600 metres thick. These deposits were compressed and became chalk or limestone. As the earth moved the rocks were pushed upwards and formed hills. The Downs of the South East of England are examples of chalk hills. Fig. 25.1 shows where chalk and limestone deposits are in Great Britain.

Both chalk and limestone are **sedimentary** rocks. This means that they were made from compressed bits of older rocks and shells. It is possible to find the remains of these sea creatures in chalk or limestone as **fossils.**

When limestone is heated to high temperatures and further compressed, it melts and crystallises forming marble. Marble is a **metamorphic** rock. It is much harder than chalk or limestone. It is found particularly in volcanic regions, e.g. Italy.

25.3 Reactions of calcium carbonate

All forms of calcium carbonate – chalk, limestone and marble – react in similar ways. Calcium carbonate does not dissolve in pure distilled water. However, calcium carbonate dissolves slightly in water in the presence of carbon dioxide. Calcium hydrogencarbonate is formed in solution and this causes temporary hardness in water (Unit 15).

calcium carbonate + water + carbon dioxide ⇌ calcium hydrogencarbonate

Dissolving of calcium carbonate leads to the formation of underground caverns. Stalagmites and stalactites are formed when calcium hydrogencarbonate decomposes (Unit 15).

Calcium carbonate does not easily decompose on heating. A temperature of about 900°C is needed to decompose it.

When calcium carbonate is heated strongly it decomposes forming calcium oxide and carbon dioxide gas:

calcium carbonate → calcium oxide + carbon dioxide

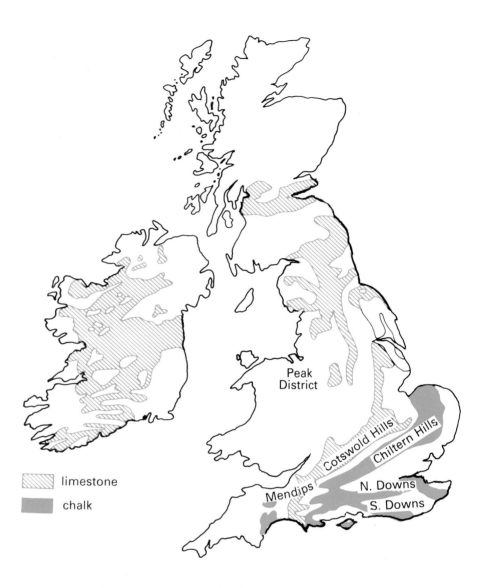

Fig. 25.1 Distribution of chalk and limestone in Great Britain

- ▨ limestone
- ▩ chalk

This reaction is accompanied by the loss of a dim white light. Originally theatres were built outdoors to use daylight. The first indoor theatres were lit by fires in baskets on stage. Lumps of lime were placed on these fires and the dim light given out by this lime decomposing lit the theatre. The light was not very good but the expression 'in the limelight', for somebody in a position to be seen, still exists in our everyday language.

Fig. 25.2 shows how a lump of calcium carbonate can be heated in the laboratory to turn it into calcium oxide. Calcium oxide is sometimes called 'quicklime'.

In industry calcium carbonate is converted into calcium oxide in a limekiln.

When cold water is added to some cold calcium oxide, a violent reaction takes place. A great deal of steam is produced and the mixture becomes very hot. The white solid remaining is calcium hydroxide, sometimes called 'slaked lime':

$$\text{calcium oxide } + \text{ water } \rightarrow \text{ calcium hydroxide}$$

This reaction is **exothermic** and the heat produced causes some of the water to boil.

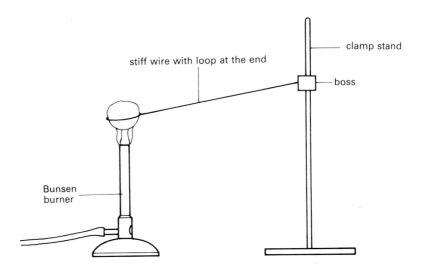

Fig. 25.2 Heating marble (calcium carbonate) in the hottest part of a Bunsen burner flame

When calcium hydroxide solid is added to water it forms a creamy-coloured suspension called 'milk-of-lime'. If this suspension is filtered, a clear solution of calcium hydroxide is produced. This is called limewater.

When carbon dioxide is bubbled through a solution of limewater, the solution first goes milky-white and then goes clear again. The milkiness is caused by the formation of insoluble calcium carbonate. Calcium hydrogencarbonate, which is soluble in water, is formed in the final clear solution:

calcium hydroxide + carbon dioxide → calcium carbonate + water

calcium carbonate + water + carbon dioxide ⇌ calcium hydrogencarbonate

Chalk, limestone and marble are attacked by acids. Carbon dioxide is a product of all reactions between calcium carbonate and acids. Examples include:

calcium carbonate + hydrochloric acid → calcium chloride + water + carbon dioxide

calcium carbonate + nitric acid → calcium nitrate + water + carbon dioxide

The reaction between calcium carbonate and sulphuric acid is much slower because the product, calcium sulphate, is not very soluble.

Limestone containing fossils of sea creatures.

TOP The chalk white cliffs of Dover.

ABOVE Concrete being used for building. The steel rods are for reinforcing the concrete blocks to make them stronger.

ABOVE Glass bottles on a production line in a drinks factory. What are the advantages and disadvantages of using glass containers in the food industry? What alternatives are there?

25.4 Uses of chalk, limestone and marble

Chalk, limestone and marble are very widely used raw materials in industry. Marble is used for statues. It is hard to shape but, being very hard, it is very long-lasting.

Limestone is used as a building material. Blocks of limestone can be used to construct buildings. It is not, however, as resistant as brick to conditions such as atmospheric pollution.

Mortar is a mixture of calcium hydroxide (slaked lime), sand and water. It is mixed to a thick paste and used to fix bricks together when building. It sets by losing water and by absorbing carbon dioxide from the air. Long crystals of calcium carbonate form and give strength to the mortar.

Cement is a more advanced material used in building. It is made by heating limestone with sand and clay (containing silicates). A complex mixture of calcium and aluminium silicates is formed and this is called cement.

On adding water, complex reactions occur producing calcium hydroxide. The setting of cement is similar to the setting of mortar.

Cement is used with sand, small stones and water to make concrete. The properties of concrete depend upon the proportions of the different ingredients. Concrete is not very strong. It can be strengthened by rods of steel or steel meshing.

Ordinary glass is made by mixing calcium carbonate, silicon dioxide (sand) and sodium carbonate together and melting them. The resulting mixture of sodium and calcium silicates, on cooling, produces glass. This type of glass is used for windows. Hardened glass, such as *Pyrex*, contains boron. This 'borosilicate' glass can be cooled quickly without cracking. Lead added to glass makes it very hard and suitable for making 'cut glass'.

Glass is often coloured and this is due to the presence of impurities such as metal oxides. When glass is collected in 'bottle-banks' for recycling it is necessary to collect glass of different colours in different containers (see page 70).

Calcium carbonate is used as a raw material in the manufacture of a number of important industrial chemicals. Sodium hydrogencarbonate and sodium carbonate are produced in the Solvay process (Unit 26). Calcium carbide, CaC_2, is also produced from calcium carbonate. Large quantities of calcium carbonate are used in iron extraction (Unit 9) to remove unwanted materials from the furnace.

Calcium carbonate and calcium hydroxide are used widely in agriculture. They neutralise excess acidity in the soil.

Calcium carbonate can be used to remove sulphur dioxide from gases escaping from power stations. This will reduce acid rain (Unit 13). The calcium carbonate can be converted into calcium sulphate which can be used for making plasterboard.

ACTIVITY ▼

Examine closely gravestones in your local cemetery. Often the headstones are made of marble. Examine the way the stones have weathered. Perhaps you can compare headstones in different areas. The decay of the headstones is often related to air pollution.

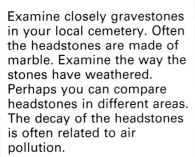

NEWS BRIEF NEWS BRIEF NEWS BRIEF NEWS BRIEF NEWS

Road engineers have been caught out by salt attack on concrete bridges. The steel rods used to give added strength to bridges are being eaten away by salt used for de-icing roads in winter (see page 181).

As salt and surface water seep into bridges, the steel rods rust and expand, causing the surrounding concrete to split. Surveys are now being carried out to find the extent of the problem on elevated sections of motorway in Britain.

QUESTIONS ON UNIT 25

Domain I: Knowledge and understanding

1. (a) Complete the following table:

Chemical name	Common name	Formula
Calcium oxide	quicklime	
	limestone	$CaCO_3$
Calcium hydrogencarbonate		
		$Ca(OH)_2$

(b) Which calcium compound in the table:
   - i) is the raw material in cement making?
   - ii) contains only two elements?
   - iii) is the major rock through which the Channel Tunnel must be drilled?
   - iv) is present in hard water?
   - v) is the major chemical in limescale left in a kettle?
   - vi) contains the greatest percentage of calcium?
   - vii) produces a great deal of heat when added to water?
   - viii) is an alkali?

2. Complete the following passage:

> When a piece of marble was heated strongly
> . . . . was given off and the
> mass . . . . The shiny surface of
> the marble disappeared and the hard marble
> turned . . . .
>
> After the solid had cooled down, a few
> drops of water were added to it. The solid
> seemed to expand and steam was given off
> showing that the reaction was
> . . . . and gave off . . . .
> When the solid was tested with Universal
> indicator paper, the paper turned . . . .
> showing that the substance was an
> . . . .

Domain II: Handling information and solving problems

3. calcium oxide, calcium, calcium chloride, calcium carbonate, calcium hydroxide, calcium hydrogencarbonate

   Complete the flow diagram below by putting in the names of the chemicals in the list above:

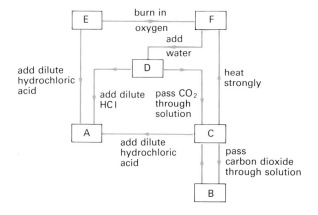

4. A friend suggests that egg shells are pure calcium carbonate. You have a supply of AR calcium carbonate. Suggest a method to prove whether the statement is true. You can use any common apparatus or chemicals.

5. A colourless solid (V) was melted and electrolysed. A brown gas was produced at the anode. A grey solid (W) was produced at the cathode.
   The grey solid reacted with water to produce a colourless gas (X) which burnt in air with a squeaky pop. A colourless solution (Y) was left.
   The colourless solution turned cloudy on standing exposed to the atmosphere. This solution was then found to contain a white solid (Z).
   A flame test carried out on V gave a brick red flame.
   From the information above:

   (a) identify W, X, Y and Z;
   (b) suggest a solid which would fit the description of V;
   (c) explain why W is not formed when an aqueous solution of V is electrolysed.

Mining in the Peak District National Park

Read the extract below which is part of an article from the Sunday Times Colour Supplement, 19th October 1986.

AT 1700 FT ON RUSHUP EDGE THE Pennine wind is keen. No hill was ever more truly named than this giant crest of grassy shale. Nor is there a more dramatic viewpoint from which to look out over the Peak District, Britain's oldest National Park. North beyond Edale lie the gritstone moors and desolate peat hags of Kinder Scout – hallowed ground for ramblers and the scene of the great trespasses of the 1930s when the Peak Park dream first took root. South is limestone country; a falling away of green upland fields; and there at its centre, like a livid scar, the great, rumbling hole of Eldon Hill quarry.

For half a century, quarrymen have been blasting their way deep into the northern

[...] around Buxton which was deli[...] from the National [...] drawn up

face of this, at 1543 ft, one of the Peak's most conspicuous hills. Every year, one third of a million tonnes of limestone are removed for the construction industry. The result is an ugly chasm, some 30 acres in extent, which has earned itself the title of 'the biggest eyesore in the Peak'.

Over the past 30 years the National Park and its mineral extractors have survived in uneasy equilibrium. Now the quarry's owners want to dig deeper into the Park and extend the life of the Eldon Hill site indefinitely – a move which has plunged the Peak Park into its biggest crisis for years and thoroughly enraged conservationists.

The Peak Park is the Pennines at their

the public inquiries in 1953, by which time the Peak Park had been in existence for two years. The decision then to keep the site open was taken following under[...] the operators of the quarry [...]new the leases [...]

best. Some 542 square miles of open space and clean moorland air set aside for the 17 million people who live within 50 miles of its boundaries. But industrialists view it in a different light. They look upon it as one of the biggest, most accessible mineral fields in the country.

Derbyshire and Staffordshire together produce more limestone than anywhere else in Britain. Most comes from the enclave around Buxton which was deliberately excluded from the National Park when its boundaries were drawn up 35 years ago, and contains ICI's giant Tunstead quarry, the biggest in Europe, whose face extends for more than two miles.

But quarrying is also a major industry inside the Park – with at least four million tonnes of limestone extracted each year. Every day, some 700 lorries rumble down the Park's network of narrow roads, loaded with rock. Some goes to the chemical and steel industries; but most is roadstone. And most comes from one source: Eldon Hill.

Quarrying on Eldon Hill began in the 1930s, long before the National Park was created. However, the major workings for the site were not approved until after the public inquiries in 1953, by which time the Peak Park had been in existence for two years. The decision then to keep the site open was taken following undertakings from the operators of the quarry that they would not renew the leases when they expired in 1997. Also it was recognised that the quarry had already 'seriously damaged an important part of the National Park'. It seemed a reasonable compromise in 1953. It gave the quarry a working life of more than 40 years, at the end of which peace would be restored to Eldon Hill.

The years passed. In 1976 the quarry changed hands. Its new owners were Thos W. Ward (Roadstone) Ltd, a subsidiary of Rio Tinto Zinc – a multinational mining giant.

Then, in 1984, came a bombshell. The new operators applied for permission to bite even deeper into the hill, eating away a further 12 acres and effectively giving the quarry an indefinite life-span.

The National Park authority refused. T. W. Ward appealed. A public inquiry followed in Buxton last November.

© Times Newspapers Ltd, 1986

The Eldon Hill quarry – 'the biggest eyesore in the Peak'.

Additional information you might wish to use

1. Mining and quarrying in the National Park are traditional industries in the area. Eldon Hill for example provides sixty full-time jobs although many of the employees live outside the park.

2. Government policy in these matters can be summarised by the 'Silkin Test', after Lewis Silkin, the Minister for Town and Country Planning, who steered the 1949 National Parks Bill through Parliament. The essence of the argument is that no mineral exploitation should take place in the Parks unless there is a clear national need which cannot be met elsewhere. Recently, a similar application by Tarmac Roadstone Ltd for a 19-acre extension of another limestone quarry at Topley Pike was turned down.

3. The Peak Park is the second most-visited National Park in the world with 20 million visits a year. It is close to large numbers of people in Sheffield, Huddersfield, Manchester, Stoke, Nottingham and Derby.

4. The National Park is not owned by the Government. Most of the Land is privately owned.

5. Mining in the Peak District:

At present 4.02 million tonnes of limestone are mined in the Peak District; 2.4 million tonnes are used for aggregate (road-making materials) and 1.61 million tonnes for chemical uses. This limestone is supplied to the East Midlands, North West and Yorkshire regions.

Small quarries produce about 6000 tonnes of building stone which is sandstone.

The main mineral mined is fluorspar (calcium fluoride) which is used in various manufacturing processes including refrigerants, solvents, aerosols, anaesthetics and uranium enrichment. There are underground workings under Longstone Edge and a new drift mine is being developed at Great Hucklow. The mineral is processed at Laportes Cavendish Mill plant at Stoney Middleton, which produces about 80 000 tonnes of fluorspar a year – which represents 60% of the UK supply. The only other UK supplier is in County Durham.

Small amounts of barytes, calcite, silica sand (for refractory bricks), shale (for cement) and fireclay are mined.

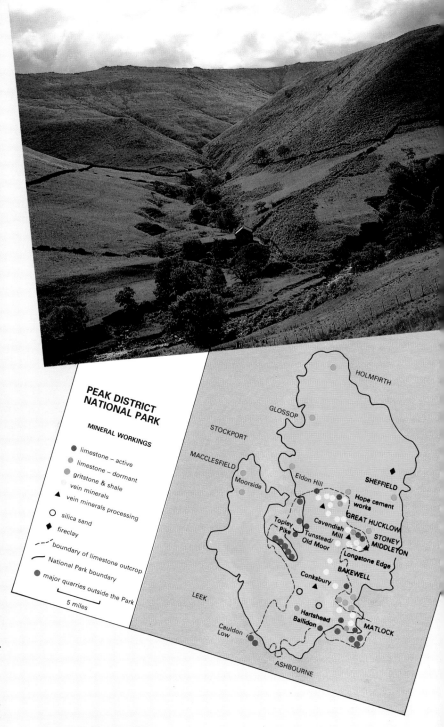

PEAK DISTRICT NATIONAL PARK

MINERAL WORKINGS

- limestone – active
- limestone – dormant
- gritstone & shale
- vein minerals
- vein minerals processing
- silica sand
- fireclay
- - - boundary of limestone outcrop
- National Park boundary
- major quarries outside the Park

5 miles

ACTIVITIES ▼

Either: Organise a debate in your group. Get two people to work together to produce the case for further mining at Eldon Hill and two people to produce the case against. Let the rest of the group come to a decision after listening to both sides of the argument.

Or: Imagine that you have been given the task of conducting the public inquiry. You have heard all of the expert evidence. You must now write a report of about 400 words which summarises the case for and against further quarrying. Your report must finish with a recommendation for or against further quarrying.

UNIT 26 Chemicals from salt

26.1 Introduction

Salt (chemical name – sodium chloride, NaCl) is a very important mineral. It is widely used in industry. It is used to make sodium, chlorine, hydrogen, sodium hydroxide, sodium carbonate and sodium hydrogencarbonate.

26.2 Mining sodium chloride

There are underground deposits of sodium chloride in various parts of Great Britain. In Winsford in Cheshire rock salt is mined from underground seams. This is then crushed and most of it is used for de-icing roads in winter.

Usually salt is not mined by conventional means. Solution mining is used (Fig. 26.1). A hole is drilled down to the deposits and then water is pumped down. The water dissolves the salt and the salt solution is pumped up to the surface. The resulting salt solution is called brine and is a raw material for the chemical industry.

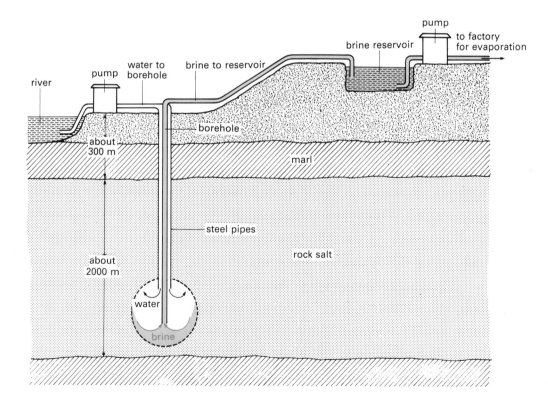

Fig. 26.1 Solution mining of salt

Underground mining of salt in Cheshire has lead to considerable subsidence of land. Also, if you compare maps of Cheshire made in the seventeenth century with modern maps you will see interesting differences. On modern maps you will find inland lakes called meres which were not there before. The meres have been formed over the last couple of centuries where land has subsided owing to salt removal.

In Mediterranean countries and similar places sodium chloride is obtained by evaporation of sea water (see page 7). Shallow lagoons of sea water are evaporated by solar energy.

A building collapses as ground above salt mines gives way – Northwich, Cheshire, 1890s. Pumping out of vast quantities of brine from bedrock led to instability and subsidence of land.

26.3 Uses of sodium chloride

Sodium chloride is a valuable raw material for the chemical industry. Most sodium compounds are made from salt. The chemical industry in North Cheshire and South Lancashire was developed because of the close proximity of the salt deposits in Cheshire.

Sodium chloride is used as rock salt for de-icing roads and preventing ice forming on roads. Salt added to water reduces the freezing point of the water. However, the salt can greatly increase the corrosion of cars and can damage concrete roads.

Sodium chloride is an important preserving agent for food. Meat and fish were preserved for the winter, centuries before refrigeration, by salting. Salt is also added in small quantities as a flavouring agent. Recently, however, concern has been expressed about effects of salt in food on heart disease.

26.4 Electrolysis of molten sodium chloride

Electrolysis of molten sodium chloride produces sodium and chlorine:

$$\text{sodium chloride} \rightarrow \text{sodium} + \text{chlorine}$$

Calcium chloride is added to the sodium chloride to lower its melting point. No water must be present. The chlorine and the sodium are collected and kept separately. The chlorine is produced at the anode and the sodium at the cathode.

Sodium does not have a wide range of uses. It is used as a coolant in nuclear reactors, as a vapour in the orange street lights that are so familiar, and as a reducing agent (for example, in the extraction of the metal titanium).

A cutting machine used in the mining of rock salt at Winsford at Cheshire – the only working salt mine in Great Britain.

Salting roads in winter with crushed rock salt. What effect does salt have on the freezing point of water?

26.5 Sodium hydrogencarbonate and sodium carbonate

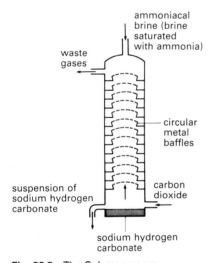

Fig. 26.2 The Solvay process

Sodium hydrogencarbonate and sodium carbonate are both produced in the Solvay process (Fig. 26.2). The raw materials in this process are sodium chloride and calcium carbonate. The products are sodium hydrogencarbonate (and sodium carbonate) and calcium chloride. Ammonia is used in the process and recycled. The overall equation can be written as:

sodium chloride + calcium carbonate → calcium chloride + sodium carbonate

The sodium carbonate produced can be in two forms – heavy and light ash. Heavy ash is denser and easier to transport. Light ash is cheaper and is purer because it contains no calcium ions. Most of the heavy ash is used in glass-making. Light ash is used for making chemicals, textiles, dyes and colours.

Sodium hydrogencarbonate is used in baking powder to produce carbon dioxide which makes cakes rise. It is also taken as an antacid for the stomach.

26.6 Sodium hydroxide

Sodium hydroxide is an important cheap industrial alkali. It is prepared from sodium chloride and there are several methods available. We will briefly look at two methods – the moving mercury method and the diaphragm cell.

The moving mercury method

This is electrolysis of brine using titanium anodes and a moving mercury cathode (Fig. 26.3). Chlorine is produced at the anode and sodium is produced at the cathode. The sodium dissolves in the mercury forming a

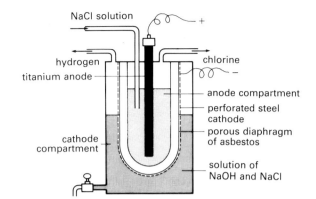

Fig. 26.3 The moving mercury method

mercury amalgam. When the mercury amalgam is added to water, sodium hydroxide and hydrogen are produced. The mercury is re-used.

sodium amalgam + water → sodium hydroxide + hydrogen + mercury

The diaphragm cell This is electrolysis of brine using a steel cathode and a titanium anode. The anode and cathode compartments are separated by a porous diaphragm (Fig. 26.4).

In the anode compartment, chlorine is produced:

$$2\,Cl^-(aq) \rightarrow Cl_2(g) + 2\,e^-$$

In the cathode compartment, hydrogen gas is produced:

$$2\,H^+(aq) + 2\,e^- \rightarrow H_2(g)$$

The solution leaving the cell contains 10% sodium hydroxide and 15% sodium chloride. On partial evaporation, most of the sodium chloride crystallises out. The sodium hydroxide produced contains some sodium chloride.

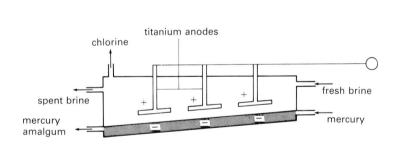

Fig. 26.4 A diaphragm cell

The mercury cell method for electrolysis of brine.

Sodium hydroxide is a most valuable product. However, the chlorine also produced is even more valuable. Sodium hydroxide is used for making household bleaches, other chemicals, man-made fibres, soaps, paper and purification of alumina.

Soap-making involves boiling natural fats and oils with alkali.

QUESTIONS ON UNIT 26

Domain I: Knowledge and understanding

1. Complete the following table which includes uses of common salt and chemicals made from salt:

Chemical	Common name	Formula	Use
	Salt		
Sodium carbonate (hydrated)			
	Heavy ash		
	Bicarbonate of soda		
		NaOH	
Chlorine	—		

2. *Electrolysis of molten sodium chloride*
   Solution mining
   Diaphragm cell method
   Moving mercury method
   Solvay process

   Which of the above methods is used to produce:

   (a) pure sodium hydroxide?
   (b) brine?
   (c) sodium carbonate?
   (d) sodium?
   (e) sodium hydrogencarbonate?

Domain II: Handling information and solving problems

3. Solution mining of sodium chloride involves pumping cold water down to salt deposits and then pumping brine to the surface. As a research chemist for a mining firm, it is suggested to you that hot water should be used instead of cold water. Using information in the Data Section (page 253), give the advantages or disadvantages of this suggestion.

4. On page 258 of the Data Section there is a graph of the world production of chlorine during this century. The pie diagram in the next column shows the major uses of chlorine. How and why has the demand for chlorine changed during this century?

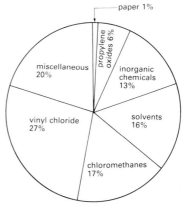

5. The map below shows an area in North Cheshire. List the reasons why a factory producing sodium hydroxide by the diaphragm method might be built at the place marked with an X. Are there any disadvantages with this site?

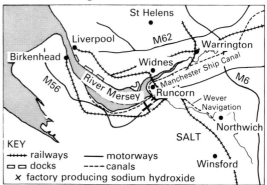

UNIT 27 The alkali metals

27.1 Introduction

The elements in group 1 of the Periodic Table (Unit 8) form a very clear family of elements. In this unit we are going to consider the chemistry of the first three members – lithium, sodium and potassium – and make some predictions about other members of the family.

Sodium chloride, NaCl is a good source of sodium and sodium compounds (Unit 26).

27.2 The alkali metals

The members of the alkali metal family are:

Lithium, Li	Rubidium, Rb
Sodium, Na	Caesium, Cs
Potassium, K	Francium, Fr

Francium is extremely rare and radioactive. This means it would be difficult to keep as it would decay.

Table 27.1 summarises the atomic numbers, melting points, boiling points and densities of the first three elements:

Table 27.1

Alkali metal	Atomic number	Melting point in °C	Boiling point in °C	Density in g per cm^3
Lithium	3	181	1331	0.54
Sodium	11	98	890	0.97
Potassium	19	63	766	0.86

All these elements have low melting points and boiling points compared to other metals. As the atomic number increases, the melting points and boiling points decrease.

The density of the alkali metals is low and this explains why some of them float on water. It is difficult to see a pattern in the densities.

All of these elements have typical metal properties. When cut, lumps of these elements show a shiny, silvery surface which rapidly corrodes. Because of this rapid corrosion, they are stored under paraffin oil which keeps them out of contact with air and water. They all conduct heat and electricity. Sodium can be used to conduct away heat in a nuclear reactor.

The oxides formed when the metals are burned are alkaline and this is the reason for the name **alkali metals.**

Humphrey Davy (1778–1829)

Davy went from being a naughty Penzance schoolboy to Sir Humphrey Davy, President of the Royal Society.

His wood-carver father died when Davy left school at 15, so the young Cornishman was apprenticed to a surgeon to earn enough money to support his mother and her four other children.

At 19 he published his first paper on Chemistry after only three months' study of the subject, and was appointed Laboratory Superintendent in Bristol, studying the effects of gases in medicine.

Two years later he wrote another paper on heat and light, but with too little research first. The terrible criticism that it received taught him to make sure that, in future, all his theories were thoroughly tested first!

Davy went on to show how nitrous oxide (laughing gas) worked as an anaesthetic – sometimes by testing it on himself!

He returned to earlier studies of electricity in 1806, five years after moving to the Royal Institution in London where he was a popular and dashing lecturer.

In 1807 he carried out the electrolysis of potash using barely-moist solids instead of a potash solution, and produced potassium for the first time. Three days later he extracted sodium from caustic soda. Later he also produced barium and strontium by electrolysis – elements all isolated for the first time.

He married a rich widow in 1812, and was knighted later the same year by the Prince Regent. In 1820 he was elected President of the Royal Society.

But he is most remembered as inventor of the **Davy Lamp** in 1815, which saved the lives of thousands of miners. The lamp worked by using a flame to detect dangerous flammable gases without igniting them, because Davy realised the flame would not pass through a fine metal gauze he built into the lamp.

A lecture demonstration being carried out at the Royal Institution in London. Humphrey Davy is the young man assisting with the experiment and holding the bellows.

27.3 Reactions of alkali metals with cold water

The alkali metals all react with cold water to form hydrogen and leave an alkaline solution (Unit 6.4). The reaction of these metals with water is a good guide to the differences in reactivity of these metals.

Lithium

When a small piece of lithium is put into a trough of cold water, the lithium floats on the surface and reacts steadily to produce hydrogen:

lithium + water → lithium hydroxide + hydrogen
(alkaline solution)

The lithium on the surface of the water remains solid. The hydrogen produced does not start to burn.

Sodium

When a piece of sodium is put into a trough of cold water, the sodium floats on the surface of the water and reacts rapidly to produce hydrogen:

sodium + water → sodium hydroxide + hydrogen
(alkaline solution)

The sodium is molten when floating on the surface. The hydrogen produced does not usually catch alight.

Potassium

When a small piece of potassium is put into a trough of cold water, the potassium floats on the surface of the water and reacts violently to produce hydrogen:

potassium + water → potassium hydroxide + hydrogen
(alkaline solution)

The potassium is molten when on the surface of the water. The hydrogen burns straight away with a lilac flame.

BELOW LEFT Potassium, being a soft metal, is cut with a knife. RIGHT A piece is then floated on water. The potassium reacts violently with the cold water to produce hydrogen. The pinkish-lilac flame is the hydrogen burning in air. The water remaining is alkaline due to the formation of potassium hydroxide. Why does potassium have to be stored under paraffin oil?

In reactions with cold water, lithium is less reactive than sodium. Sodium is less reactive than potassium. This order of reactivity applies in all reactions and not just reactions with water. Rubidium, caesium and francium are even more reactive than potassium.

27.4 Reactions of alkali metals with chlorine

Chlorine is a reactive gas which reacts with the alkali metals to form solid salts (Unit 11). The apparatus in Fig. 27.1 is suitable for burning a small piece of alkali metal in chlorine gas.

A small piece of the alkali metal is heated in the bowl of the combustion spoon until it starts to burn. The spoon is then lowered into the gas jar of chlorine.

The alkali metal continues to burn in the chlorine gas to produce white fumes of the metal chloride. These form as a white solid on the inside of the gas jar. The reactions are:

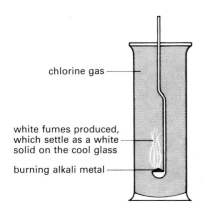

chlorine gas

white fumes produced, which settle as a white solid on the cool glass

burning alkali metal

Fig. 27.1

> lithium   + chlorine → lithium chloride
> sodium   + chlorine → sodium chloride
> potassium + chlorine → potassium chloride

NB The combustion spoon is usually made of iron. It reacts with chlorine and reddish brown fumes of iron(III) chloride may be seen.

QUESTIONS ON UNIT 27

Domain I: Knowledge and understanding

1. lithium, sodium, potassium

   Which alkali metal in the list above:

   (a) would be most expensive to buy?
   (b) has the lowest melting point?
   (c) is the most reactive?
   (d) is used in street lights?
   (e) has the greatest density?
   (f) is the least dense metal of all the metals?
   (g) has atoms with an electron arrangement 2,8,1?

2. Why are alkali metals stored under paraffin oil?

3. Write word equations for the reactions of sodium with:

   (a) oxygen
   (b) chlorine
   (c) water.

Domain II: Handling information and solving problems

4. The table below contains information about the colours and solubilities of sodium and potassium compounds in water. Use the information in the Data Section (pages 250–1) to help you complete the table:

5. Refer to Table 27.1 (page 185). Without looking up the information in the Data Section, predict the melting points, boiling points and densities of rubidium and caesium. Check your prediction in the Data Section (pages 248–9).

6. Look up the meanings of the words printed in **bold type** in the Glossary.

   Lithium chloride, LiCl, is an example of a **deliquescent** compound. Sodium carbonate crystals, $Na_2CO_3.10H_2O$, are **efflorescent**. Sodium nitrate and sodium chloride are **hygroscopic**.

   (a) How would the masses of (i) lithium chloride and (ii) sodium carbonate crystals change if samples were left on watch-glasses in a open laboratory?
   (b) What would you advise a chemical manufacturer to use for packing (i) lithium chloride, and (ii) sodium carbonate crystals?
   (c) Why is potassium nitrate preferred to sodium nitrate when making gunpowder?
   (d) Why are rice grains sometimes found in salt cellars in restaurants?

Compound	Formula	Colour	Solubility in water
Sodium chloride		white	s
Sodium manganate(vii)	$NaMnO_4$	purple	s
Sodium sulphate		white	s
Sodium nitrate		white	
Potassium manganate(vii)		purple	
Potassium chloride		white	
Potassium sulphate	K_2SO_4	white	s
Potassium iodide		white	

What can you conclude about the colour and solubility of most alkali metal compounds?

UNIT 28 The halogens

28.1 Introduction

In Unit 27 the family of metals called alkali metals was discussed. In this unit a family of non-metals called halogens will be considered. The halogens are in group 7 of the Periodic Table (Unit 8).

28.2 The halogens

Toothpaste containing fluoride for added protection against tooth decay.

The members of the halogen family are:

Fluorine, F (frequently mis-spelt flourine)
Chlorine, Cl
Bromine, Br
Iodine, I
Astatine, At

The element astatine is extremely rare. It is estimated that there is only 0.029 g in the whole Earth. It is a product of radioactive decay and itself rapidly decays.

Table 28.1 summarises the atomic number, melting point, boiling point, density and appearance of the first four halogens.

Table 28.1

Halogen	Atomic number	Melting point in °C	Boiling point in °C	Density in g per cm^3	Appearance
Fluorine	9	−220	−188	0.0016	colourless gas
Chlorine	17	−101	−35	0.003	greenish-yellow gas
Bromine	35	−7	58	3.12	reddish-brown liquid
Iodine	53	114	183	4.94	greyish-black solid

NEWS BRIEF NEWS BRIEF

Proposals to add fluoride to water in part of the Severn-Trent Water Authority region is being opposed by residents, who say they would rather drink the existing 'pure' water than have it contaminated with added fluoride.

The melting points and the boiling points of the halogen family increase with increasing atomic number. At room temperature (20°C), fluorine and chlorine are gases, bromine is a liquid and iodine is a solid.

Iodine has a shiny black appearance. Otherwise, the elements are typically non-metallic.

In all halogens, molecules are made up from pairs of atoms and so we write F_2, Cl_2, Br_2 and I_2. In solid iodine the molecules are held together by weak forces in a regular arrangement.

LEFT   Painting road lines with a specialised paint made of chlorinated rubber.

ABOVE   Chlorine used to kill the germs in a swimming pool. Sometimes chlorine cylinders are used but more often a solid or liquid is used which forms chlorine when added to the water.

28.3 Solubility of halogens in water and other solvents

The halogens do not readily dissolve in water, but they all react with water to a certain extent to form soluble products. Chlorine dissolves in water to form a solution called **chlorine water.** This consists of a mixture of hydrochloric acid, HCl, and hypochlorous acid, HOCl. This solution has bleaching and germ-killing properties. On standing in sunlight, the solution decomposes to produce oxygen.

Bromine and iodine react less with water.

The halogens dissolve in organic solvents, e.g. hexane, better than in water. They produce coloured solutions.

28.4 Reactions of halogens with metals

The halogens react with metals to form solid salt compounds. The name 'halogen' means 'salt-producer'.

Chlorine reacts with metals to form chlorides, bromine forms bromides and iodine forms iodides.

Chlorine reacts with iron to form brown crystals of iron(III) chloride. Fig. 28.1 shows apparatus suitable for this experiment. The word equation for the reaction is:

$$\text{iron} + \text{chlorine} \rightarrow \text{iron(III) chloride}$$

The iron wool glows during the reaction because the reaction is **exothermic,** i.e. energy is given out.

Bromine and iodine react with iron in a similar way.

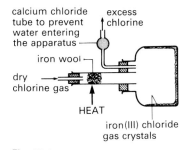

calcium chloride tube to prevent water entering the apparatus

excess chlorine

iron wool

dry chlorine gas

HEAT

iron(III) chloride gas crystals

Fig. 28.1

28.5 Reactions of halogens with hydrogen

Chlorine, bromine and iodine react with hydrogen to produce hydrogen chloride, hydrogen bromide and hydrogen iodide, respectively:

hydrogen + chlorine → hydrogen chloride
hydrogen + bromine → hydrogen bromide
hydrogen + iodine ⇌ hydrogen iodide

There are considerable differences in the rate of these reactions. The reaction between hydrogen and chlorine takes place slowly in the dark but explosively in sunlight. Hydrogen and bromine react when heated to about 200°C. Hydrogen and iodine do not react completely even when heated to 500°C. The reaction is reversible.

From these reactions and other reactions the order of reactivity shown at the left can be obtained. This order of reactivity can be used to predict reactions involving halogens.

Fluorine   most reactive
Chlorine
Bromine
Iodine   least reactive

28.6   Displacement reactions of halogens

If chlorine gas is passed into a colourless solution of potassium bromide, bromine gas is formed which colours the solution red. This is because chlorine is more reactive than bromine and therefore replaces it:

chlorine + potassium bromide → bromine + potassium chloride

No reaction would take place if bromine was added to potassium chloride solution.

28.7   Uses of halogens

The halogen elements are widely used in industry, often in compounds. Fluorine is an extremely expensive element. It is produced by the electrolysis of potassium hydrogen difluoride, KHF_2, dissolved in anhydrous hydrogen fluoride. It is a very reactive element.

Compounds of fluorine with chlorine and carbon are called CFCs. Their use in aerosols and refrigerators is included in Case Study 4 (pages 90-1).

Compounds of an element with fluorine are called fluorides. Fluorides are present in some natural water samples. It has been shown that fewer children suffer from tooth decay in areas where fluoride is present in the water. Some toothpastes contain fluorides.

Fluorine is used to make the polymer called polytetrafluoroethene (PTFE) which is the non-stick coating used for saucepans. Fluorine is also used for making solvents and in the separation of uranium-235 and 238 by gaseous diffusion of the uranium fluorides.

Chlorine is used in very large quantities. Much is used to make chloroethene which is then polymerised to make PVC (Unit 23). Chlorine is used to make solvents such as trichloroethene used as a dry cleaning fluid. Chlorine is used for killing germs in water (e.g. in swimming pools) and making household bleaches.

Bromine is added to petrol in the form of 1,2-dibromoethane (CH_2BrCH_2Br). The additive ensures that all of the lead in petrol leaves the engine. Lead reacts with bromine to form lead(II) bromide which vaporises easily from the car exhaust. Other uses for bromine include making pesticides, dyestuffs and flame retardant treatments for materials.

Iodine is very expensive and so its uses are few. It is used to make medicines, photographic chemicals, additives for animal feeds and catalysts for the chemical industry.

QUESTIONS ON UNIT 28

Domain I: Knowledge and understanding

1. fluorine, chlorine, bromine, iodine

   Which of the halogens in the list above:

   (a) contains the smallest atoms?
   (b) is most reactive?
   (c) is used as a solution in ethanol as an antiseptic to kill germs?
   (d) is used to kill germs in water in swimming baths?
   (e) is used to make a compound with sodium which is used in toothpastes?
   (f) has the highest boiling point?
   (g) has an electron arrangement of 2,7?

2. Complete the following table:

Halogen	Symbol	State at room temperature	Colour
Fluorine	Cl	liquid	grey-black

3. What is a displacement reaction?

4. Complete the following word equations.

   sodium + chlorine → ....

   iron + chlorine → ....

   hydrogen + bromine → ....

   bromine + potassium iodide → ....

Domain II: Handling information and solving problems

5. Using the information in Table 28.1 (page 190), predict the melting point, boiling point and density of the halogen astatine (atomic number 85). How would the reactivity of astatine compare with the reactivities of the other halogens?

6. Complete the table at the top of the next column, which records results for reactions between halogens and potassium halides:

Reaction takes place ✓   No reaction takes place x

Halogen \ Solutions	Potassium chloride solution	Potassium bromide solution	Potassium iodide solution
Fluorine	✓		
Chlorine	x		
Bromine	x		
Iodine			

7. The element tin (Sn) reacts with dry chlorine to produce tin(IV) chloride, $SnCl_4$. This is a liquid at room temperature. It has to be kept away from water because it reacts forming hydrogen chloride gas.

   (a) Write a word and symbol equation for the reaction taking place when tin(IV) chloride is formed.
   (b) Draw a labelled diagram of apparatus suitable for preparation of a small sample of tin(IV) chloride.
   (c) A 25 g sample of tin(IV) chloride has to be sent from Manchester to Southampton. What advice would you give about packaging, labelling and method of transport? Give reasons for your answer.

8. At a recent public meeting local residents objected to plans to add fluorides to drinking water.
   The following points were made:

   — Fluorides can be poisonous.
   — Fluorides are produced in industrial waste.
   — If fluorides are added to water, nobody can choose to use fluoride-free water.
   — If we allow fluorides to be added to water, what will be added next?
   — Fluoride is a very reactive element and is highly toxic.

   Imagine you are a chemist working for the local Water Authority.

   (a) Write a letter to the Secretary of the Residents' Action Committee, Mrs Waterson, explaining the reasons why fluoridation of water should be introduced.

   (b) Outline the steps you would propose to show that fluorides in water in Easthampton cause less dental decay than in the town of Westhampton where there is no fluoride in the water.

UNIT 29 Sulphur and sulphuric acid

29.1 Sources of sulphur and sulphur compounds

The source of the sulphur that we use in industry has changed in recent years. Originally sulphur was obtained from the inside of volcanos. Until recently the most important source of sulphur was underground deposits in Texas and Louisiana in the United States. Superheated water (at 170°C) was pumped underground to melt the sulphur. Hot, compressed air was then pumped down to force the mixture of molten sulphur and water to the surface. The impurities do not melt and therefore remain underground. The sulphur produced by this method is very pure.

Now most sulphur is obtained from natural gas and petroleum, which contain small quantities of sulphur compounds. These have to be removed otherwise, on burning, sulphur dioxide would be produced and this is a serious pollutant.

In Great Britain our sulphur is usually imported as a liquid. The sulphur is kept above 120°C so that it remains molten. It can then just be pumped off the ship into storage tanks. Some of our sulphur comes from Poland.

ABOVE Ships transporting liquid sulphur to a factory in the United States for turning into sulphuric acid. What conditions must the sulphur be kept under if it is to remain liquid? Why is it an advantage to transport liquid sulphur rather than solid sulphur?

RIGHT Volcanic deposits of sulphur formed when sulphur gases from deep inside the Earth cool as they leave the volcano.

29.2 Allotropes of sulphur

There are two crystalline forms of sulphur: α–sulphur and β–sulphur. Fig. 29.1 shows the different shapes of the crystals. They are both made from different arrangements of sulphur molecules (Fig. 29.2). These molecules are made up of eight sulphur atoms in a ring. Table 29.1 summarises the properties of the two allotropes of sulphur.

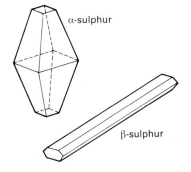

Fig. 29.1   Crystals of α and β sulphur

Table 29.1 The properties of α-sulphur and β-sulphur

	α-sulphur	β-sulphur
Appearance	Bright yellow crystals	Orange-brown needle shaped crystals
Density in g per cm³	2.02	1.96
Volume of 32 g of sulphur in cm³	15.8	16.3
Solubility	Insoluble in water. Soluble in organic solvents like methylbenzene (toluene) and carbon disulphide	
Effect of heat	Rapidly heated it melts at 113°C	Melts at 119°C
Range of stability	More stable below 96°C	More stable above 96°C
Burning in oxygen	Burns to produce sulphur dioxide. No residue. Equal masses of both allotropes produce equal masses of sulphur dioxide	

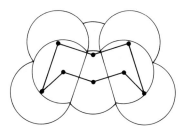

Fig. 29.2   Sulphur molecule

Plastic sulphur is a non-crystalline form of sulphur made when molten sulphur is poured into cold water. It resembles brown chewing gum. It is made up of long chains of sulphur atoms tangled together. After a few minutes it changes and goes hard and yellow. It forms α–sulphur.

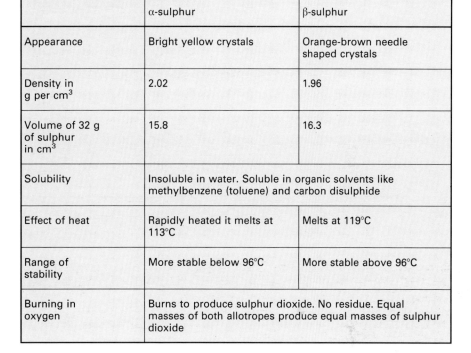

RIGHT   Molten sulphur being poured into cold water. The brown plastic sulphur which forms soon goes hard and brittle as it turns into α-sulphur. In front of the beaker is a lump of roll sulphur, which is the usual way of buying sulphur.

29.3 Action of heat on sulphur

Table 29.2 summarises the changes which take place when crushed sulphur is heated. You will notice that a number of changes take place. These are due to changes in the arrangement of sulphur atoms.

Table 29.2 Effect of heat on powdered sulphur

Temperature	State	Colour	Ease of pouring out of the test tube	Structure
Up to 113°C	Solid	Yellow	–	A regular arrangement of S_8 rings
113°C –180°C	Liquid	Amber	Easy to pour	Irregular arrangement of S_8 rings Rings are free to move
180°C –220°C	Liquid	Dark reddish brown	Difficult to pour	Rings open and short chains join together to produce long chains Long chains are tangled up
220°C –444°C	Liquid	Black	Easy to pour	Long chains break up to form short chains
At 444°C	Turns to gas	Colourless	–	Pairs of sulphur atoms

29.4 Uses of sulphur

Most sulphur is used to make sulphuric acid. Another use is for vulcanising rubber. This is a process developed by Charles Goodyear in the last century. Natural rubber is soft, slightly sticky and quickly becomes unsuitable for making tyres. The rubber contains long chains. Vulcanising is a process where the natural rubber is mixed with up to 30% sulphur. The result is a much harder and more suitable material. The sulphur forms links joining the chains together.

29.5 Burning sulphur in air and oxygen

Sulphur burns in air or oxygen with a blue flame producing sulphur dioxide gas:

$$\text{sulphur} + \text{oxygen} \rightarrow \text{sulphur dioxide}$$

The sulphur dioxide produced is an acid gas. Sulphur dioxide dissolves in water forming sulphurous acid.

Sulphur trioxide, SO_3, is not produced when sulphur or sulphur compounds burn in air or oxygen.

29.6 Manufacturing sulphuric acid in the contact process

The Contact process for the manufacture of sulphuric acid was first invented by Peregrine Phillips in 1831. However, because of the difficulties in understanding the chemical reactions taking place, the first factory was not opened until 1875, in London.

The process involves three stages:

Stage 1 Sulphur dioxide is produced by burning sulphur in air or from burning sulphur-containing compounds:

sulphur + oxygen → sulphur dioxide

The sulphur dioxide is then purified. All of the impurities, especially arsenic compounds, are removed otherwise they damage the catalyst in the next stage.

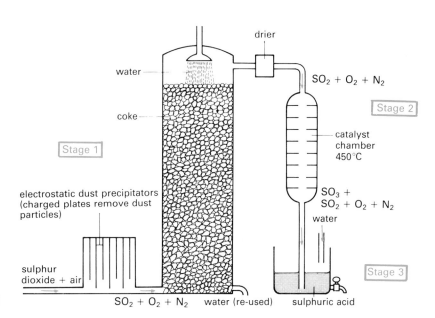

Fig. 29.3 The Contact process for manufacturing sulphuric acid

Stage 2 This is the important stage. Success in this stage will ensure a good yield of sulphuric acid at the end of the process.

Sulphur dioxide and air are passed over a heated catalyst at about 450°C. The catalyst used today is vanadium(v) oxide. About 99.5% of the sulphur dioxide is converted to sulphur trioxide:

sulphur dioxide + oxygen ⇌ sulphur trioxide

The original catalyst for this reaction was platinum metal. This is very expensive and easily ruined by impurities.

Stage 3 All that theoretically has to be done now is to dissolve the sulphur trioxide in water:

sulphur trioxide + water → sulphuric acid

This was the original method used, but this process gives out a great deal of heat and the sulphuric acid boils. The droplets of sulphuric acid condense in the factory. This reduces the yield of sulphuric acid and also makes unbearable and unsafe working conditions.

Now the sulphur trioxide is dissolved in concentrated sulphuric acid forming oleum (sometimes called fuming sulphuric acid), $H_2S_2O_7$:

sulphur trioxide + sulphuric acid → oleum

The oleum is then carefully diluted with the correct quantity of water to make concentrated sulphuric acid:

oleum + water → concentrated sulphuric acid

Because all of the impurities have been removed during manufacture, the sulphuric acid is very pure. Other methods do not make pure sulphuric acid.

The waste gases escaping from the process are cleaned up and only between 0.18 and 0.05% sulphur dioxide escapes into the atmosphere.

The Contact process is summarised in Fig. 29.3 (previous page).

LEFT   Sulphur being used to vulcanise rubber in the manufacture of tyres.

ABOVE   A sulphuric acid plant at Runcorn in Cheshire.

29.7 Possible sites for a sulphuric acid plant

It would be advisable to site the factory on the coast because:

1. Sulphur is imported and so transport costs are reduced.
2. Sulphuric acid could be exported more cheaply.
3. Any sulphur dioxide gas escaping can disperse over the sea.

It is not sited on the coast so that waste products can be pumped into the sea or so that water is available for the process. Sea water is, in fact, highly unsuitable even as cooling water because it is so corrosive.

There are other considerations when siting a sulphuric acid plant. These include:

(a) a supply of labour to build and operate the factory
(b) possible customers for sulphuric acid in the area
(c) communications – road and rail
(d) grants from Government or Local Authorities towards setting up a factory
(e) possible complaints about noise and risk of factory explosion.

In addition to providing jobs connected with the factory, a sulphuric acid factory will encourage the growth of other firms in supply and service industries.

29.8 Safe transport and dilution of concentrated sulphuric acid

Concentrated sulphuric acid is a very corrosive and dangerous material to transport. It has always been transported in large glass bottles called carboys packed in wire baskets with straw. Now it is transported in tankers. The tankers must display a card giving the name of the chemical being transported and how it should be treated in case of spillage (see Unit 2).

If sulphuric acid is spilled from a tanker, it has to be neutralised with an alkali and diluted with a large volume of water. This is a similar procedure to that which we would follow if sulphuric acid was spilt in the laboratory.

If a spillage occurs it is most important to check rivers and water courses close-by for possible pollution.

If concentrated sulphuric acid is diluted it is important to follow a safe procedure. It is most unwise to just add water to acid. The acid is likely to spit all over the place as considerable amounts of heat are given out.

If you are given this task in the laboratory you should put on protective clothing and goggles. Small volumes of acid should be added to water in a large beaker. After each addition the solution should be stirred. Remember – add acid to water and not water to acid!

29.9 Uses of sulphuric acid

It used to be said that the prosperity of a country could be judged by the amount of sulphuric acid that it used each year. This certainly was true when most industry was heavy industry – ship-building, car-making, etc. However, modern technology relies much less on sulphuric acid and this guide to prosperity is no longer true.

Fig. 29.4 shows a pie diagram giving the percentages of sulphuric acid used in different industries.

The most important use of sulphuric acid is in agriculture, in the manufacture of ammonium sulphate fertiliser and in the manufacture of calcium superphosphate – a phosphorus fertiliser. Calcium phosphate, the natural material, is virtually insoluble in water. Treating it with concentrated sulphuric acid produces calcium superphosphate which is more soluble.

Another important use of sulphuric acid is in the manufacture of soapless detergents. Soapless detergents lather equally well in hard and soft water. Soapless detergents are made by reacting hydrocarbon wastes from petroleum refining with concentrated sulphuric acid.

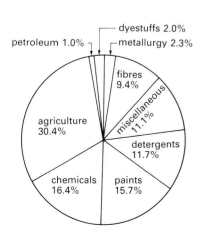

Fig. 29.4 Uses of sulphuric acid

QUESTIONS ON UNIT 29

Domain I: Knowledge and understanding

1. blue, yellow, black, amber, darker, lighter, atoms, molecules, ions, mobile, viscous, melts, boils, burns, solid, liquid, vapour

Complete the following passage about the structure of sulphur and the changes which take place on heating, by putting in the most suitable words from the list above:

Sulphur is a . . . . solid which is made up from an arrangement of sulphur . . . . each containing eight . . . . Sulphur melts at a temperature just above the boiling point of water and forms an . . . . coloured liquid. This liquid is . . . . which means it is easy to pour.

When it is heated further the liquid goes . . . . in colour and becomes . . . . which means it is difficult to pour.

On further heating the sulphur goes black and becomes easy to pour again. Finally, at 444°C the liquid sulphur . . . . and sulphur . . . . is formed.

If the sulphur catches alight during this heating it burns with a . . . . coloured flame.

2. Complete the following passage about the Contact process:

Sulphuric acid is made by the Contact process. First, sulphur or some sulphur-containing mineral is burned in air to produce . . . . gas. This gas is then purified and dried to prevent . . . . the catalyst at a later stage.

This gas and air are then passed over a heated catalyst made of . . . . There the gases react to produce sulphur trioxide. The sulphur trioxide dissolves in . . . . to produce oleum which, when diluted with the correct amount of . . . ., produces concentrated sulphuric acid.

3. Complete the following word equations:

magnesium + sulphuric acid (dilute) → . . . . + ...

sodium hydroxide + sulphuric acid → . . . . + ...

copper(II) oxide + sulphuric acid → . . . . + ...

sodium carbonate + sulphuric acid → . . . . + ... + ...

copper + sulphuric acid (conc) → . . . . + water + sulphur dioxide

Domain II: Handling information and solving problems

4. Below is a flow diagram for the Contact process. Study the diagram and answer the following questions:

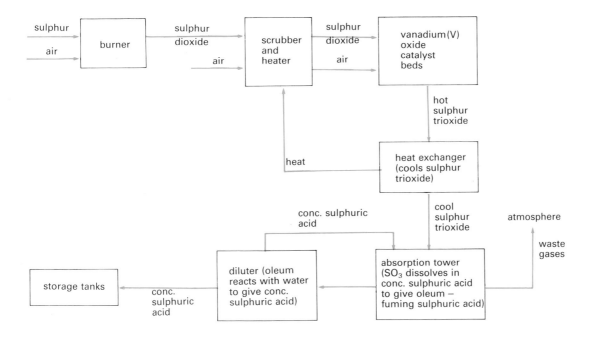

(a) Explain why the heat exchanger helps to make the production of sulphuric acid an economical process.

(b) Why must care be taken to monitor the gases entering the atmosphere?

(c) Why are most sulphuric acid factories in Great Britain built on the coast?

(d) The imaginary country of Asbootoland is a poor country with little mineral wealth and little industry. Its agriculture is under-developed and it is unable to feed its whole population. In the north of the country there is a volcanic region with sulphur deposits.

Why might Asbootoland wish to develop its own means of producing sulphuric acid? Does it have any advantages over a factory in Great Britain producing sulphuric acid and selling it to Asbootoland?

5. Burning sulphur in air produces sulphur dioxide:

$$\text{sulphur} + \text{oxygen} \rightarrow \text{sulphur dioxide}$$
$$\text{S(s)} + \text{O}_2\text{(g)} \rightarrow \text{SO}_2\text{(g)}$$

Sulphur dioxide is a gas which dissolves in water to form a solution with a pH of 2.

(a) Outline a method of removing sulphur dioxide from waste gases escaping from a factory chimney.

(b) Give an economic advantage of recovering sulphur dioxide.

6. Design apparatus for comparing the amount of sulphur dioxide in air in different places. Explain the working of the apparatus and any measurements you would make.

UNIT 30 Chemical testing

30.1 Introduction

A chemist spends a lot of time carrying out tests to identify substances. In this unit some of the important chemical tests are given. You will have met some of these tests in earlier units.

30.2 Testing for gases

Table 30.1 gives the information about properties and tests for common gases.

Nitrogen is a particularly difficult gas to test for because it does not give any simple positive test.

Table 30.1 Tests for common gases

Gas	Formula	Colour	Smell	Test with moist litmus	Test with lighted splint	Other tests
Hydrogen	H_2	×	×	×	Squeaky pop splint extinguished	–
Oxygen	O_2	×	×	×	Relights glowing splint	–
Nitrogen	N_2	×	×	×	Extinguished	Forms compound with magnesium
Chlorine	Cl_2	Greenish-yellow	√	Blue → red then bleaches	Extinguished	–
Hydrogen chloride	HCl	×	√	Blue → red	Extinguished	White fumes with ammonia
Carbon dioxide	CO_2	×	×	Little change	Extinguished	Turns limewater milky
Carbon monoxide	CO	×	×	×	Burns with blue flame	–
Ammonia	NH_3	×	√	Red → blue	Extinguished	White fumes with hydrogen chloride
Sulphur dioxide	SO_2	×	√	Blue → red	Extinguished	Turns potassium dichromate green. No effect on lead nitrate
Hydrogen sulphide	H_2S	×	√	Blue → slightly red	Burns producing sulphur dioxide	Lead nitrate paper turns black
Nitrogen dioxide	NO_2	Brown	√	Blue → red	Extinguished	–
Dinitrogen monoxide	N_2O	×	√	×	Relights glowing splint	Quite soluble
Nitrogen monoxide	NO	×	–	–	–	Forms brown fumes in air

30.3 Testing for water

Many colourless liquids look like water. There are two sets to show that a liquid contains water:

1. Add blue cobalt(II) chloride paper to the liquid. If it turns pink the liquid contains water.
2. Add white anhydrous copper(II) sulphate powder to the liquid. It turns blue if water is there.

To show a liquid is *pure* water, it is necessary to show that it boils at 100°C and freezes at 0°C.

30.4 Testing for carbon and hydrogen in a compound

Organic compounds contain carbon and hydrogen. When they are burned, carbon dioxide and water are formed. Burning them, however, can be a messy business!

A cleaner way of burning or oxidising an organic compound involves heating a mixture of the compound and copper(II) oxide. The products include carbon dioxide (test with limewater) and water (test with cobalt(II) chloride or anhydrous copper(II) sulphate). Brown copper will also be seen in the final mixture.

compound + copper(II) oxide → carbon dioxide + water + copper

30.5 Testing for starch

Many everyday substances contain starch, e.g. potatoes, bread. It is easy to test for starch by adding a drop of iodine solution. If starch is present a dark-blue colour is formed.

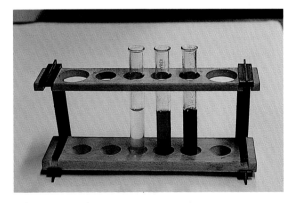

Testing for starch. The three test tubes contain, from left to right: (i) starch solution; (ii) iodine solution; (iii) the dark blue-black complex formed when starch solution and iodine solution are mixed.

30.6 Testing for reducing sugars

Sugars are carbohydrates. Some sugars can act as reducing agents and are called **reducing sugars**. These include glucose, fructose and maltose. To test for a reducing sugar, either Fehling's or Benedict's solution is added to the solution and the solution is boiled. A brick-red precipitate of copper(I) oxide is formed if a reducing sugar is present.

30.7   Testing for negative ions

Much of the testing is used to identify sulphates, chlorides, carbonates, nitrates, etc. These are called negative ions or anions.

Carbonate

When dilute hydrochloric acid is added to a carbonate, carbon dioxide gas is produced. No heat is required. The carbon dioxide turns limewater milky.

Chloride

When a solution of a chloride is treated with dilute nitric acid (to make the solution acid) and silver nitrate solution, a white precipitate of silver chloride is formed at once. This precipitate slowly turns purplish in sunlight and dissolves completely in ammonia solution.

When a solid chloride is treated with concentrated sulphuric acid, steamy colourless fumes of hydrogen chloride are formed. These fumes turn blue litmus red and form dense white fumes with ammonia gas.

Bromide and iodide

The same test is used to test for a bromide or iodide as was used for a chloride in solution. Instead of a white precipitate of silver chloride, either a cream precipitate of silver bromide or a yellow precipitate of silver iodide is formed.

Sulphate

When dilute hydrochloric acid and barium chloride solution are added to a solution of a sulphate, a white precipitate of barium sulphate is formed immediately.

Nitrate

Sodium hydroxide solution is added to a solution believed to contain a nitrate and aluminium powder is added. The mixture is warmed and hydrogen gas is produced. If a nitrate is also present, ammonia gas will also be produced, which turns red litmus blue.

30.8   Testing for positive ions

There are three tests which can be used to identify positive ions (cations):

Flame tests

A small quantity of the compound is taken and a couple of drops of concentrated hydrochloric acid are added. A clean piece of platinum wire is dipped into the mixture and put into a hot Bunsen burner flame. Certain positive ions (or metal ions) colour the flame. Common flame colours are shown in Table 30.2.

Flame colour	Cation
Orange-yellow	Sodium Na^+
Lilac-pink	Potassium K^+
Brick red	Calcium Ca^{2+}
Bright red	Strontium Sr^{2+}
Pale green	Barium Ba^{2+}
Green	Copper(II) Cu^{2+}
Blue	Lead Pb^{2+}

Table 30.2 Flame tests for identifying cations

Tests with sodium hydroxide solution

If a small quantity of the compound in solution is treated with sodium hydroxide solution, an insoluble hydroxide may be precipitated. If a precipitate is formed it may re-dissolve in excess sodium hydroxide solution. Table 30.3 summarises the results.

Table 30.3 Precipitation of metal hydroxides with sodium hydroxide

Cation	Addition of sodium hydroxide solution	
	A couple of drops	Excess
Potassium K^+	No precipitate	No precipitate
Sodium Na^+	No precipitate	No precipitate
Calcium Ca^{2+}	White precipitate	Precipitate insoluble
Magnesium Mg^{2+}	White precipitate	Precipitate insoluble
Aluminium Al^{3+}	White precipitate	Precipitate soluble – colourless solution
Zinc Zn^{2+}	White precipitate	Precipitate soluble – colourless solution
Iron(II) Fe^{2+}	Green precipitate	Precipitate insoluble
Iron(III) Fe^{3+}	Red-brown precipitate	Precipitate insoluble
Lead Pb^{2+}	White precipitate	Precipitate soluble – colourless solution
Copper(II) Cu^{2+}	Blue precipitate	Precipitate insoluble
Silver Ag^+	Grey-brown precipitate	Precipitate insoluble

If no precipitate is formed, the solution should be warmed. If the ammonium ion (NH_4^+) is present, ammonia gas is produced, which turns red litmus blue.

Tests with aqueous ammonia solution (ammonium hydroxide)

If a small quantity of the compound in solution is treated with ammonia solution, an insoluble hydroxide may be precipitated. The precipitate may re-dissolve in excess ammonia solution. The possible results are summarised in Table 30.4.

Table 30.4 Precipitation of metal hydroxides with ammonia solution

Cation	Addition of ammonia solution	
	A couple of drops	Excess
Potassium	No precipitate	No precipitate
Sodium	No precipitate	No precipitate
Calcium	No precipitate	No precipitate
Magnesium	White precipitate	Precipitate insoluble
Aluminium	White precipitate	Precipitate insoluble
Zinc	White precipitate	Precipitate soluble – colourless solution
Iron(II)	Green precipitate	Precipitate insoluble
Iron(III)	Red-brown precipitate	Precipitate insoluble
Lead	White precipitate	Precipitate insoluble
Copper	Blue precipitate	Precipitate soluble – blue solution
Silver	Brown precipitate	Precipitate soluble

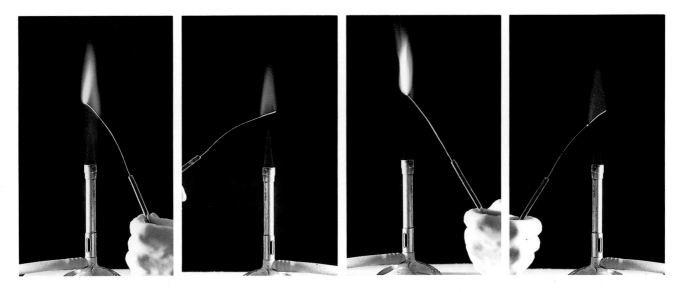

Flame tests can be used to test for the presence of metal ions. Can you identify the metal ions present from the colours of the flames produced? You will need to refer to Table 30.2.

Robert Wilhelm Bunsen (1811–1899)

The invention of the **Bunsen burner** was just one part of this German chemist's varied, and occasionally hazardous, work. At the end of his 88-year life he had a string of discoveries – and a blind eye – as evidence of his years of dedicated study in the laboratory.

Robert Bunsen was born in Gottingen and studied Chemistry, Physics and Zoology there before moving on to study in Paris, Berlin and Vienna. In 1852 he became Professor of Chemistry in Heidelberg.

Bunsen investigated the different colours produced when substances are put into a hot Bunsen burner flame. We still use those 'flame tests' to identify certain metals. As a result of his work in this field in 1861 two new elements were discovered, caesium and rubidium.

He also invented the ice calorimeter which shows how much heat chemical reactions give off by measuring their effect on ice, and an efficient carbon-zinc **Bunsen battery**.

He studied the highly-poisonous arsenic compounds, and having studied poison, worked out that the antidote to arsenic poisoning is iron oxide. It is not recorded whether he ever needed to take that antidote!

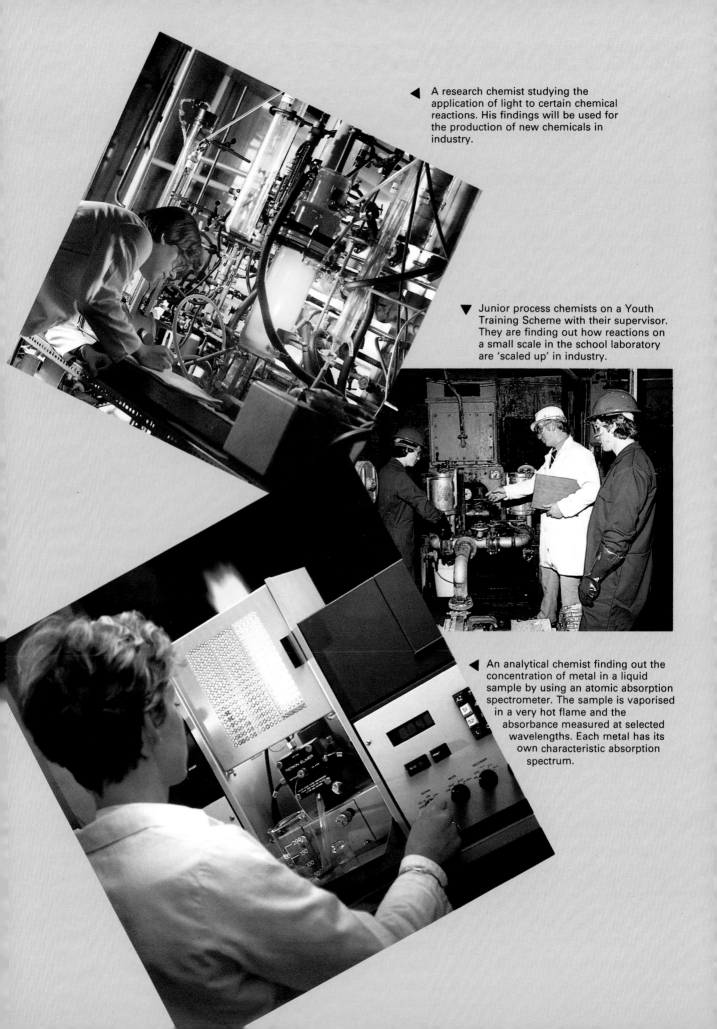

◀ A research chemist studying the application of light to certain chemical reactions. His findings will be used for the production of new chemicals in industry.

▼ Junior process chemists on a Youth Training Scheme with their supervisor. They are finding out how reactions on a small scale in the school laboratory are 'scaled up' in industry.

◀ An analytical chemist finding out the concentration of metal in a liquid sample by using an atomic absorption spectrometer. The sample is vaporised in a very hot flame and the absorbance measured at selected wavelengths. Each metal has its own characteristic absorption spectrum.

QUESTIONS ON UNIT 30

Domain I: Knowledge and understanding

1. hydrogen, oxygen, nitrogen, chlorine, carbon dioxide, ammonia

   Which gas in the list above:

   (a) puts out a lighted splint and turns limewater milky?
   (b) puts out a lighted splint and does not turn limewater milky?
   (c) is a greenish-yellow gas?
   (d) is a gas which turns blue litmus red and then bleaches it?
   (e) relights a glowing splint?
   (f) burns with a squeaky pop when a lighted splint is put in?
   (g) turns red litmus blue?

2. cobalt(II) chloride paper, Universal indicator paper, Fehling's solution, iodine solution, dilute hydrochloric acid

   Which of the above reagents is used to test for:

   (a) starch?
   (b) water?
   (c) a reducing sugar?
   (d) a carbonate?
   (e) an alkali?

3. Name the substance precipitated when:

   (a) a mixture of dilute nitric acid and silver nitrate solution is added to sodium chloride solution;
   (b) a mixture of dilute hydrochloric acid and barium chloride solution is added to sodium sulphate solution;
   (c) sodium hydroxide solution is added to copper(II) sulphate solution.

4. Which positive ion:

   (a) gives a lilac flame test?
   (b) produces ammonia gas when heated with sodium hydroxide solution?
   (c) gives a brick-red flame test?
   (d) produces a green precipitate when sodium hydroxide solution is added?
   (e) produces a white precipitate when sodium hydroxide solution is added and the precipitate re-dissolves in excess alkali? Also, a white precipitate is formed when ammonia solution is added but this time the precipitate does not re-dissolve in excess alkali.

5. ammonium chloride, potassium carbonate, hydrated cobalt(II) chloride, zinc oxide, copper(II) oxide, anhydrous sodium carbonate, sodium nitrate

   Name a compound from the list above which:

   (a) loses oxygen on heating
   (b) loses water on heating
   (c) forms a blue solution when warmed with dilute sulphuric acid
   (d) sublimes of heating
   (e) forms bubbles of gas when dilute hydrochloric acid is added.

Domain II: Handling information and solving problems

6. Hazel was asked to identify a compound by carrying out qualitative tests. The results are shown below:

Test	Observations
Appearance	White solid
Heat compound	No change
Flame test	Orange flame
Add dilute hydrochloric acid	Solid dissolves, no effervescence
Add dilute hydrocholoric acid and barium chloride solution to a solution of the substance	No precipitate
Add dilute nitric acid and silver nitrate solution to a solution of the unknown substance	White precipitate

Identify the white solid she was using.

UNIT 31 Chemical calculations

31.1 Introduction

In most Chemistry courses, especially if a grade C or above is the target, it is necessary to attempt some simple chemical calculations. The understanding of the quantities of chemicals used and produced in chemical reactions can be extremely important in the chemical industry. It enables a manufacturer, for example, to work out costs and therefore the price that has to be charged for the product if a profit is to be made. A manufacturer would also have to work out how much energy is required and include this in the pricing.

31.2 Relative atomic mass

In Unit 8 the idea of **relative atomic mass** was introduced. Atoms of an element are extremely small and copper atoms, for example, are different from iron atoms.

The relative atomic mass A_r of an element tells you how much heavier one atom is than another. In fact, the A_r is the number of times the mass of one atom of an element is heavier than one twelfth of the mass of a carbon-12 atom:

$$\text{relative atomic mass} = \frac{\text{mass of one atom of the element}}{\text{mass of one twelfth of a carbon-12 atom}}$$

NB The relative atomic mass is a ratio or number and therefore has no units.

The relative atomic masses of some of the common elements are shown at the foot of each page in this unit to help you with the questions in this section.

QUESTIONS TO TRY

1. How many times heavier is:

(a) one atom of helium than one atom of hydrogen?
(b) one atom of bromine than one atom of calcium?
(c) one atom of mercury than one atom of calcium?
(d) one atom of copper than two atoms of oxygen?

2. Which one of each of the following pairs contains the larger number of atoms?

(a) 12 g of magnesium or 12 g of carbon
(b) 25 g of sulphur or 25 g of phosphorus
(c) 15 g of sodium or 30 g of calcium
(d) 10 g of nickel or 20 g of tin

3. A krypton atom is seven times heavier than a carbon-12 atom. What is the relative atomic mass of krypton?

31.3 The mole

The relative atomic masses of hydrogen and helium are 1 and 4 respectively. This means that:

> 1 atom of helium weighs 4 times as much as 1 atom of hydrogen.
>
> 2 atoms of helium weigh 4 times as much as 2 atoms of hydrogen.
>
> 1000 atoms of helium weigh 4 times as much as 1000 atoms of hydrogen.

In fact, providing *equal numbers of helium and hydrogen atoms* are considered, the helium atoms will always weigh four times as much as the hydrogen atoms.

It would be useful to have a measure which enabled us to compare a *fixed number* of atoms of different elements. This is where the idea of the **mole** comes in.

A mole is that amount of a substance which contains 600 000 000 000 000 000 000 000 particles. This number is more easily written as 6×10^{23} and is sometimes called **Avogadro's number** (L) after the famous nineteenth-century Italian chemist Avogadro. It is a very large number indeed, so large that it is difficult for us to imagine. Here are two ways of thinking about this number:

1. If the whole population of the world was to sit down and count up to this number, sharing the job between us, it would take us six million years to finish – providing we did not have breaks!
2. A line 6×10^{23} millimetres long would stretch from the earth to the sun and back two million times.

Why do we choose such a large number? It just happens that 6×10^{23} atoms of the lightest element, hydrogen (relative atomic mass = 1) weigh

H = 1, He = 4, C = 12, N = 14, O = 16, Na = 23, Mg = 24, Al = 27, P = 31, S = 32, Cl = 35.5,

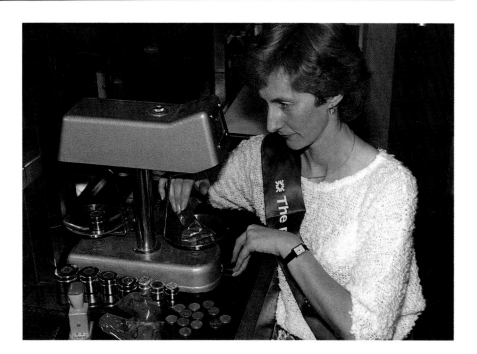

A bank teller weighs bags of coins and can work out from the weighings how many coins are in the bag without having to count them. Similarly, a chemist can work out how many particles are present in a sample using the weight of the sample and Avogadro's number.

exactly 1 g, so choosing this number enables us to translate the relative atomic mass of any element into an equivalent mass in grams. Hence 6×10^{23} atoms (1 mole) of oxygen atoms (relative atomic mass = 16) will weigh 16 g, while 6×10^{23} (one mole) of sulphur atoms (relative atomic mass = 32) will weigh 32 g. This means that the *ratio* of the relative atomic masses of any two elements is the same as the ratio of their masses of one mole.

One mole of each element therefore contains the same number of particles (i.e. 6×10^{23}).

This is further proof of the very small size of atoms. Twelve grams of carbon is a very small handful but it contains a very large number of carbon atoms (6×10^{23}). How many carbon atoms are there in a tonne of coal?

QUESTIONS TO TRY

4. How many grams do each of the following weigh?

(a) 6×10^{23} atoms of helium
(b) 6×10^{23} atoms of aluminium
(c) 12×10^{23} atoms of iron
(d) 3×10^{23} atoms of sulphur
(e) 6×10^{22} atoms of mercury

5. 6×10^{23} atoms of barium weigh 137 g. What is the relative atomic mass of barium?

6. One mole of carbon atoms weighs 12 g. If a mole of titanium atoms weighs four times as much as one of carbon atoms, what is the relative atomic mass of titanium?

K = 39, Ca = 40, Fe = 56, Ni = 59, Cu = 63.5, Br = 80, Ag = 108, Sn = 119, Hg = 200, Pb = 207

31.4 Moles of molecules and moles of ions

In Unit 31.3 we dealt with moles of atoms of an element, but we can also calculate moles of molecules or ions.

Most gases contain pairs of atoms. They are said to be **diatomic**. Hydrogen, for example, is written as H_2, while oxygen, nitrogen and chlorine are written as O_2, N_2 and Cl_2 respectively.

One mole of hydrogen molecules has a mass of $1 \times 2 = 2$ g, while a mole of oxygen molecules weighs $16 \times 2 = 32$ g.

We can also work out the mass of a mole of molecules in a compound providing we know the formula of the compound.

Example Sulphuric acid has a formula H_2SO_4. The mass of 1 mole of sulphuric acid consists of:

Calculation	2×1 g $=\ $ 2 g of hydrogen
	$+$
	1×32 g $=$ 32 g of sulphur
	$+$
	4×16 g $=$ 64 g of oxygen
	————————————
	98 g of H_2SO_4

Example Similarly, we can calculate the mass of 0.5 moles of nitrate ions, NO_3^-:

Calculation	$1 \times 14 = 14$ g of nitrogen
	$+$
	$3 \times 16 = 48$ g of oxygen
	————————————
	1 mole of nitrate ions $= 62$ g
	0.5 moles of nitrate ions $= 31$ g (i.e. half of 62 g)

NB The fact that the nitrate ion is charged does not matter. Electrons, which produce the negative charge, have negligible mass.

If you wish to calculate the number of moles of a substance in a given sample, the following equation can be used:

$$\text{number of moles} = \frac{\text{mass of the sample}}{\text{mass of 1 mole}}$$

Example Calculate the number of moles present in 28 g of calcium oxide, CaO:

Calculation

1 mole of calcium oxide has a mass of 56 g (i.e. $40 + 16$)

number of moles of calcium oxide $= {}^{28}\!/_{56} = 0.5$

H = 1, He = 4, C = 12, N = 14, O = 16, Na = 23, Mg = 24, Al = 27, P = 31, S = 32, Cl = 35.5,

7. Work out the mass of:

 (a) 1 mole of sodium atoms (Na)
 (b) 1 mole of chlorine atoms (Cl)
 (c) 1 mole of chlorine molecules (Cl_2)
 (d) 1 mole of chloride ions (Cl^-)
 (e) 0.5 moles of carbon atoms (C)
 (f) 0.1 moles of bromine atoms (Br)
 (g) 0.1 moles of bromine molecules (Br_2)
 (h) One third of a mole of aluminium atoms (Al)

8. Work out how many moles of atoms are present in each of these masses:

 (a) 64 g of sulphur atoms (S)
 (b) 3.9 g of potassium atoms (K)
 (c) 0.14 g of nitrogen atoms (N)
 (d) 400 g of mercury atoms (Hg)

9. Calculate the mass of 1 mole of:

 (a) nitrogen dioxide molecules (NO_2)
 (b) nitric acid (HNO_3)
 (c) calcium hydroxide ($Ca(OH)_2$)
 (d) carbonate ions (CO_3^{2-})
 (e) ammonia (NH_3)
 (f) sulphur atoms (S)
 (g) sulphur molecules (S_8)
 (h) hydrochloric acid (HCl)

31.5 Molar volume of gases

One mole of molecules of any gas occupies a volume of 24 dm^3 (24 000 cm^3) at room temperature and atmospheric pressure. The volume of the gas would change, however, if temperature or pressure are changed. For example:

 a cube of side 29 cm (0.29 m) has a volume of approximately 24 dm^3.

If the volume of a gas at room temperature and atmospheric pressure is known, the number of moles of gas can be calculated.

Example Calculate the number of moles of carbon dioxide molecules present in 240 cm^3 of gas at room temperature and atmospheric pressure:

Calculation

1 mole of carbon dioxide would occupy 24 000 cm^3

$1/100$th mole of carbon dioxide would occupy 240 cm^3

number of moles of carbon dioxide = 0.01 moles

K = 39, Ca = 40, Fe = 56, Ni = 59, Cu = 63.5, Br = 80, Ag = 108, Sn = 119, Hg = 200, Pb = 207

QUESTIONS TO TRY

10. Work out how many moles of molecules each of the following gases would contain:

(a) 12 dm^3 of hydrogen (H$_2$)
(b) 1.2 dm^3 of ammonia (NH$_3$)
(c) 100 cm^3 of carbon monoxide (CO)

All volumes are measured at room temperature and pressure.

11. In an experiment to find the mass of 1 mole of sulphur dioxide gas, a corked, glass round-bottom flask was used. The results are shown below:

Mass of corked flask filled with dry air = 190.85 g
Mass of corked flask with all the air removed = 190.25 g
Mass of corked flask filled with sulphur dioxide = 191.58 g

(a) What was the mass of the air in the flask?
(b) If 1000 cm^3 of dry air has a mass of 1.2 g, what is the volume of the flask?
(c) What was the mass of sulphur dioxide filling the flask?
(d) What would be the mass of 1 dm^3 of sulphur dioxide?
(e) What would be the mass of 24 dm^3 of sulphur dioxide?
(f) What would be the mass of 1 mole of sulphur dioxide molecules?
(g) Given that the formula of sulphur dioxide is SO$_2$, what mass would you have expected from the experiment?
(h) Why do you think the calculated and experimental values were not the same?

31.6 Working out the formula of a compound

One mole of *any* substance contains *the same number of particles*. Fig. 31.1 shows two piles. One pile contains 0.1 moles of copper atoms and the other 0.1 moles of sulphur atoms. Though the pile of sulphur atoms is bigger, the pile of copper atoms weighs more. Both piles contain the same number of particles.

In Fig. 31.2 there are, again, two piles. One pile consists of 0.1 moles of carbon atoms and the other 0.2 moles of iron atoms. Although the two piles look the same, there are twice as many iron atoms as carbon atoms. You cannot judge the number of moles present just by looking at the size of a pile. We will use these ideas in working out the formula of a compound.

In theory, the formula of any compound can be obtained by an experiment involving a series of weighings. Three examples are given on the pages which follow.

        sulphur   copper   carbon   iron

Fig. 31.1   **Fig. 31.2**

H = 1, He = 4, C = 12, N = 14, O = 16, Na = 23, Mg = 24, Al = 27, P = 31, S = 32, Cl = 35.5,

1. Magnesium oxide   The formula of magnesium oxide can be found by burning a known mass of magnesium ribbon in a crucible (Fig. 31.3).

A crucible and lid are weighed and then weighed again with a piece of magnesium ribbon inside. The crucible is then heated until all the magnesium has burned. The lid is lifted from time to time to let the air in but care must be taken that smoke does not escape.

The crucible is then left to cool and finally the crucible, lid and magnesium oxide residue are weighed.

Sample result: (1) Mass of crucible + lid = 25.15 g
(2) Mass of crucible + lid + magnesium = 25.27 g
(3) Mass of crucible· + lid + magnesium oxide = 25.35 g

Calculation   From these results we can calculate:

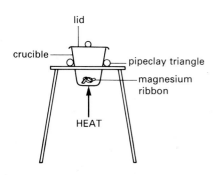

Fig. 31.3

> Calculation
>
> the mass of magnesium (2) − (1) = 25.27 g − 25.15 g = 0.12 g
> the mass of magnesium oxide (3) − (1) = 25.35 g − 25.15 g = 0.20 g
> 0.12 g of magnesium combine with (0.20 − 0.12)g of oxygen to form
>   0.20 g of magnesium oxide
> 0.12 g of magnesium combines with 0.08 g of oxygen

These masses then have to be converted in numbers of moles using the formula in Unit 31.4. This involves dividing the mass by the appropriate relative atomic mass:

> Calculation
>
> $^{0.12}/_{24}$ moles of magnesium atoms combine with $^{0.08}/_{16}$ moles of
>   oxygen atoms
> 0.005 moles of magnesium atoms combine with 0.005 moles of
>   oxygen atoms

Remember that 0.005 moles of magnesium and oxygen contain the same number of atoms.

The simplest formula of magnesium oxide is, therefore, MgO.

If this experiment is carried out often the answer obtained is uncertain. There are so many possible inaccuracies in the experiment. Usual errors result from:

(a) all of the magnesium not burning
(b) some of the magnesium oxide escaping as smoke
(c) nitrogen in the air also reacts with magnesium and so the solid produced contains some magnesium nitride.

Good results can be obtained by groups of students doing a series of reactions with different masses of magnesium ribbon. The results can be recorded on a graph (Fig. 31.4). A straight line is drawn on the graph and the mass of oxygen reacting with 0.12 g of magnesium can be found.

Burning a known mass of magnesium in air to produce magnesium oxide.

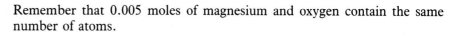

K = 39, Ca = 40, Fe = 56, Ni = 59, Cu = 63.5, Br = 80, Ag = 108, Sn = 119, Hg = 200, Pb = 207

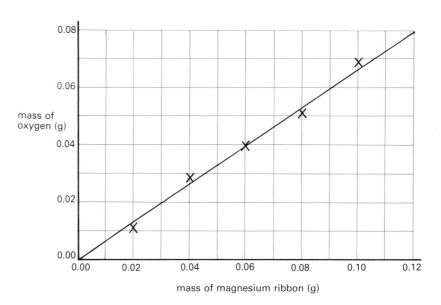

Fig. 31.4

2. Copper(ɪɪ) oxide   A known mass of copper(ɪɪ) oxide is reduced to copper by hydrogen in the apparatus shown in Fig. 31.5. (See photograph on page 218.)

$$\text{copper(ɪɪ) oxide} + \text{hydrogen} \rightarrow \text{copper} + \text{water}$$

Sample results   (1) Mass of combustion boat = 12.20 g
(2) Mass of boat + copper(ɪɪ) oxide = 13.80 g
(3) Mass of boat + copper = 13.48 g

Calculation   From these results we can calculate:

Calculation

mass of copper(ɪɪ) oxide used (2) − (1) = 1.60 g

mass of copper produced (3) − (1) = 1.28 g

1.28 g of copper combines with (1.60 − 1.28 g) of oxygen to form 1.60 g of copper(ɪɪ) oxide

1.28 g of copper combines with 0.32 g of oxygen

$^{1.28}/_{64}$ moles of copper atoms combine with $^{0.32}/_{16}$ moles of oxygen atoms

0.02 moles of copper atoms combine with 0.02 moles of oxygen atoms

---

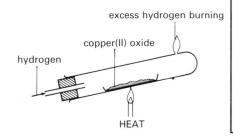

Fig. 31.5

The simplest formula is, therefore, CuO.

H = 1, He = 4, C = 12, N = 14, O = 16, Na = 23, Mg = 24, Al = 27, P = 31, S = 32, Cl = 35.5,

3. Iron(III) oxide   In a similar way an experiment could be carried out and the results obtained could be processed as before.

Calculation

1.12 g of iron combines with 0.48 g of oxygen to form 1.60 g of iron oxide

$^{1.12}/_{56}$ moles of iron atoms combine with $^{0.48}/_{16}$ moles of oxygen atoms.

0.02 moles of iron atoms combine with 0.03 moles of oxygen atoms.

This time, for every two atoms of iron present there are thre atoms of oxygen.

The simplest formula is, therefore, Fe_2O_3.

QUESTIONS TO TRY

12. Calculate the simplest formula of mercury chloride from the following results of an experiment in which a known mass of mercury chloride is reduced to mercury:

    Mass of beaker = 45.23 g
    Mass of beaker + mercury chloride = 47.94 g
    Mass of beaker + mercury = 47.23 g

13. Calculate the simplest formulae from the following data:

    (a) 2.0 g of sulphur combines with 3.0 g of oxygen
    (b) 6 g of carbon combines with 1 g of hydrogen
    (c) 0.09 g of hydrogen combines with 4.2 g of nitrogen
    (d) 4.14 g of lead combines with 0.64 g of oxygen to form lead oxide
    (e) 0.7 g of nitrogen combines with oxygen to form 1.5 g of nitrogen oxide.

31.7 Calculating the simplest formula from percentages

Example   A hydrocarbon contains 75% carbon and 25% hydrogen. Calculate the simplest formula of the hydrocarbon from this information.

Calculation

	C	H
percentage	75	25
relative atomic mass	12	1
percentage/relative atomic mass	6.25	25
divide by the smallest, i.e. 6.25	1	4

The simplest formula is CH_4.

K = 39, Ca = 40, Fe = 56, Ni = 59, Cu = 63.5, Br = 80, Ag = 108, Sn = 119, Hg = 200, Pb = 207

31.8 Calculating the percentages of elements in a compound

Example   Calculate the percentage of nitrogen in ammonium nitrate NH_4NO_3.

A known mass of wire-form copper(II) oxide being reduced to form copper.

> **Calculation**
>
> mass of 1 mole of ammonium nitrate =
> $14 + (4 \times 1) + 14 + (3 \times 16) = 80$ g
>
> each 80 g of ammonium nitrate contains (2×14)g of nitrogen,
>   i.e. 28 g
>
> percentage of nitrogen = $\frac{28}{80} \times 100 = 35\%$

QUESTIONS TO TRY

14. Calculate in each case the simplest formula from the percentages given:

(a) sulphur 50%, oxygen 50%
(b) iron 28%, sulphur 24%, oxygen 48%
(c) carbon 84%, hydrogen 16%

15. Calculate the percentage of each element present in calcium carbonate, $CaCO_3$.

16. Calculate the percentage of:

(a) potassium in potassium hydrogencarbonate, $KHCO_3$
(b) magnesium in magnesium oxide, MgO
(c) nitrogen in ammonium sulphate, $(NH_4)_2SO_4$

31.9 Calculations from equations

Balanced symbol equations (see Appendix) give a summary of the chemicals reacting and produced in a chemical reaction. However, they do more than this. A balanced symbol equation will enable a manufacturer to work out the quanities required and the masses of the products that can be expected.

Example   The equation for the reaction between calcium carbonate and hydrochloric acid is:

$$CaCO_3(s) + 2HCl(aq) \rightarrow CaCl_2(aq) + CO_2(g) + H_2O(l)$$

The equation tells us that 1 mole of calcium carbonate reacts with 2 moles of hydrochloric acid to produce 1 mole of calcium chloride, 1 mole of

H = 1, He = 4, C = 12, N = 14, O = 16, Na = 23, Mg = 24, Al = 27, P = 31, S = 32, Cl = 35.5,

carbon dioxide and 1 mole of water. If we translate this information into masses we get:

100 g of calcium carbonate reacts with 73 g of hydrochloric acid to produce 111 g of calcium chloride, 44 g of carbon dioxide and 18 g of water.

NB The sum of the masses of the reacting substances should equal the sum of the masses of the substances produced.

This information can then be used in calculations.

Example Calculate the mass of calcium chloride produced when 40 g of calcium carbonate reacts with excess hydrochloric acid:

> Calculation
>
> 100 g of calcium carbonate produces 111 g of calcium chloride
> 1 g of calcium carbonate produces $^{111}/_{100}$ g of calcium chloride
> 40 g of calcium carbonate produces $40 \times {}^{111}/_{100}$ of calcium chloride, i.e. 44.4 g.

QUESTIONS TO TRY

17. $Mg(s) + H_2SO_4(aq) \rightarrow MgSO_4(aq) + H_2(g)$

(a) Calculate the mass of magnesium sulphate produced when 4.8 g of magnesium reacts with excess dilute sulphuric acid.
(b) Calculate the volume of hydrogen which would be produced if 4.8 g of magnesium reacts with excess dilute sulphuric acid. The volume of hydrogen is measured at room temperature and atmospheric pressure.
(Hint: Look back to Unit 31.5).

18. $C_2H_4(g) + H_2(g) \rightarrow C_2H_6(g)$

Calculate the mass of ethane, C_2H_6, produced when 28 tonnes of ethene, C_2H_4, reacts with hydrogen.

19. $N_2(g) + 3H_2(g) \rightarrow 2\,NH_3(g)$

What volume of ammonia would be produced if 10 cm³ of nitrogen and 30 cm³ of hydrogen are converted completely into ammonia? (All volumes measured at room temperature and atmospheric pressure.)

K = 39, Ca = 40, Fe = 56, Ni = 59, Cu = 63.5, Br = 80, Ag = 108, Sn = 119, Hg = 200, Pb = 207

MORE QUESTIONS FOR YOU TO TRY

You will need to refer to the Data Section (pages 245–260).

20. Calculate the cost of:

(a) 1 kg of AR sodium chloride
(b) 100 g of Technical grade ammonium nitrate.
(c) 1 mole of Laboratory grade sodium hydroxide.

21. Complete the following table:

Name	Formula	State	Mass of 1 mole in g
Methane Butane Propan-1-ol Glucose	CH_4	g	16

22. Calculate the volume of 1 mole of atoms of the following elements:

(a) neon
(b) phosphorus
(c) mercury.

23. Calculate the percentage of mercury in mercury(I) chloride, $HgCl$ and mercury(II) chloride, $HgCl_2$.

24. Sometimes the solubility of a substance is given in mole per dm^3. Calculate the solubility in water, in mole per dm^3, of:

(a) sodium chloride at 20°C
(b) copper(II) sulphate at 80°C
(c) ammonia at 20°C.

25. $2NaOH(aq) + H_2SO_4(aq) \rightarrow Na_2SO_4(aq) + 2H_2O(l)$

(a) Calculate the mass of:
  (i) 1 mole of sodium hydroxide
  (ii) 1 mole of sulphuric acid
  (iii) 1 mole of anhydrous sulphuric acid
  (iv) 1 mole of water.

(b) Calculate the mass of sodium hydroxide which would react with 9.8 g of sulphuric acid.

(c) Calculate the mass of sodium hydroxide which must be dissolved in water to make 500 cm^3 of solution of concentration of 0.1 mole per dm^3.

(d) Calculate the mass of sulphuric acid which must be dissolved in water to make 250 cm^3 of solution of concentration 0.1 mole per dm^3.

(e) What volume of sulphuric acid (0.1 mole per dm^3) would exactly react with 25.0 cm^3 of sodium hydroxide solution (0.1 mole per dm^3)?

H = 1, He = 4, C = 12, N = 14, O = 16, Na = 23, Mg = 24, Al = 27, P = 31, S = 32, Cl = 35.5,

PAST GCSE QUESTIONS

You may need to use information in the Data Section to answer these questions.

1. The table below shows how certain substances affect the rusting of steel. A tick (✓) indicates that the substance is present. A cross (x) indicates that the substance is absent.

Speed of rusting	Substances present			
	Water	Air	Salt	Mud
Nil	✓	x	x	x
Nil	x	✓	x	x
Slow	✓	✓	x	x
Fast	✓	✓	✓	x
Very fast	✓	✓	✓	✓

(a) Using the table, answer the following questions.

   i) Which two substances are needed for rusting to occur?
   ii) Which substances together produce very fast rusting?
   iii) Mr and Mrs Thomas, who live on a farm by the seaside, said that there was no point in washing their car during the winter because it became muddy as soon as it was taken out again.
        Say whether or not you agree with the statement, giving a reason for your answer.
   iv) The door of the Thomas's car became dented and some of the paint covering the door was scraped off. The exposed metal rusted very quickly. Give a reason.

(b) Why do you think that the exhaust system of a car rusts more rapidly than the body?

(c) In view of the fact that iron and steel rust, suggest suitable alternative materials for each of the following:

   i) a household bath
   ii) a Coca Cola can.

Midland Examining Group (1375/2) 1988

2.

Metal solution	1 Silver	2 Magnesium	3 Zinc	4 Copper
A Copper(II) sulphate	No reaction	Copper displaced	Copper displaced	No reaction
B Magnesium chloride	No reaction	No reaction	No reaction	No reaction
C Silver nitrate	No reaction		Silver displaced	Silver displaced
D Zinc sulphate	No reaction	Zinc displaced	No reaction	

(a) Some metals displace others from solutions of their salts. The results of a set of experiments are given above, e.g. in column 2, line A, magnesium is placed into a solution of copper(II) sulphate and copper is displaced.

   i) Complete lines C and D in the table.
   ii) Use the table to arrange the metals in order of reactivity, placing the most reactive first.

(b) Copper and aluminium are good conductors of electricity and are used for overhead power cables. Silver is an excellent conductor of electricity. Suggest why silver is not used for overhead power cables.

(c) The chart below shows the approximate dates by which the main ores of some metals will have been used up at the present rate of use.

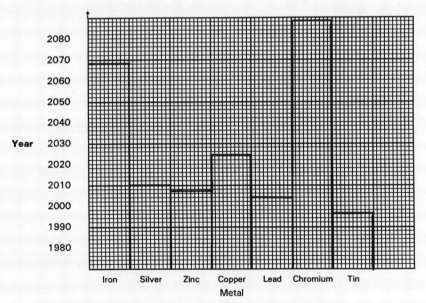

Use the chart to answer the following questions.

   i) Which metal ore will be used up first?
   ii) Which two metals will not rise in price as quickly as the others? Give a reason for your answers.

Midland Examining Group (1375/2) 1988

3. The equation for the production of sulphur trioxide in the Contact Process from sulphur dioxide and oxygen is given below:

$$2SO_2 + O_2 \rightleftharpoons 2SO_3$$

(a) What does the sign $\rightleftharpoons$ indicate?

(b) What effect does each of the following have on the reaction:

    i) a catalyst?
    ii) increasing the temperature?

(c)

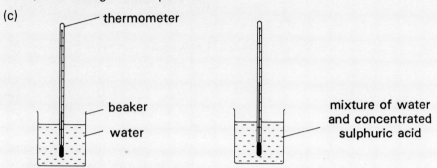

Concentrated sulphuric acid was diluted by carefully adding it to water. The temperature of the water was recorded before the acid was added and the final temperature of the mixture was also recorded. The results are given below.

Final temperature of the mixture	=	54°C
Temperature of the water	=	21°C
		___
Difference in temperature	=	
		___

    i) Complete the table of results.
    ii) What kind of heat change has occurred?
    iii) What do you think would happen to the temperature if more concentrated sulphuric acid was added?
    iv) Give one major industrial use of sulphuric acid.

(d) The diagram below shows part of the pictorial hazard sign on a tanker used to carry sulphuric acid.

    i) Give one property of the material used to make the container which holds the acid.
    ii) Give one advantage of using pictorial hazard warnings on chemical containers.
    iii) The word underneath the 'picture' has been covered by dirt from the road. What does this picture symbol indicate?

Midland Examining Group (1375/2) 1988

4. (a) The fertiliser *Fastgrow* contains ammonium sulphate. The method shown is used to find out if ammonium sulphate would be washed out of soil by rain.

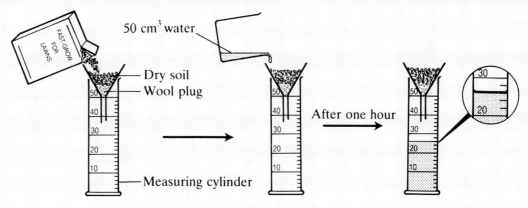

i) How much water has run through the soil after one hour?

ii) Explain how you could test the acidity of the water that has run through the soil.

iii) A sample of this water is heated with some sodium hydroxide solution, as shown below.

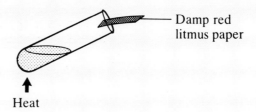

What happens to the damp red litmus paper if ammonium sulphate is in the water?

iv) Give a reason for your answer to (iii).

v) If ammonium sulphate is in this water how would you test the water to show that a sulphate is present?

Test	Results

(b) How could you find out how much ammonium sulphate is washed out of the soil shown in the diagram? Assume that there are **no** other dissolved substances in the water.

(c) Ammonia is manufactured by making nitrogen and hydrogen react together at 350°C and at high pressure in the presence of iron.

i) Put numbers in to balance the equation for this reaction.

$$N_2 \quad + \quad H_2 \quad \rightarrow \quad NH_3$$

ii) Why is iron needed for this reaction?

(d) The electronic arrangement of an atom of nitrogen and an atom of hydrogen are shown below.

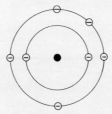

Nitrogen atom   Hydrogen atom

  i) Name the region of the atom shown by ● in the diagrams.
 ii) Draw a diagram to show the electronic arrangement in a molecule of ammonia.
iii) What type of bonding is present in the ammonia molecule?

(e) Most of the ammonia that is manufactured is used to make ammonium salts. Describe how you could change an ammonia solution into a solution of ammonium sulphate. You must name any **other** substances that you use for the chemical change.

Southern Examining Group (A/1GEW) 1988

5. The electronic arrangement of atoms with atomic numbers 4 and 12 are shown below.

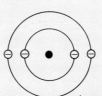 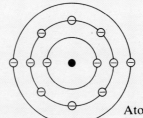

Atomic number 4   Atomic number 12

(a) Name the particle represented by ⊝.

(b) Complete the diagram below to show the electronic arrangement of the atom with atomic number 20.

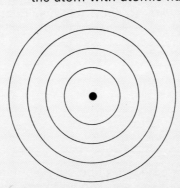

(c) Use the Periodic Table on pages 246–7 to help you to answer these questions.
  i) What is the name of the element with atomic number 20?
 ii) Why do all three elements with atomic numbers 4, 12 and 20 have similar chemical properties?

Southern Examining Group (A/1GEW) 1988

6. An excess of marble chips was added to 10 cm³ of hydrochloric acid (concentration 1 mole per dm³). The volume of carbon dioxide given off was measured every 30 seconds.

Time in seconds	0	30	60	90	120	150	180	210
Volume of carbon dioxide in cm³	0	30	52	78	80	88	91	91

(a) i) Plot these results on the grid below:

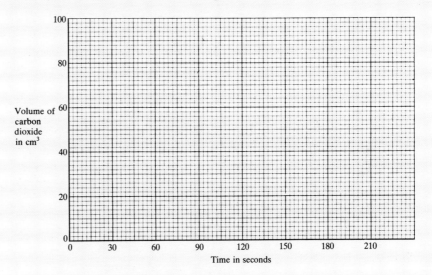

ii) Draw the best curve possible for these results.
iii) Why did the reaction stop?

(b) i) Which **one** of the results seems to be wrong?
ii) At what time was the reaction going fastest?

(c) What is **one** way of making this reaction go faster?

(d) Complete the diagram of the apparatus on the left which could be used to measure the volume of gas given off.

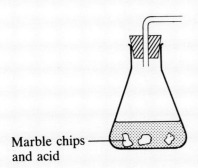

Marble chips and acid

(e) How could you investigate the rate of this reaction, without measuring the volume of gas given off?

Southern Examining Group (B/2GEW) 1988

7.   The table below shows the ideal soil conditions for growing three crops.

Crop	Soil pH	Soil nitrogen	Soil phosphorus	Soil potassium
Wheat	6	medium	high	low
Potatoes	9	medium	medium	high
Sugar beet	7	medium	medium	high

(a) Which crop grows best in an:
  i) acidic soil?
  ii) alkaline soil?

(b) A gardener wanted to grow sugar beet. When the soil was tested it was found to have a pH of 5.

  i) Name a substance that could be added to the soil to make its pH more suitable for growing sugar beet.
  ii) Explain why this substance changes the pH of the soil.

(c) A farmer bought the following fertiliser:

Common name	Chemical formula
Sulphate of potash	K_2SO_2
Triple superphosphate	$Ca(H_2PO_4)_2$
Sulphate of ammonia	$(NH_4)_2SO_4$

Samples of soil from two fields, A and B, were analysed. The results are in the following table:

Field	Nitrogen	Phosphorus	Potassium
A	low	high	low
B	medium	medium	medium

  i) Which of the fertilisers should the farmer add to the soil in field A to make it more suitable for growing wheat?
  Explain why you have chosen this fertiliser.
  ii) Which of the fertilisers should the farmer add to the soil of field B to make it more suitable for growing sugar beet?
  Explain why you have chosen this fertiliser.

(d) Why could it be an advantage for a farmer to use the fertiliser ammonium hydrogenphosphate, $(NH_4)_2HPO_4$?

Midland Examining Group (Salters' 1377/2) 1988

8.   Starch is a carbohydrate. It can be broken down into glucose and into alcohol by enzymes. The following experiment demonstrates how changing the temperature affects the action of enzymes on starch.

Iodine gives a blue colour with starch. The presence or absence of starch is detected using iodine indicator.

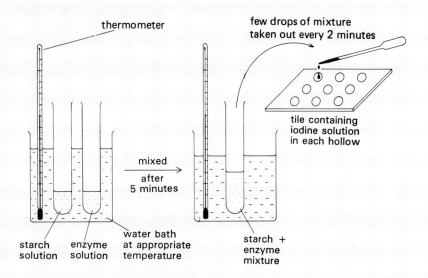

(a)   i) What is a carbohydrate?
      ii) Why are the carbohydrates important food substances?

The results of the experiment are in the table below:

Temperature/°C	20	25	30	35	40	45	50	55	60	65 70
Time taken until no blue colour is formed/mins	10	8	8	6	6	8	10	16	30	blue colour remains

(b) Why are the starch and enzyme solutions placed in the water bath for 5 minutes before mixing?

(c) Plot a graph of the results.

(d) What does the graph indicate about the effect of temperature on enzyme activity?

(e) How could you change the experiment to investigate how the enzyme activity varied with pH?

(f) The glucose produced from starch can be converted into an alcohol by fermentation.

   i) Give the chemical name of the alcohol formed in this process.
   ii) State **two** different types of uses for this alcohol.

Midland Examining Group (Salters' 1377/2) 1988

9. Biogas can be made by allowing manure to rot in tanks called biogas digestors:

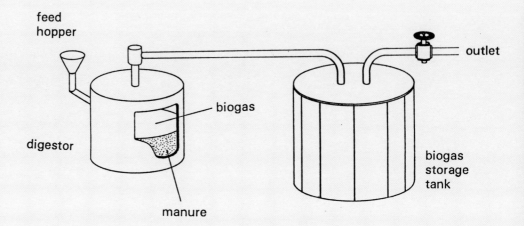

Biogas is 60% methane. The rest is carbon dioxide.

(a) Methane has the formula CH_4.

    i) How many hydrogen atoms does one molecule of methane contain?

    ii) Complete the word equation for the burning of methane in air:

methane + oxygen → .... + ...

    iii) Give one advantage and one disadvantage of using biogas as a fuel.

    iv) What type of micro-organisms change the manure into biogas?

    v) Why are biogas digestors run at temperatures which are slightly above room temperature?

    vi) Suggest one use for the waste sludge left in the digestor.

(b) A group of students wanted to investigate which would give the most biogas – chicken manure or horse manure.

    The students used this apparatus as an experimental biogas generator:

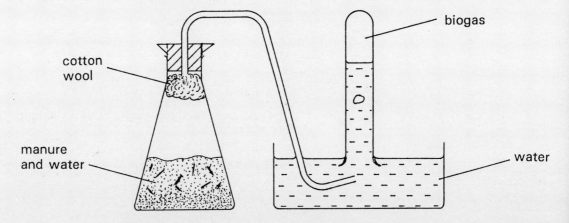

Suggest **two** things that the students should do to make the experiment a fair test of the two types of manure.

Midland Examining Group (Salters' 1377/1) 1988

10. (a) Iron is extracted from its ores in the blast furnace.

RAW MATERIALS   PRODUCTS

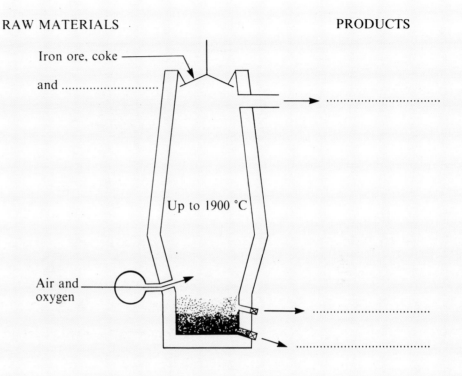

Iron ore, coke

and ....

Up to 1900 °C

Air and
oxygen

      i) Complete the diagram above labelling the one missing raw
material and the three missing products.
     ii) Name one ore from which iron is extracted.

(b) Why are metals like iron, aluminium and magnesium not found as
pure metals in the earth's crust?

(c) In the blast furnace the iron ore is reduced to iron by carbon
monoxide. The equation below shows how carbon monoxide is
formed.

$$2C(s) \; + \; O_2(g) \; \rightarrow \; 2CO(g)$$

Use this information to write the word equation for the reaction
between carbon and oxygen.

.... + ... → ....

(d) The equation for the reduction of iron oxide is given below.

$$Fe_2O_3(s) \; + \; 3CO(g) \; \rightarrow \; 2Fe(l) \; + \; 3CO_2(g)$$

      i) What is oxidation?
     ii) Which material is oxidised in this reaction?

(e) Most of the best quality iron ore comes to Britain from North Africa, Australia and America. Britain has to import large quantities of iron ore because the ores found locally are low in iron content. You are given the job of selecting two new sites for iron works in Britain.

    i) On the map below clearly mark with an X and a Y the position of the two sites you would select.

Coalfields   ⬤

Iron ore deposits   ▨

   ii) Give your reasons for selecting your sites.

(f) Give two reasons for building a steel-making plant very close to an iron works.

(g) Suggest two advantages and two disadvantages of building an iron and steel works close to a major town.

(h) What is the major disadvantage of building bridges and seaside piers from iron?

London and East Anglian Group (1077/2) 1988

11. There are two chlorides of mercury. The table below gives some of the properties of these chlorides.

Property	Mercury(I) chloride	Mercury(II) chloride
Melting point	400°C (sublimes)	276°C
Boiling point	Sublimes	302°C
Solubility in water	Insoluble	Slightly soluble in cold water, quite soluble in hot
Conductivity of solution	None	Conducts

Both chlorides of mercury are poisonous. The symbol for mercury is Hg.

(a) There are three states of matter: solid, liquid and gas. What state are the following at room temperature?

  i) Mercury(I) chloride.
  ii) Mercury(II) chloride.

(b) How does the information in the table indicate that mercury(II) chloride has ionic bonding?

(c) Both chlorides of mercury were present in industrial waste that was dumped into the Sea of Japan. Many people earn their living fishing in the Sea of Japan. What are the likely consequences of dumping this waste into the sea?

(d) One of these chlorides was converted into mercury in a laboratory experiment. The results of the experiment are given below.

Mass of beaker	=	54.25 g
Mass of beaker + mercury chloride	=	59.69 g
Mass of mercury chloride used	=	.... g
Mass of beaker + mercury	=	58.27 g
Mass of mercury produced	=	.... g
Mass of chlorine in the mercury chloride	=	.... g

  i) Complete the results table above.
  ii) How many moles of mercury atoms were produced in the experiment? (Relative atomic mass Hg = 201)
  iii) How many moles of chlorine atoms were present in the mercury chloride? (Relative atomic mass Cl = 35.5)
  iv) How many moles of chlorine atoms combined with one mole of mercury atoms?
  v) What was the formula of the mercury chloride used?
  vi) The experiment was carried out in a fume cupboard. Why was this necessary?

London and East Anglian Group (1077/2) 1988

12. (a) Complete the passage below by putting words from the following list into the gaps. Each word may be used once, more than once or not at all.

saturated   soluble   solute
solution   solvent

At the dry cleaners an organic .... is used to dissolve grease

from clothes. The .... containing the dissolved grease is

distilled to get back pure .... and separate it from the grease.

If this is not done more and more grease becomes dissolved until

a .... is formed.

(b) Water does not dissolve grease but it will dissolve many compounds. The graph shows how many grams (g) of three different compounds dissolve in 100 g of water at different temperatures.

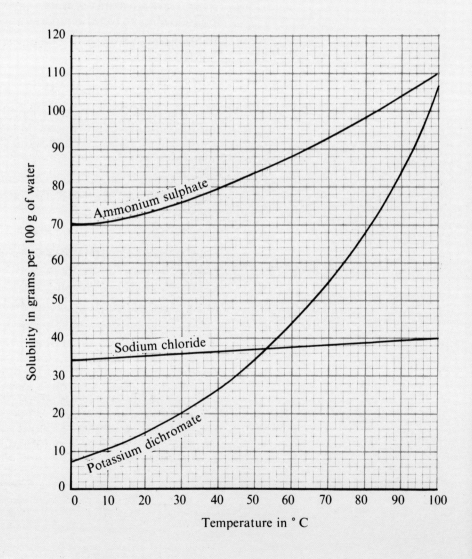

i) Give the name of the substance which is *most* soluble at (a) 20°C and (b) 70°C.

    ii) Give the name of the substance which is *least* soluble at (a) 20°C and (b) 70°C.

    iii) For which substance is the solubility *least* affected by changes in temperature?

(c) Why do you think that the temperature axis only goes up to 100°C?

(d) A student wanted to purify some potassium dichromate. The student added the compound to 100 cm^3 of water and heated gently while stirring. The compound *just* dissolved at 90°C. The solution was then allowed to cool to 50°C.

    i) What mass of potassium dichromate was added (ignore impurities)?

    ii) What mass of potassium dichromate would still be dissolved when the solution had cooled to 50°C?

    iii) What mass of crystals would be produced after the solution had stopped crystallising at 50°C?

    iv) How could the student obtain a sample of dry crystals of potassium dichromate from this experiment?

(e) Two of the three substances named on the graph are used in large amounts in many countries. Name these substances and give an important use for each.

London and East Anglian Group (1075/2, 6075/2) 1988

13. This question is about air pollution.

(a) i) When a hydrocarbon fuel is burned, one of the main products is a *slightly* acidic gas, G. What is the name of the gas G?

    ii) Give two ways in which the gas G is involved in nature.

(b) Fuels often contain an impurity, X. X burns to form a pollutant, Y.

X	BURN $-\rightarrow$	POLLUTANT Y	RAIN $-\rightarrow$ AIR	ACID RAIN

    i) Give the name of one fuel which can cause acid rain.

    ii) What is the name of the element X?

    iii) What is the name of the compound Y?

    iv) Write a balanced chemical equation for the combustion of X, showing state symbols.

    v) Give the chemical name of the acid in 'acid rain'.

(c) Read the following, which is part of a report published by the Southern Electricity Board in the Winter of 1986.

> The Loch Fleet Project is a project to restore fish to an acidified loch in south west Scotland.
> The aim of the project is to determine the most effective methods for improving the water quality of acidified lakes and streams so that they might be able to sustain a healthy fish population.
> Within months of the application of limestone powder to parts of the Loch Fleet catchment area, the water quality has improved to a level suitable for the survival of brown trout.

NOTE: A *loch* is a lake or stretch of water.
A *catchment area* is all the land around the loch from which water drains into the loch.
The *brown trout* is a fish which the project wanted to put back into the loch.

  i) What is the chemical name of limestone?
 ii) How does limestone improve water quality?
iii) Why is the limestone powdered?
 iv) How did the pH *change* in the loch as the water improved?
  v) What simple test could you do to the water in the loch to show this?

London and East Anglian Group (1075/2, 6075/2) 1988

14. Aluminium is an extremely important metal with widespread uses. Much of our aluminium is imported; only relatively small quantities of the metal being extracted in the UK.

(a) State **two** reasons why the UK output of aluminium is relatively small.

(b)

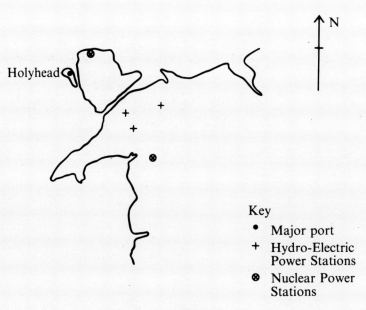

Key
• Major port
+ Hydro-Electric Power Stations
⊗ Nuclear Power Stations

Figure 1

Figure 1 shows a map of North Wales. State **two** reasons why North Wales is a suitable location for aluminium extraction plants.

(c) Figure 2 on the next page shows the type of cell used for the extraction of aluminium from alumina. Alumina is purified aluminium oxide.

(c)

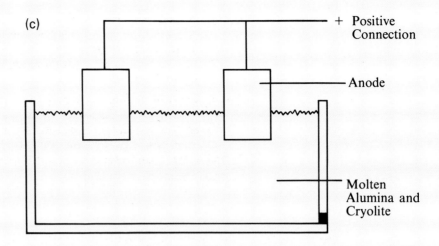

Figure 2

    i) Name the material from which the anodes are made.
   ii) On the diagram label the negative electrode (cathode).
  iii) On the diagram label the position where the molten aluminium produced collects.
  iv) Oxygen is released at the anode. This results in the anode requiring frequent replacement. Explain carefully why this is necessary.
   v) In this process alumina is dissolved in molten cryolite (another aluminium containing substance). Explain why alumina is not used on its own.

(d) Give **two** reasons, in each case, why aluminium is used to make:
    i) overhead power cables.
   ii) saucepans.

London and East Anglian Group (5075/2, 5076/2) 1988

15. (a) You are the Managing Director of the Brimstone Company which manufactures and markets sulphuric acid.

The company has recently discovered extensive deposits of sulphur on the surface of the island of Smallbrook and purchased the rights to mine the sulphur. The island lies about 50 km west of the industrial mainland.

Apart from a range of hills in the north-east the island is mainly flat. The roads are poor and there is no railway. The prevailing wind blows from the east.

A, B and C are tiny fishing villages. D is a small market town. The rest of the island is largely uninhabited with a few small farms. The price of land is low compared with that on the mainland.

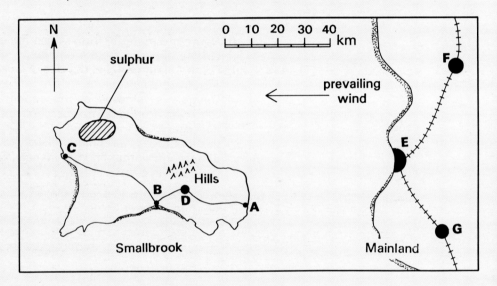

On the mainland, E is a major port with good road and rail communications to all main industrial centres, such as F and G. Your company has no buildings or trade in this area.

To exploit the deposits your company proposes to build a new sulphuric acid plant.

Write a short report to the Board of Directors recommending a site for the new plant. You should indicate clearly where the plant is to be built (it may be on the island or on the mainland), listing the advantages and disadvantages of your chosen site under the following headings:

  i) Other chemical resources
 ii) Pollution problems
iii) Economic/transport aspects.

(b) It is the first time your company has had any activity near the sea. List two mineral resources to be found in the sea and the uses to which they might be put.

Midland Examining Group (1375/3) 1988

16. Hydrogen chloride is a gas which is denser than air and dissolves easily in water.

(a) Describe how you could show that hydrogen chloride is very soluble in water.

(b) Give the tests you could use to show that when hydrogen chloride reacts with water the resulting solution contains both hydrogen ions (H^+(aq)) and chloride ions (Cl^-(aq)).

	Test	Result
Hydrogen ions (H^+(aq)) Chloride ions (Cl^-(aq))		

(c) Hydrochloric acid is formed when hydrogen chloride is bubbled through water. Describe an experiment in which hydrochloric acid acts as a typical acid. You should name any reagents used, give any observations and write a balanced chemical equation for the reaction.

Southern Examining Group (A/3EW) 1988

17. (a) One way of getting zinc from the mineral sphalerite is outlined below:

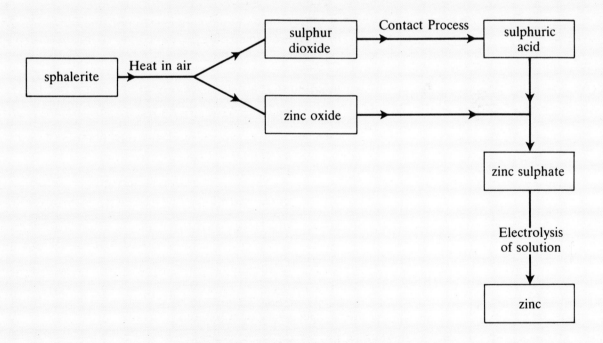

i) Apart from zinc, name another element that is present in sphalerite.

ii) Which element from the air reacts with the heated sphalerite?

iii) Explain why the sulphur dioxide formed should **not** be allowed to escape into the air for economic and environmental reasons.

iv) In the process zinc is produced by the electrolysis of zinc sulphate solution. State the electrode at which the zinc is deposited.

v) Why is the formation of zinc at the electrode called a *reduction*?

(b) Zinc can also be obtained from zinc sulphate solution by displacement with another metal **M**.

$$\mathbf{M} \;+\; ZnSO_4 \;\rightarrow\; \mathbf{MSO_4} \;\rightarrow\; Zn$$

  i) From the Reactivity Series (see page 37) choose **one** metal that could be used as metal **M**.
  ii) Why could the metals sodium and copper **not** be used for this displacement reaction?
  iii) Why is this method of displacement **not** used for the industrial extraction of zinc from zinc sulphate solution?

(c) The amount of metal ores in the Earth's crust is limited. The number of ingots shows how long known reserves will last:

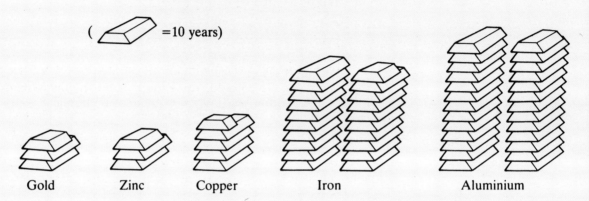

(= 10 years)

Gold   Zinc   Copper   Iron   Aluminium

  i) About how many years reserve of zinc remain?
  ii) New resources may be found before this reserve of zinc runs out. Suggest **two** other possible ways of overcoming the shortage of zinc.

(d) Imagine that a new discovery of sphalerite has been found under farmland. One major problem is that the mining of this mineral will produce large quantities of waste rock.

  i) Give one advantage and one disadvantage to the local population of mining the sphalerite.

Advantage	Disadvantage

  ii) Give **one** advantage to the national government of this new discovery of sphalerite.
  iii) What should be done to the land once all the sphalerite has been mined?

Southern Examining Group (A/3EW) 1988

18. A student investigated the burning of a candle under an upturned beaker.

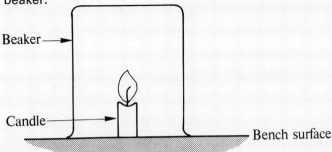

Beaker

Candle

Bench surface

The table below shows the results of the student's experiment to test a theory.

Experiment	Volume of beaker (cm^3)	Time the candle stayed lit (seconds)
1	200	20
2	250	25
3	500	50
4	600	60
5	750	90
6	1000	100

(a) What theory was the student testing?

(b) Draw a graph of the results on the grid below.

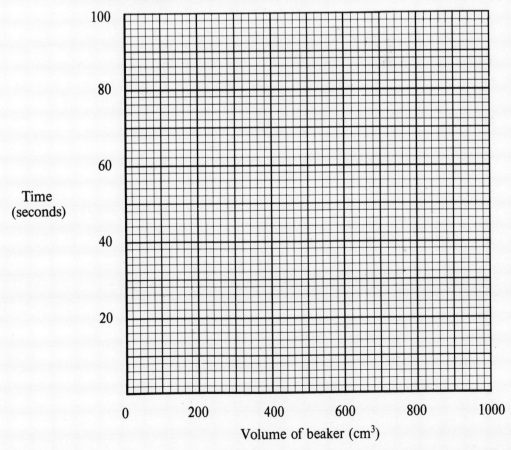

Time (seconds)

Volume of beaker (cm^3)

(c) Which result does not fit the pattern?

(d) Use the graph to find out how long a candle would burn in a beaker with a volume of
   i) 400 cm^3
   ii) 100 cm^3.

(e) Which of the values in (d) is likely to be less accurate? Explain your answer.

(f) Describe how you would change the experiment to find the approximate percentage of oxygen in a sample of air.

Northern Examining Association (2023/1) 1988

19. Domestic bleach is a mixture of compounds formed by the reaction of chlorine with sodium hydroxide solution. One of these compounds is sodium chlorate(ı), NaOCl, which causes the bleaching action.

When an acid is added to bleach, chlorine is released. The concentration of a bleach can be calculated from the amount of chlorine produced when it reacts with an acid .

$$NaOCl\ (aq) + 2HCl\ (aq) \rightarrow NaCl\ (aq) + H_2O(l) + Cl_2(g)$$

In an investigation of three domestic bleaches, separate measured samples of three different brands of bleach were reacted with 10 cm^3 of 2M hydrochloric acid and the volume of chlorine given off was measured.

The results were:

Brand tested	Volume of bleach used in cm^3	Volume of chlorine produced in cm^3	Cost of bleach in pence per litre
A	2	64	60
B	4	58	52
C	4	66	42

(a) Draw a diagram of the apparatus you could use to carry out the investigation described above.

(b) What precautions would you take whilst carrying out this experiment?

(c) i) Which brand contained the most sodium chlorate(ı) per litre? Explain how you arrived at your answer.
   ii) Show by calculation or with reasons, which of the three bleaches would offer the most chlorine per penny.

(d) Some household cleaners contain acids to remove limescale. Why is there a warning on packs of these cleaners that they should not be mixed with bleach?

(e) Suggest a use of domestic bleach other than for bleaching.

London and East Anglian Group (1077/3) 1988

20. The diagram shows some ways in which air plays an important part in industry.

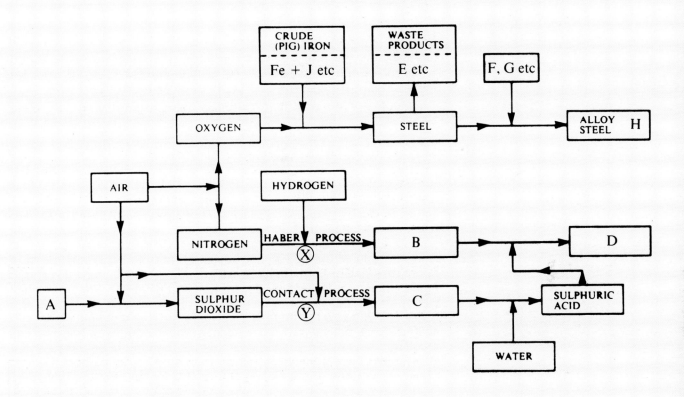

(a) i) Give the name of the process by which air is separated into oxygen and nitrogen.

ii) Give the name of one other important product of this process.

(b) Give the names of possible substances which might be represented by the letters A to D.

(c) What are the catalysts X and Y used in the two named processes?

i) Give the name of a possible waste product E.

ii) Give the names of two metallic elements, F and G, which might be used to make alloy steel.

iii) Give an example of an alloy steel H.

(e) Give one **other** industrial or commercial use for nitrogen and oxygen, and in each case explain why air is not a suitable substitute.

London and East Anglian Group (1075/3, 6075/3) 1988

21. Washing soda is often used for degreasing sink waste pipes and drains. A one kilogramme (1 kg) packet costs 45 pence. The chemical name of washing soda is sodium carbonate-10-water; it formula is $Na_2CO_3.10H_2O$.

(1 Tonne = 1000 kg; Relative atomic masses: H = 1.0, C = 12.0, O = 16.0, Na = 23.0)

(a) Calculate the mass of washing soda which can be made from 1 tonne of anhydrous sodium carbonate Na_2CO_3.

(b) The cost of 1 tonne of anhydrous sodium carbonate is £160. What is the cost of the sodium carbonate used to produce a 1 kg packet of washing soda?

(c) On the basis of these two calculation, how much profit is made on each packet of washing soda?

(d) Give **four** reasons why, in practice, the manufacturer's profit is much less than this.

London and East Anglian Group (1075/3, 6075/3) 1988

22. A local manufacturer asks your advice on how to electroplate a large supply of small brass medallions with copper. Describe how this should be done and include in your description a fully labelled diagram which clearly shows the circuit to be used.

If, when you saw the first results, you found that the medallions were coated with a patchy covering of copper, how would you interpret this result and how would you suggest that the fault might be rectified? (i.e. What might have gone wrong and what could be done about it?)

London and East Anglian Group (1075/3, 6075/3) 1988

23. Starch solution can be hydrolysed:

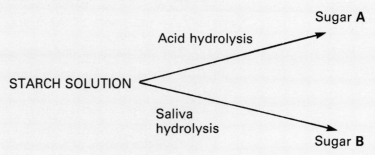

(a) Name sugar **A** and sugar **B**.

(b) For the acid hydrolysis of starch, describe how:

   i) the experiment could be carried out in the laboratory,
   ii) the presence of a reducing sugar could be detected in the reaction mixture,
   iii) the time taken for all the starch to be hydrolysed could be determined.

(c) Describe how sugars **A** and **B** could be identified by chromatography.

London and East Anglian Group 1077/3 1988

Data Section

The Periodic Table

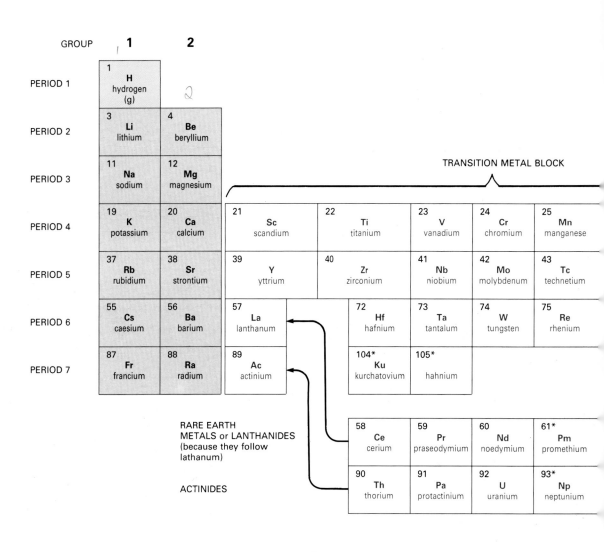

TRANSITION METAL BLOCK

GROUP	1	2					
PERIOD 1	1 **H** hydrogen (g)						
PERIOD 2	3 **Li** lithium	4 **Be** beryllium					
PERIOD 3	11 **Na** sodium	12 **Mg** magnesium					
PERIOD 4	19 **K** potassium	20 **Ca** calcium	21 Sc scandium	22 Ti titanium	23 V vanadium	24 Cr chromium	25 Mn manganese
PERIOD 5	37 **Rb** rubidium	38 **Sr** strontium	39 Y yttrium	40 Zr zirconium	41 Nb niobium	42 Mo molybdenum	43 Tc technetium
PERIOD 6	55 **Cs** caesium	56 **Ba** barium	57 La lanthanum	72 Hf hafnium	73 Ta tantalum	74 W tungsten	75 Re rhenium
PERIOD 7	87 **Fr** francium	88 **Ra** radium	89 Ac actinium	104* Ku kurchatovium	105* Ta hahnium		

RARE EARTH METALS or LANTHANIDES (because they follow lathanum)

ACTINIDES

58 Ce cerium	59 Pr praseodymium	60 Nd noedymium	61* Pm promethium
90 Th thorium	91 Pa protactinium	92 U uranium	93* Np neptunium

Key

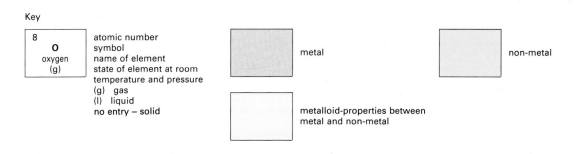

8 **O** oxygen (g)	atomic number symbol name of element state of element at room temperature and pressure (g) gas (l) liquid no entry – solid

metal

non-metal

metalloid-properties between metal and non-metal

					3	**4**	**5**	**6**	**7**	**0**
										2 **He** helium (g)
					5 **B** boron	6 **C** carbon	7 **N** nitrogen (g)	8 **O** oxygen (g)	9 **F** fluorine (g)	10 **Ne** neon (g)
					13 **Al** aluminium	14 **Si** silicon	15 **P** phosphorus	16 **S** sulphur	17 **Cl** chlorine (g)	18 **Ar** argon (g)
26 **Fe** iron	27 **Co** cobalt	28 **Ni** nickel	29 **Cu** copper	30 **Zn** zinc	31 **Ga** gallium	32 **Ge** germanium	33 **As** arsenic	34 **Se** selenium	35 **Br** bromine (l)	36 **Kr** krypton (g)
44 **Ru** ruthenium	45 **Rh** rhodium	46 **Pd** palladium	47 **Ag** silver	48 **Cd** cadmium	49 **In** indium	50 **Sn** tin	51 **Sb** antimony	52 **Te** tellurium	53 **I** iodine	54 **Xe** xenon (g)
76 **Os** osmium	77 **Ir** iridium	78 **Pt** platinum	79 **Au** gold	80 **Hg** mercury (l)	81 **Tl** thallium	82 **Pb** lead	83 **Bi** bismuth	84 **Po** polonium	85* **At** astatine	86 **Rn** radon (g)

62 **Sm** samarium	63 **Eu** europium	64 **Gd** gadolinium	65 **Tb** terbium	66 **Dy** dysprosium	67 **Ho** holmium	68 **Er** erbium	69 **Tm** thulium	70 **Yb** ytterbium	71 **Lu** lutetium
94* **Pu** plutonium	95* **Am** americium	96* **Cm** curium	97* **Bk** berkelium	98* **Cf** californium	99* **Es** einsteinium	100* **Fm** fermium	101* **Md** mendelevium	102* **No** nobelium	103* **Lw** lawrencium

Elements in the main block of the Periodic table are printed in black.

* - element does not occur naturally
- man-made element

The chemical elements

Atomic number	Element	Symbol	Approximate relative atomic mass	Melting point in °C	Boiling point in °C	Density in g per cm³	Date of discovery
1	Hydrogen	H	1	−259	−253	0.00008	1766
2	Helium	He	4	−270	−269	0.00017	1868
3	Lithium	Li	7	180	1330	0.53	1817
4	Beryllium	Be	9	1280	2700	1.9	1827
5	Boron	B	11	2000	3000	2.3	1808
6	Carbon	C	12		4200	2.2	*
7	Nitrogen	N	14	−210	−196	0.00117	1772
8	Oxygen	O	16	−219	−183	0.00132	1774
9	Fluorine	F	19	−220	−188	0.0016	1886
10	Neon	Ne	20	−249	−246	0.0008	1898
11	Sodium	Na	23	98	890	0.97	1807
12	Magnesium	Mg	24	650	1110	1.7	1808
13	Aluminium	Al	27	660	2060	2.7	1825
14	Silicon	Si	28	1410	2700	2.4	1823
15	Phosphorus	P	31	44	280	1.8	1669
16	Sulphur	S	32	119	445	2.1	*
17	Chlorine	Cl	35.5	−101	−35	0.003	1774
18	Argon	Ar	40	−189	−189	0.0017	1894
19	Potassium	K	39	64	760	0.86	1807
20	Calcium	Ca	40	850	1440	1.6	1808
21	Scandium	Sc	45	1400	2500	3.1	1879
22	Titanium	Ti	48	1670	3300	4.5	1789
23	Vanadium	V	51	1900	3400	6.0	1801
24	Chromium	Cr	52	1900	2500	7.2	1797
25	Manganese	Mn	55	1250	2000	7.4	1774
26	Iron	Fe	56	1540	3000	7.9	*
27	Cobalt	Co	59	1490	2900	8.9	1735
28	Nickel	Ni	59	1450	2800	8.9	1751
29	Copper	Cu	63.5	1080	2500	9.0	*
30	Zinc	Zn	65.5	419	910	7.1	17th Century
31	Gallium	Ga	70	30	2200	5.9	1875
32	Germanium	Ge	72.5	950	2800	5.4	1886
33	Arsenic	As	75		615	5.7	13th Century
34	Selenium	Se	79	217	690	4.8	1817
35	Bromine	Br	80	−7	58	3.1	1826
36	Krypton	Kr	84	−157	−153	0.0035	1898
37	Rubidium	Rb	85.5	39	700	1.5	1861
38	Strontium	Sr	88	770	1380	2.6	1808
39	Yttrium	Y	89	1500	3000	4.5	1794
40	Zirconium	Zr	91	1900	4000	6.5	1789
41	Niobium	Nb	93	2500	4800	8.5	1801
42	Molybdenum	Mo	96	2620	5000	10.2	1782
43	Technetium	Tc	99	2200	4600	11.5	1937
44	Ruthenium	Ru	101	2500	4000	12.2	1845
45	Rhodium	Rh	103	1960	3700	12.4	1803
46	Palladium	Pd	106	1550	3000	12.0	1803
47	Silver	Ag	108	961	2200	10.5	*
48	Cadmium	Cd	112	320	765	8.7	1817
49	Indium	In	115	156	2000	7.3	1861
50	Tin	Sn	119	232	2600	7.3	*
51	Antimony	Sb	122	630	1400	6.6	*
52	Tellurium	Te	128	450	990	6.2	1782
53	Iodine	I	127	114	183	4.9	1811

*These elements have been known for thousands of years

Atomic number	Element	Symbol	Approximate relative atomic mass	Melting point in °C	Boiling point in °C	Density in g per cm³	Date of discovery
54	Xenon	Xe	131	−112	−108	0.005	1898
55	Caesium	Cs	133	29	680	1.9	1861
56	Barium	Ba	137	710	1600	3.5	1805
57	Lanthanum	La	139	920	3500	6.2	1839
58	Cerium	Ce	140	800	3000	6.7	1803
59	Praseodymium	Pr	141	935	3100	6.8	1885
60	Neodymium	Nd	144	1020	3100	7.0	1885
61	Promethium	Pm	147	1030	2700		1945
62	Samarum	Sm	150	1080	1600	7.6	1879
63	Europium	Eu	152	830	1430	5.3	1901
64	Gadolinium	Gd	157	1320	3000	7.9	1886
65	Terbium	Tb	159	1400	2600	8.3	1843
66	Dysprosium	Dy	162.5	1500	2400	8.5	1886
67	Holmium	Ho	165	1500	2500	8.8	1879
68	Erbium	Er	167	1500	2700	9.0	1843
69	Thulium	Tm	169	1550	2000	9.3	1879
70	Ytterbium	Yb	173	824	1500	7.0	1878
71	Lutetium	Lu	175	1700	3330	9.9	1907
72	Hafnium	Hf	179	2000	5000	13.1	1923
73	Tantalum	Ta	181	3000	5400	16.6	1802
74	Tungsten	W	184	3400	6000	19.3	1789
75	Rhenium	Re	186	3200	5630	21.0	1925
76	Osmium	Os	190	2700	5000	22.6	1804
77	Iridium	Ir	192	2440	5300	22.5	1804
78	Platinum	Pt	195	1770	4000	21.4	1735
79	Gold	Au	197	1060	2700	19.3	*
80	Mercury	Hg	200	−39	357	13.6	*
81	Thallium	Tl	204	300	1460	11.8	1861
82	Lead	Pb	207	327	1744	11.3	*
83	Bismuth	Bi	209	270	1560	9.8	16th Century
84	Polonium	Po	210	254	1000	9.3	1898
85	Astatine	At	210	302			1940
86	Radon	Rn	222	−71	−62	0.009	1900
87	Francium	Fr	223	30	650		1936
88	Radium	Ra	226	700	1500	5.0	1898
89	Actinium	Ac	227	1050	3000		1899
90	Thorium	Th	232	1700	4000	11.6	1929
91	Protactinium	Pa	231	1200	4000	15.4	1917
92	Uranium	U	238	1130	3800	19.0	1789
93	Neptunium	Np	237	640		19.5	1940
94	Plutonium	Pu	242	640	3200	19.6	1940
95	Americium	Am	243	1200	2600	11.7	1944
96	Curium	Cm	247				1944
97	Berkelium	Bk	247				1949
98	Californium	Cf	251				1950
99	Einsteinium	Es	254				1952
100	Fermium	Fm	253				1953
101	Mendelevium	Md	256				1955
102	Nobelium	No	254				1958
103	Lawrencium	Lw	257				1961
104	Kurchatovium	Ku					1969
105	Hahnium						1970

*These elements have been known for thousands of years

Data about common compounds

The table below gives chemical formulae, melting point and boiling points of some common inorganic compounds. Those marked * are usually hydrated (i.e. containing water of crystallisation). The state at room temperature and atmospheric pressure is given by **s** (solid), **l** (liquid) or **g** (gas). If the substance decomposes or sublimes on heating it is shown by **dec.** or **sub.** in the table. The solubility in water at room temperature is classified:

i	insoluble
ss	slightly soluble
s	soluble
vs	very soluble
r	reacts with water

Compound	Formula	State	Melting point in °C	Boiling point in °C	Solubility
aluminium chloride	$AlCl_3$	s	sub.		r
aluminium oxide	Al_2O_3	s	2015	2980	i
ammonium chloride	NH_4Cl	s	sub.		s
ammonium nitrate	NH_4NO_3	s	170	dec.	vs
ammonium sulphate	$(NH_4)_2SO_4$	s	dec.		s
barium chloride*	$BaCl_2$	s	963	1560	s
barium oxide	BaO	s	1923	2000	r
barium sulphate	$BaSO_4$	s	1580		i
boron trichloride	BCl_3	g	−107	12	r
boron hydride	B_2H_6	g	−165	−92	r
boron oxide	B_2O_3	s	460	1860	i
caesium chloride	$CsCl$	s	645	1300	vs
calcium carbonate	$CaCO_3$	s	dec.		i
calcium chloride*	$CaCl_2$	s	782	2000	s
calcium hydroxide	$Ca(OH)_2$	s	dec.		ss
calcium nitrate*	$Ca(NO_3)_2$	s	561	dec.	vs
calcium oxide	CaO	s	2600	3000	r
carbon monoxide	CO	g	−205	−191	i
chromium(III) chloride*	$CrCl_3$	s	1150	1300	i
chromium(III) oxide	Cr_2O_3	s	2435	4000	i
cobalt(II) chloride*	$CoCl_2$	s	730	1050	s
copper(II) chloride*	$CuCl_2$	s	620	dec.	s
copper(II) nitrate*	$Cu(NO_3)_2$	s	114	dec.	vs
copper(I) oxide	Cu_2O	s	1235		i
copper(II) oxide	CuO	s	1326		i
copper(II) sulphate*	$CuSO_4$	s	dec.		s

Compound	Formula	State	Melting point in °C	Boiling point in °C	Solubility
hydrogen bromide	HBr	g	−87	−67	vs
hydrogen chloride	HCl	g	−114	−85	vs
hydrogen fluoride	HF	g	−93	20	s
hydrogen iodide	HI	g	−51	−35	s
hydrogen oxide (water)	H_2O	l	0	100	
hydrogen peroxide	H_2O_2	l	0	150	vs
hydrogen sulphide	H_2S	g	−85	−60	ss
iron(II) chloride	$FeCl_2$	s	677	sub.	s
iron(III) chloride*	$FeCl_3$	s	307	dec.	s
iron(III) oxide	Fe_2O_3	s	1565		i
iron(II) sulphate*	$FeSO_4$	s	dec.		s
iron(II) sulphide	FeS	s	1196	dec.	i
lead(II) bromide	$PbBr_2$	s	370	914	i
lead(II) chloride	$PbCl_2$	s	501	950	ss
lead(II) nitrate	$Pb(NO_3)_2$	s	dec.		s
lead(II) oxide)	PbO	s	886	1472	i
lead(IV) oxide	PbO_2	s	dec.		i
lead(II) sulphate	$PbSO_4$	s	1170		i
lithium chloride	LiCi	s	614	1382	s
lithium fluoride	LiF	s	877	1677	r
lithium hydride	LiH	s	680		r
lithium oxide	Li_2O	s	1700		r
magnesium chloride*	$MgCl_2$	s	714	1418	s
magnesium nitrate*	$Mg(NO_3)_2$	s	89		vs
magnesium oxide	MgO	s	2800	3600	i
magnesium(IV) oxide	MnO_2	s	dec.		i
mercury(II) chloride	$HgCl_2$	s	276	302	ss
mercury(II) oxide	HgO	s	dec.		i
nickel(II) sulphate*	$NiSO_4$	s			s
nitric acid	HNO_3	l	−42	83	vs
nitrogen hydride (ammonia)	NH_3	g	−78	−34	vs
nitrogen oxide	NO	g	−163	−151	ss
nitrogen dioxide	NO_2	g	−11	21	s
phosphorus trichloride	PCl_3	l	−112	76	r
phosphorus pentachloride	PCl_5	s	dec.		r
phosphorus hydride	PH_3	g	−133	−90	i
phosphorus pentoxide	P_4O_{10}	s	sub.		r
potassium bromide	KBr	s	730	1435	s
potassium chloride	KCl	s	776	1500	s
potassium hydroxide	KOH	s	360	1322	vs
potassum iodide	KI	s	686	1330	vs
potassium manganate(VII)	$KMnO_4$	s	dec.		s
potassium nitrate	KNO_3	s	334	dec.	vs
rubidium chloride	RbCl	s	715	1390	s
silicon tetrachloride	$SiCl_4$	l	−70	58	r
silicon hydride	SiH_4	g	−185	−112	i
silicon dioxide	SiO_2	s	1610	2230	i
silver bromide	AgBr	s	432	dec.	i
silver chloride	AgCl	s	455	1550	i
silver iodide	AgI	s	558	1506	i
silver nitrate	$AgNO_3$	s	212	dec.	vs
sodium bromide	NaBr	s	755	1390	s
sodium carbonate*	Na_2CO_3	s	851	dec.	s
sodium chloride	NaCl	s	808	1465	s
sodium hydroxide	NaOH	s	318	1390	s
sodium nitrate	$NaNO_3$	s	307	dec.	s
sodium oxide	Na_2O	s	sub.		r
sodium sulphate*	Na_2SO_4	s	890		s
sodium thiosulphate*	$Na_2S_2O_3$	s	dec.		vs
sodium dioxide	SO_2	g	−75	−10	vs
sulphur trioxide	SO_3	l	−17	43	r
sulphuric acid	H_2SO_4	l	10	330	vs
zinc chloride	$ZnCl_2$	s	283	732	vs
zinc oxide	ZnO	s	1975		i
zinc sulphate*	$ZnSO_4$	s	740	dec.	vs

Physical properties of some organic compounds

The table below shows the formulae, state at room temperature and atmospheric pressure, melting points and boiling points of some common organic compounds.

Compound	Formula	State	Melting point in °C	Boiling point in °C
Alkanes				
methane	CH_4	g	−182	−161
ethane	C_2H_6	g	−183	−88
propane	C_3H_8	g	−188	−42
butane	C_4H_{10}	g	−138	−0.5
pentane	C_5H_{12}	l	−130	36
hexane	C_6H_{14}	l	−95	69
decane	$C_{10}H_{22}$	l	−30	174
hexadecane	$C_{16}H_{34}$	l	18	287
eicosane	$C_{20}H_{42}$	s	37	344
Alkenes				
ethene	C_2H_4	g	−169	−104
propene	C_3H_6	g	−185	−48
Alcohols				
methanol	CH_3OH	l	−98	65
ethanol	C_2H_5OH	l	−114	78
propan-1-ol	C_3H_7OH	l	−126	97
butan-1-ol	C_4H_9OH	l	−89	118
water	H_2O	l	0	100
Carboxylic acids				
methanoic (formic) acid	HCO_2H	l	9	101
ethanoic (acetic) acid	CH_3CO_2H	l	17	118
propanoic acid	$C_2H_5CO_2H$	l	−21	141
octadecanoic (stearic) acid	$C_{17}H_{35}CO_2H$	s	71	375
Esters				
ethyl ethanoate (acetate)	$CH_3CO_2C_2H_5$	l	−84	77
ethyl propanoate	$C_2H_5CO_2C_2H_5$	l	−74	99
methyl ethanoate	$CH_3CO_2CH_3$	l	−98	57
methyl propanoate	$C_2H_5CO_2CH_3$	l	−87	80
Halogen-containing compounds				
chloromethane	CH_3Cl	g	−98	−24
trichloromethane (chloroform)	$CHCl_3$	l	−63	61
tetrachloromethane	CCl_4	l	−23	77
1,1,1-trichloroethane	CH_3CCl_3	l	−30	74
Miscellaneous				
glucose	$C_6H_{12}O_6$	s	146	dec.
naphthalene	$C_{10}H_8$	s	80	218
propanone (acetone)	CH_3COCH_3	l	−95	56
sucrose	$C_{12}H_{22}O_{11}$	s	186	dec.

Common acid–base indicators

An indicator changes colour as pH changes. The table at the top of the next page shows the pH at which each indicator changes colour and the colour of the indicator in acid and alkaline solutions.

Indicator	pH range	Colour in	
		acid	alkali
litmus	6.5 – 7.5	red	blue
methyl orange	3.1 – 4.4	red	yellow
bromophenol blue	3.0 – 4.6	yellow	blue
bromocresol green	3.8 – 5.4	yellow	blue
methyl red	4.2 – 6.3	red	yellow
bromothymol blue	6.0 – 7.6	yellow	blue
phenol red	6.8 – 8.4	yellow	red
phenolphthalein	8.3 – 10.0	colourless	red
thymolphthalein	9.3 – 10.5	colourless	blue

Solubilities of salts at different temperatures

The table below shows the mass of solute, in grams, which will dissolve in 100 g of water at different temperatures to produce a saturated solution.

Salt	Formula	Temperature in °C						
		0	10	20	40	60	80	100
ammonium chloride	NH_4Cl	29.4	33.3	37.2	45.8	55.2	65.6	77.3
copper(II) sulphate	$CuSO_4.5H_2O$	14.3	17.4	20.7	28.5	40.0	55.0	75.4
potassium chloride	KCl	28.1	31.2	34.2	40.0	45.8	51.3	56.3
potassium bromide	KBr	53.5	59.5	65.2	75.5	85.5	95.0	104
potassium nitrate	KNO_3	13.3	20.9	31.6	63.9	110	169	246
sodium chloride	$NaCl$	35.7	35.8	36.0	36.6	37.3	38.4	39.8

Solubility of gases in water

The solubilities given are the mass of gas, in grams, dissolving in 1000 g of water when the total pressure of gas is 1 atmosphere.

Gas	Temperature in °C					
	0	20	40	60	70	80
ammonia NH_3	895	531	307			
carbon dioxide CO_2	3.35	1.69	0.97	0.57		
chlorine Cl_2		7.0	4.1	2.5		
hydrogen H_2	0.0019	0.0016	0.0013	0.0012	0.0010	0.0008
hydrogen chloride HCl	823	721	633	561		
hydrogen sulphide H_2S	7.07	3.85	2.36	1.48	1.10	0.76
nitrogen H_2	0.029	0.019	0.014	0.011	0.008	0.006
oxygen O_2	228	113	54.1			

Hardness of water

In the table below, the hardness of water is shown on a 5-point scale. 1 means soft water and 5 means very hard water.

The hardness of water varies considerably depending on the source. In Nottingham, water from Derbyshire used by the city is much harder than water from the sandstone below the city.

Aberdeen	1	Coventry	4–5	Manchester	1
Belfast	2	Derby	2	Newcastle-upon-Tyne	4
Birmingham	variable	Edinburgh	2–3	Norwich	5
Bournemouth	5	Exeter	2	Nottingham	variable
Bradford	1	Glasgow	1	Oxford	5
Bristol	5	Hull	4–5	Sheffield	1
Burton-on-Trent	4	Leeds	2	Southampton	4
Cambridge	3	Leicester	3	Stoke-on-Trent	3–4
Cardiff	1	Liverpool	1	York	4
Carlisle	2	London	4–5		

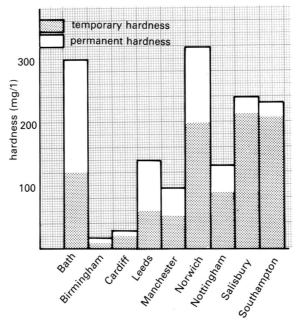

Comparison of temporary and permanent hardness of water from different places

Sources of energy

Insert Graph (data b), pie chart (data c) and pie chart (data d)

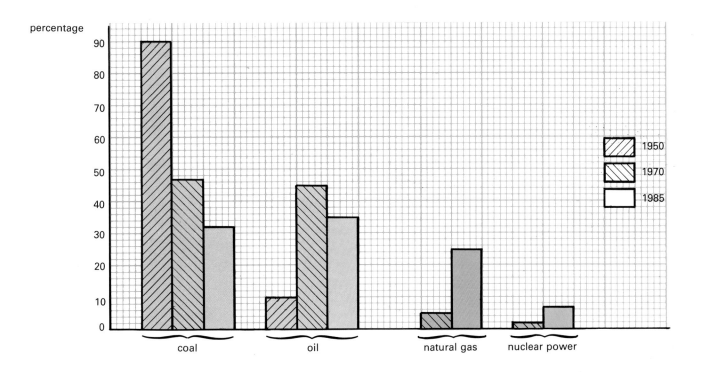

Sources of energy in the UK in 1950, 1970 and 1985

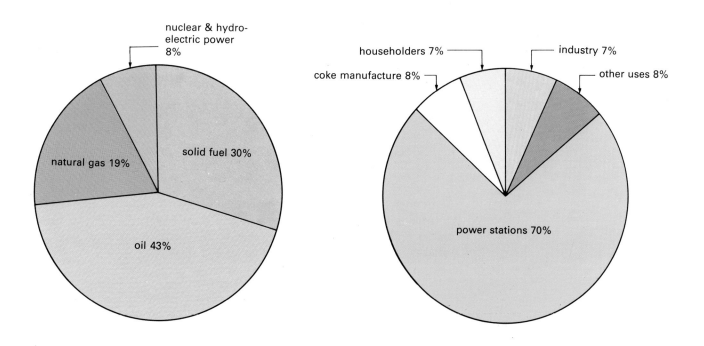

World energy sources (1985)   Uses of coal

Metal, alloys and their uses

Metals are obtained from metal ores. Some of these are listed in the table below:

Metal	Common ore	Formula	% Metal in ore as found (typical value)
Aluminium	bauxite	$Al_2O_3.3H_3O$	28
Copper	chalcopyrite	$CuFeS_2$	0.5
Gold	native	Au	0.001
Iron	haematite	FE_2O_3	30–60
Lead	galena	PbS	5–10
Mercury	cinnabar	HgS	0.3
Nickel	pentlandite	$NiS.(FeS)_2$	2.0
Platinum	cooperite	PtS (also native)	0.01
Silver	argenite	Ag_2S	0.6
Tin	cassiterite	SnO_2	1.5
Titanium	rutile	TiO_2	2.5–25
Uranium	uranium oxide	U_3O_8	0.1–0.9
Zinc	zinc blende	ZnS	10–30

Pure metals have a wide range of uses, as summarised in the table below:

Metal	Use	A reason for use
Copper	Electricity cables	Excellent conductor of electricity/very ductile
Tin	Coating tin cans	Not poisonous
Aluminium	Kitchen foil	Very malleable
Iron	Wrought iron gates	Easy to forge and resists corrosion
Lead	Flashing on roofs	Soft, easy to shape, does not corrode

Many metals are used in mixtures called **alloys**. An alloy often has better properties for a particular use than any pure metal. An alloy is usually harder and stronger than a pure metal. The table on the next page gives information about some common alloys and their uses.

Alloy	Constituent elements	Uses
Steel	Iron + between 0.15% and 1.5% carbon. The properties of steel depend on the percentage of carbon. Other metals may be present, e.g. chromium in stainless steel	Wide variety of uses including cars, ships, tools, reinforced concrete, tinplate (coated with tin)
Brass	Copper and zinc	Ornaments, buttons, screws
Duralumin	Aluminium, magnesium copper and manganese	Lightweight uses e.g. aircraft, bicycles
Solder	Tin and lead	Joining metals (NB importance of low melting point)
Coinage bronze	Copper, zinc and tin	1p and 2p coins
Bronze	Copper and tin	Ornaments

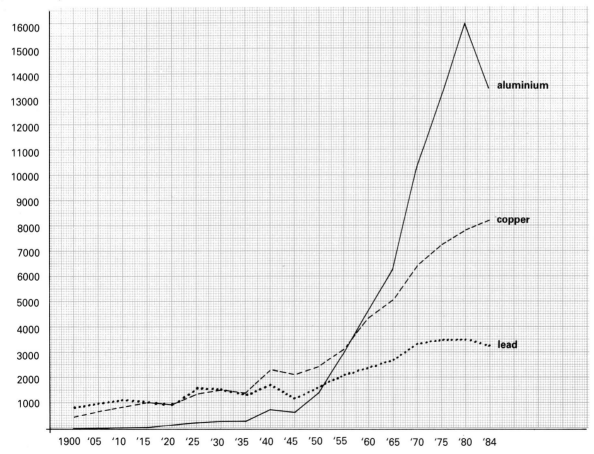

amount used
('000 tonnes)

Amounts of metals used this century

Miscellaneous data

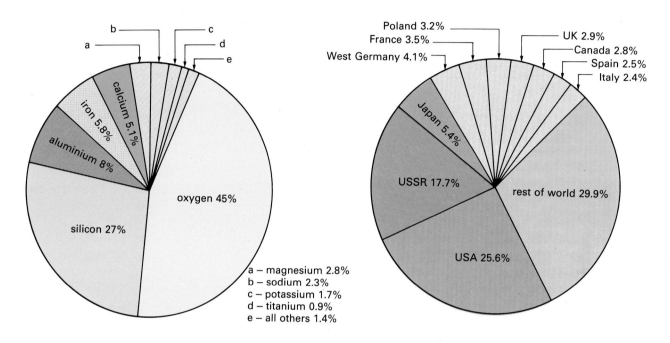

a – magnesium 2.8%
b – sodium 2.3%
c – potassium 1.7%
d – titanium 0.9%
e – all others 1.4%

Elements of the Earth

Countries producing sulphuric acid

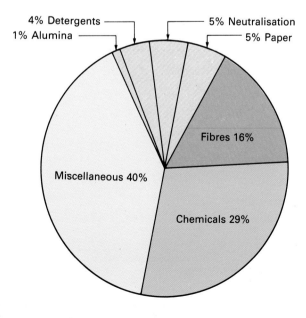

Uses of sodium hydroxide

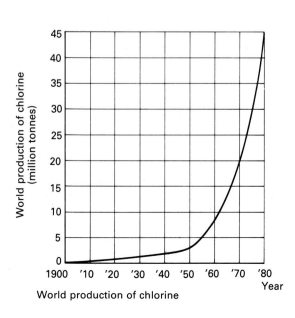

World production of chlorine

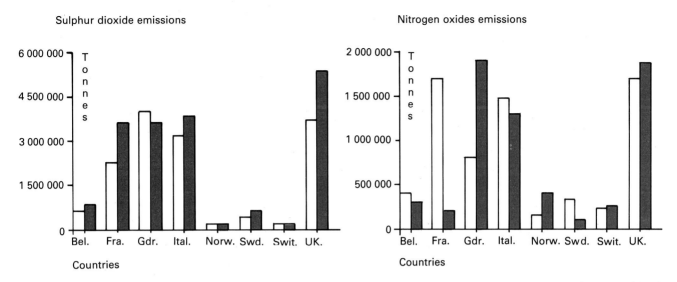

Sulphur dioxide emissions

Nitrogen oxides emissions

ABOVE A comparison of official (white) and independent (black) figures for emissions of sulphur dioxide and nitrogen oxides in different European countries (1984 figures).

Sulphur dioxide emissions

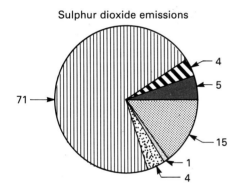

Nitrogen oxide emissions

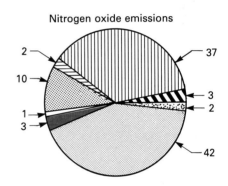

KEY

Domestic	Industry
Commerce	Road
Power Stations	Rail
Refineries	Other

Sources of acid rain emissions

The use of recycled materials in the UK (1987)

Material	Per cent (weight) of the total production accounted for by reclaimed material
Iron and steel	52
Copper	40
Aluminium	30
Zinc	25
Lead	65
Glass	22
Paper products	42
Wood fibres	10.5
Cotton and man-made fibres	14.5

Costs of laboratory chemicals

Costs of laboratory chemicals (January 1989)

Chemical	Formula	Quantity	Technical grade	Laboratory grade	Analar (AR) grade
Ammonium carbonate	$(NH_4)_2CO_3$	500 g		£2.65	£7.36
Ammonium chloride	NH_4Cl	500 g		£2.61	£7.63
Ammonium nitrate	NH_4NO_3	500 g	£1.60	£3.10	£7.27
Ammonium sulphate	$(NH_4)_2SO_4$	500 g		£2.25	£6.33
Barium chloride-2-water	$BaCl_2.2H_2O$	500 g		£2.90	£8.50
Barium hydroxide-8-water	$Ba(OH)_2.8H_2O$	500 g		£2.35	£6.48
Calcium carbonate	$CaCO_3$	500 g		£1.55	£18.80
Calcium nitrate-4-water	$Ca(NO_3)_2.4H_2O$	500 g		£3.00	
Copper(ii) oxide	CuO	500 g		£4.20	£50.00
Copper(ii) sulphate-5-water	$CuSO_4.5H_2O$	500 g	£2.15	£2.55	£10.00
Copper(ii) sulphate, anhydrous	$CuSO_4$	500 g		£7.00	
Hydrochloric acid (conc)	HCl	2½ l	£3.25	£3.37	£8.47
Hydrogen peroxide (6% soln)	H_2O_2	1 l		£2.18	£9.20
Hydrogen peroxide (30% soln)	H_2O_2	500 cm³		£4.60	
Iron(ii) sulphate-7-water	$FeSO_4.7H_2O$	500 g		£2.42	£11.00
Lead(ii) nitrate	$Pb(NO_3)_2$	500 g		£4.35	
Lithium chloride	$LiCl$	100 g		£3.95	
Magnesium ribbon	Mg	25 g		£4.25	
Magnesium chloride-6-water	$MgCl_2.6H_2O$	500 g		£3.80	
Magnesium sulphate-7-water	$MgSO_4.7H_2O$	500 g		£1.30	£7.95
Mercury(i) chloride	Hg_2Cl_2	25 g		£3.19	
Mercury(ii) chloride	$HgCl_2$	50 g		£3.50	£8.00
Nitric acid	HNO_3	2½ l	£4.71	£4.77	£11.56
Potassium bromide	KBr	500 g		£3.71	£15.00
Potassium chloride	KCl	500 g		£2.55	£10.70
Potassium fluoride	KF	100 g		£3.14	
Potassium hydroxide	KOH	500 g		£2.35	£5.38
Potassium iodide	KI	500 g		£13.30	£21.75
Potassium nitrate	KNO_3	500 g		£2.18	
Potassium sulphate	K_2SO_4	500 g		£1.71	£6.78
Sodium carbonate, anhydrous	Na_2CO_3	500 g		£2.03	£6.38
Sodium carbonate-10-water	$Na_2CO_3.10H_2O$	2 kg		£3.36	
Sodum chloride	$NaCl$	1 kg	£1.98	£2.36	£10.50
Sodium hydrogencarbonate	$NaHCO_3$	500 g		£1.82	£4.27
Sodium hydroxide	$NaOH$	500 g		£2.20	
Sulphuric acid	H_2SO_4	2½ l		£3.75	£8.73
Zinc oxide	ZnO	500 g		£3.69	£7.20
Zinc sulphate-7-water	$ZnSO_4.7H_2O$	500 g		£4.25	£10.00

APPENDIX
Chemical formulae and chemical equations

Introduction

Earlier in this book you will have seen written chemical shorthand to represent chemical elements. We called these **symbols.** For example, the symbols for oxygen, magnesium and lead are O, Mg and Pb. Also we can use these symbols to write **chemical formulae,** e.g. NaCl for sodium chloride. You will find examples of chemical formulae throughout the book.

Each chemical formula could be found by experiment (see Unit 31). However, you may want to write chemical formulae correctly. This appendix will show you how.

Throughout this book also you will find word equations written. For example:

magnesium + hydrochloric acid → magnesium chloride + hydrogen

Each word equation summarises a chemical reaction which takes place. The same reaction can be written as a **symbol equation.** For example, the above reaction can be written as:

$$Mg(s) + 2HCl(aq) \rightarrow MgCl_2(aq) + H_2(g)$$

This appendix will show you how to write equations like this. You should be able to understand this type of equation but, if you are aiming at a grade C or above, you should be able to *write* this type of equation too.

This appendix includes symbol equations for all of the reactions you have met in this book. You should incorporate them in your notes as you go along and try to learn some of them.

Writing chemical formulae

You can work out the formula of a compound using the ions which make it up. The table below lists some common positive and negative ions.

Positive ions		Negative ions	
Sodium	Na^+	Chloride	Cl^-
Potassium	K^+	Bromide	Br^-
Silver	Ag^+	Iodide	I^-
Copper(II)	Cu^{2+}	Hydroxide	OH^-
Lead	Pb^{2+}	Nitrate	NO_3^-
Magnesium	Mg^{2+}	Nitrate	NO_2^-
Calcium	Ca^{2+}	Hydrogencarbonate	HCO_3^-
Zinc	Zn^{2+}	Sulphate	SO_4^{2-}
Barium	Ba^{2+}	Sulphite	SO_3^{2-}
Iron(II)	Fe^{2+}	Carbonate	CO_3^{2-}
Iron(III)	Fe^{3+}	Oxide	O^{2-}
Aluminium	Al^{3+}	Sulphide	S^{2-}
Ammonium	NH_4^+	Phosphate	PO_4^{3-}
Hydrogen	H^+		

Let us look at two ions in more detail.

Pb^{2+} a lead ion with a two plus charge. This was formed when a lead metal atom lost two electrons.

SO$_4{}^{2-}$ a sulphate ion is a negatively charged ion. Each ion is made up of a group of one sulphur atom and four oxygen atoms. This group of atoms has gained two electrons to become negatively charged with a two minus charge.

Now let us look at the writing of five chemical formulae.

(1) Potassium chloride

This is made up from potassium ions, K$^+$, and chloride ions, Cl$^-$. The number of positive charges must be equal to the number of negative charges. In this case they are, and so writing the formula is easy:

$$K^+ \quad Cl^- \qquad KCl \text{ is the formula}$$

(NB The formula does not show the charges on the ions.)

(2) Magnesium oxide

This is made up from magnesium ions, Mg^{2+}, and oxide ions, O^{2-}. Again, the number of positive and negative charges are the same:

$$Mg^{2+} \quad O^{2-} \qquad MgO \text{ is the formula}$$

(3) Calcium chloride

This is made up from Ca^{2+} and Cl$^-$ ions. This time each calcium ion has twice as much charge as each chloride ion. The final formula must show two chloride ions for each calcium ion.
The formula is CaCl$_2$.

(4) Sodium sulphate

Ions present – Na$^+$ and SO$_4{}^{2-}$. There must be two sodium ions for each sulphate ion. Therefore the formula is Na$_2$SO$_4$.

(5) Aluminium sulphate

Ions present – Al^{3+} and SO$_4{}^{2-}$. For each two aluminium ions there must be three sulphate ions. The formula is written Al$_2$(SO$_4$)$_3$.

There are some simple formulae that are best remembered. The common gases hydrogen, oxygen, nitrogen and chlorine are composed of molecules each made up of two atoms. We therefore write H$_2$, O$_2$, N$_2$ and Cl$_2$.
Common gaseous compounds include:

carbon dioxide	CO$_2$
ammonia	NH$_3$
hydrogen chloride	HCl
sulphur dioxide	SO$_2$
sulphur trioxide	SO$_3$

The formula for water is H$_2$O.
The three common mineral acids are:

sulphuric acid	H$_2$SO$_4$
hydrochloric acid	HCl
nitric acid	HNO$_3$

Writing symbol equations

The first step in writing a symbol equation is to get a correct word equation. For example:

$$\text{magnesium} + \text{oxygen} \rightarrow \text{magnesium oxide}$$

The arrow shows the direction of the reaction. Reacting substances (called **reactants**) are on the left-hand side and the substances produced (called **products**) are on the right-hand side of the equation.

Each substance in the word equation is written correctly in symbols:

$$Mg + O_2 \rightarrow MgO$$

The equation is not, however, balanced. There must be the same number of each kind of atom on each side of the equation. In this example you have:

left-hand side	right-hand side
one magnesium	one magnesium
two oxygen	one oxygen

You cannot alter the formula of anything. You *cannot* therefore write:

$$Mg + O \rightarrow MgO$$

$$\text{or} \quad Mg + O_2 \rightarrow MgO_2$$

All you can do is to alter the proportions of the different reactants and products. You can double the amount of magnesium and magnesium oxide and get:

$$2\,Mg + O_2 \rightarrow 2\,MgO$$

This is now balanced, and you can check it:

left-hand side	right-hand side
two magnesium	two magnesium
two oxygen	two oxygen

Finally, the equation is finished off by putting in **state symbols.** These are:

(g) for gas
(l) for liquid
(s) for solid
(aq) for an aqueous solution, i.e. a solution where the solvent is water

The final symbol equation for the reaction between magnesium and oxygen is therefore:

$$\textbf{2 Mg(s)} + \textbf{O}_2\textbf{(g)} \rightarrow \textbf{MgO(s)}$$

List of equations for reactions used in this book

Unit 3

ammonia + hydrogen chloride → ammonium chloride
$NH_3(g) + HCl(g) \rightarrow NH_4Cl(s)$

Unit 5

iron + sulphur → iron(II) sulphide
$Fe(s) + S(s) \rightarrow FeS(s)$

hydrogen + oxygen → water
$2H_2(g) + O_2(g) \rightarrow 2H_2O(l)$

nitrogen + hydrogen ⇌ ammonia
$N_2(g) + 3H_2(g) \rightleftharpoons 2NH_3(g)$

Unit 6

potassium + water → potassium hydroxide + hydrogen
$2K(s) + 2H_2O(l) \rightarrow 2KOH(aq) + H_2(g)$

sodium + water → sodium hydroxide + hydrogen
$2Na(s) + 2H_2O(l) \rightarrow 2NaOH(aq) + H_2(g)$

magnesium + steam → magnesium oxide + hydrogen
$Mg(s) + H_2O(g) \rightarrow MgO(s) + H_2(g)$

zinc + steam → zinc oxide + hydrogen
$Zn(s) + H_2O(g) \rightarrow ZnO(s) + H_2(g)$

magnesium + hydrochloric acid → magnesium chloride + hydrogen
$Mg(s) + 2HCl(aq) \rightarrow MgCl_2(aq) + H_2(g)$

magnesium + sulphuric acid → magnesium sulphate + hydrogen
$Mg(s) + H_2SO_4(aq) \rightarrow MgSO_4(aq) + H_2(g)$

aluminium + hydrochloric acid → aluminium chloride + hydrogen
$2Al(s) + 6HCl(aq) \rightarrow 2AlCl_3(aq) + 3H_2(g)$

aluminium + sulphuric acid → aluminium sulphate + hydrogen
$2Al(s) + 3H_2SO_4(aq) \rightarrow Al_2(SO_4)_3(aq) + 3H_2(g)$

zinc + hydrochloric acid → zinc chloride + hydrogen
$Zn(s) + 2HCl(aq) \rightarrow ZnCl_2(aq) + H_2(g)$

zinc + sulphuric acid → zinc sulphate + hydrogen
$Zn(s) + H_2SO_4(aq) \rightarrow ZnSO_4(aq) + H_2(g)$

iron + hydrochloric acid → iron(II) chloride + hydrogen
$Fe(s) + 2HCl(aq) \rightarrow FeCl_2(aq) + H_2(g)$

iron + sulphuric acid → iron(II) sulphate + hydrogen
$Fe(s) + H_2SO_4(aq) \rightarrow FeSO_4(aq) + H_2(g)$

copper(II) sulphate + iron → iron(II) sulphate + copper
$CuSO_4(aq) + Fe(s) \rightarrow FeSO_4(aq) + Cu(s)$

aluminium + iron(III) oxide → aluminium oxide + iron
$2Al(s) + Fe_2O_3(s) \rightarrow Al_2O_3(s) + 2Fe(s)$

Unit 9

carbon + oxygen → carbon dioxide
$$C(s) + O_2(g) \rightarrow CO_2(g)$$

carbon dioxide + carbon → carbon monoxide
$$CO_2(g) + C(s) \rightarrow 2CO(g)$$

iron(III) oxide + carbon monoxide → iron + carbon dioxide
$$Fe_2O_3(s) + 3CO(g) \rightarrow 2Fe(l) + 3CO_2(g)$$

calcium carbonate → calcium oxide + carbon dioxide
$$CaCO_3(s) \rightarrow CaO(s) + CO_2(g)$$

calcium oxide + silicon dioxide → calcium silicate
$$CaO(s) + SiO_2(s) \rightarrow CaSiO_3(s)$$

aluminium oxide → aluminium + oxygen
$$Al_2O_3(s) \rightarrow 2Al(s) + 3O_2(g)$$

Unit 11

magnesium + sulphuric acid → magnesium sulphate + hydrogen
$$Mg(s) + H_2SO_4(aq) \rightarrow MgSO_4(aq) + H_2(g)$$

zinc + hydrochloric acid → zinc chloride + hydrogen
$$Zn(s) + 2HCl(aq) \rightarrow ZnCl_2(aq) + H_2(g)$$

sodium carbonate + hydrochloric acid → sodium chloride + carbon dioxide + water
$$Na_2CO_3(s) + 2HCl(aq) \rightarrow 2NaCl(aq) + CO_2(g) + H_2O(l)$$

ammonium chloride + sodium hydroxide → sodium chloride + ammonia + water
$$NH_4Cl(s) + NaOH(aq) \rightarrow NaCl(aq) + NH_3(g) + H_2O(l)$$

copper(II) oxide + sulphuric acid → copper(II) sulphate + water
$$CuO(s) + H_2SO_4(aq) \rightarrow CuSO_4(aq) + H_2O(l)$$

sodium hydroxide + hydrochloric acid → sodium chloride + water
$$NaOH(aq) + HCl(aq) \rightarrow NaCl(aq) + H_2O(l)$$

calcium carbonate + nitric acid → calcium nitrate + water + carbon dioxide
$$CaCO_3(s) + 2HNO_3(aq) \rightarrow Ca(NO_3)_2(aq) + H_2O(l) + CO_2(g)$$

lead(II) nitrate + sodium sulphate → lead(II) sulphate + sodium nitrate
$$Pb(NO_3)_2(aq) + Na_2SO_4(aq) \rightarrow PbSO_4(s) + 2NaNO_3(aq)$$

Unit 12

copper + oxygen → copper(II) oxide
$$2Cu(s) + O_2(g) \rightarrow 2CuO(s)$$

carbon dioxide + water → sugars + oxygen
$$6CO_2(g) + 6H_2O(l) \rightarrow C_6H_{12}O_6(aq) + 6O_2(g)$$

Unit 13

sulphur dioxide + water → sulphurous acid
$$SO_2(g) + H_2O(l) \rightarrow H_2SO_3(aq)$$

Unit 14

sulphur + oxygen → sulphur dioxide
$$S(s) + O_2(g) \rightarrow SO_2(g)$$

magnesium + oxygen → magnesium oxide
$$2Mg(s) + O_2(g) \rightarrow 2MgO(s)$$

mercury(II) oxide → mercury + oxygen
$$2HgO(s) \rightarrow 2Hg(l) + O_2(g)$$

copper(II) oxide + hydrogen → copper + water
$$CuO(s) + H_2(g) \rightarrow Cu(s) + H_2O(l)$$

Unit 15

calcium carbonate + water + carbon dioxide $\rightleftharpoons$ calcium hydrogencarbonate
$CaCO_3(s) + H_2O(l) + CO_2(g) \rightleftharpoons Ca(HCO_3)_2(aq)$

Unit 17

nitrogen + hydrogen $\rightleftharpoons$ ammonia
$N_2(g) + 3H_2(g) \rightleftharpoons 2NH_3(g)$

ammonium chloride + sodium hydroxide $\rightarrow$ sodium chloride + ammonia + water
$NH_4Cl(s) + NaOH(aq) \rightarrow NaCl(aq) + NH_3(g) + H_2O(l)$

ammonia + oxygen $\rightarrow$ nitrogen dioxide + steam
$4NH_3(g) + 7O_2(g) \rightarrow 4NO_2(g) + 6H_2O(g)$

nitrogen dioxide + water + oxygen $\rightarrow$ nitric acid
$4NO_2(g) + 2H_2O(l) + O_2(g) \rightarrow 4HNO_3(l)$

Unit 19

calcium carbonate + hydrochloric acid $\rightarrow$ calcium chloride + water + carbon dioxide
$CaCO_3(s) + 2HCl(aq) \rightarrow CaCl_2(aq) + H_2O(l) + CO_2(g)$

sodium thiosulphate + hydrochloric acid $\rightarrow$ sodium chloride + water + sulphur dioxide + sulphur
$Na_2S_2O_3(aq) + 2HCl(aq) \rightarrow 2NaCl(aq) + H_2O(l) + SO_2(g) + S(s)$

hydrogen peroxide $\rightarrow$ water + oxygen
$2H_2O_2(aq) \rightarrow 2H_2O(l) + O_2(g)$

copper(II) sulphate crystals $\rightleftharpoons$ anhydrous copper(II) sulphate + water
$CuSO_4.5H_2O(s) \rightleftharpoons CuSO_4(s) + 5H_2O(l)$

Unit 21

carbon + oxygen $\rightarrow$ carbon dioxide
$C(s) + O_2(g) \rightarrow CO_2(g)$

carbon + oxygen $\rightarrow$ carbon monoxide
$2C(s) + O_2(g) \rightarrow 2CO(g)$

lead(II) oxide + carbon $\rightarrow$ lead + carbon monoxide
$PbO(s) + C(s) \rightarrow Pb(s) + CO(g)$

Unit 24

glucose $\rightarrow$ ethanol + carbon dioxide
$C_6H_{12}O_6(aq) \rightarrow 2C_2H_5OH(aq) + 2CO_2(g)$

Unit 25

calcium carbonate + water + carbon dioxide $\rightleftharpoons$ calcium hydrogencarbonate
$CaCO_3(s) + H_2O(l) + CO_2(g) \rightleftharpoons Ca(HCO_3)_2(aq)$

calcium carbonate $\rightarrow$ calcium oxide + carbon dioxide
$CaCO_3(s) \rightarrow CaO(s) + CO_2(g)$

calcium oxide + water $\rightarrow$ calcium hydroxide
$CaO(s) + H_2O(l) \rightarrow Ca(OH)_2(s)$

calcium hydroxide + carbon dioxide $\rightarrow$ calcium carbonate + water
$Ca(OH)_2(aq) + CO_2(g) \rightarrow CaCO_3(s) + H_2O(l)$

calcium carbonate + nitric acid $\rightarrow$ calcium nitrate + water + carbon dioxide
$CaCO_3(s) + 2HNO_3(aq) \rightarrow Ca(NO_3)_2(aq) + H_2O(l) + CO_2(g)$

Unit 26

sodium chloride → sodium + chlorine
$$2NaCl(l) → 2Na(l) + Cl_2(g)$$

sodium chloride + calcium carbonate ⇌ calcium chloride + sodium carbonate
$$2NaCl(aq) + CaCO_3(s) ⇌ CaCl_2(aq) + Na_2CO_3(aq)$$

sodium amalgam + water → sodium hydroxide + hydrogen + mercury
$$2Na/Hg(l) + 2H_2O(l) → 2NaOH(aq) + H_2(g) + 2Hg(l)$$

Unit 27

lithium + water → lithium hydroxide + hydrogen
$$2Li(s) + 2H_2O(l) → 2LiOH(aq) + H_2(g)$$

sodium + water → sodium hydroxide + hydrogen
$$2Na(s) + 2H_2O(l) → 2NaOH(aq) + H_2(g)$$

potassium + water → potassium hydroxide + hydrogen
$$2K(s) + 2H_2O(l) → 2KOH(aq) + H_2(g)$$

lithium + chlorine → lithium chloride
$$2Li(s) + Cl_2(g) → 2LiCl(s)$$

sodium + chlorine → sodium chloride
$$2Na(s) + Cl_2(g) → 2NaCl(s)$$

potassium + chlorine → potassium chloride
$$2K(s) + Cl_2(g) → 2KCl(s)$$

Unit 28

iron + chlorine → iron(III) chloride
$$2Fe(s) + 3Cl_2(g) → 2FeCl_3(s)$$

hydrogen + chlorine → hydrogen chloride
$$H_2(g) + Cl_2(g) → 2HCl(g)$$

hydrogen + bromine → hydrogen bromide
$$H_2(g) + Br_2(g) → 2HBr(g)$$

hydrogen + iodine ⇌ hydrogen iodide
$$H_2(g) + I_2(g) ⇌ 2HI(g)$$

chlorine + potassium bromide → bromine + potassium chloride
$$Cl_2(g) + 2KBr(aq) → Br_2(g) + 2KCl(aq)$$

Unit 29

sulphur + oxygen → sulphur dioxide
$$S(s) + O_2(g) → SO_2(g)$$

sulphur dioxide + oxygen ⇌ sulphur dioxide
$$2SO_2(g) + O_2(g) ⇌ 2SO_3(g)$$

sulphur trioxide + water → sulphuric acid
$$SO_3(g) + H_2O(l) → H_2SO_4(l)$$

sulphur trioxide + sulphuric acid → oleum
$$SO_3(g) + H_2SO_4(l) → H_2S_2O_7(l)$$

oleum + water → sulphuric acid
$$H_2S_2O_7(l) + H_2O(l) → 2H_2SO_4(l).$$

Glossary

Absolute temperature   There is a minimum temperature below which it will never be possible to cool anything. This is called **absolute zero** and is $-273°C$. This is the starting point for the **Kelvin** or absolute temperature scale: e.g. $0°C$ is the same as 273 K on the absolute temperature scale.

Acid   A substance that dissolves in water to form a solution with a pH below 7. An acid contains hydrogen which can be replaced by a metal to form a salt. The three mineral acids are sulphuric acid H_2SO_4, hydrochloric acid HCl and nitric acid HNO_3.

Alcohol   An alcohol is an organic compound containing an OH group. A common alcohol is ethanol C_2H_5OH.

Alkali   A base that dissolves in water to form a solution with a pH above 7. Alkalis are neutralised by acids to form salts. Common alkalis include sodium hydroxide $NaOH$, potassium hydroxide KOH and calcium hydroxide $Ca(OH)_2$.

Alkali metal   A metal in group 1 of the Periodic Table. Common alkali metals include lithium, sodium and potassium.

Alkaline earth metal   A metal in group 2 of the Periodic Table. Common alkaline earth metals include calcium and magnesium.

Alkane   A family of hydrocarbons with a general formula C_nH_{2n+2}. The simplest alkane is methane CH_4. This is the main ingredient of natural gas.

Alkene   A family of hydrocarbons with a general formula C_nH_{2n}. The simplest alkene is ethene C_2H_4. This is a most important chemical in industry.

Allotropy   When an element can exist in two or more forms in the same physical state, it is said to show allotropy. The different forms are called **allotropes.** Diamond and graphite are two solid allotropes of carbon. Different allotropes exist because of different arrangements of atoms.

Alloy   A metal made by mixing two or more metals together, e.g. brass is an alloy of copper and zinc.

Amalgam   Many metals form alloys when mixed with mercury. These alloys are called amalgams. The mixture used to fill teeth is an amalgam.

Amorphous   Without definite or regular shape.

Analysis   Finding out the elements present in a substance is called **qualitative analysis. Quantitative analysis** is finding out how much of each element is present.

Anhydride   An anhydride (sometimes called an acid anhydride) is an oxide of a non-metal which dissolves in water to form an acid. Carbon dioxide is an anhydride, dissolving in water to form carbonic acid.

Anhydrous   A substance without water. Often used to describe salts which have lost water of crystallisation.

Anion	A negatively charged ion which moves towards the anode during electrolysis, e.g. Cl^-.
Anode	A positively charged electrode in electrolysis.
Aqueous solution	A solution made by dissolving a substance in water. The solvent in an aqueous solution is always water.
Atom	The smallest part of an element that can exist.
Atomic number	The atomic number is the number of protons in the nucleus of an atom. It is equal to the number of electrons in the atom. The elements in the Periodic Table are arranged in order of atomic number.
Base	A substance which reacts with an acid to form a salt and water only. Metal oxides are bases. A base which is soluble in water forms an alkaline solution.
Battery	A battery is a source of electricity. A carbon-zinc battery is the type of battery used in a torch. The battery in a car is a lead-acid battery which stores electricity. It can be recharged.
Boiling	When a liquid turns rapidly to its vapour at a fixed temperature called the **boiling point.** The boiling point of a liquid varies with pressure. The lower the pressure the lower the boiling point.
Calorimeter	Apparatus used for measuring heat.
Carbohydrates	Compounds of carbon, hydrogen and oxygen. The number of hydrogen atoms in each molecule is twice the number of oxygen atoms. These compounds are energy foods, e.g. glucose $C_6H_{12}O_6$.
Catalyst	A substance which alters the rate of a chemical reaction but is not used up in the reaction.
Cathode	The negatively charged electrode in electrolysis.
Cation	A positively charged ion which moves towards the cathode in electrolysis, e.g. H^+.
Chemical change	A change which results in the formation of new substances. A chemical reaction is not easily reversed.
Chromatography	A way of separating mixtures, especially of coloured substances, by letting them spread across filter paper or through a powder.
Combination	The joining together of atoms of different elements to form a compound (see **synthesis**).
Combustion	Burning is a combination of a substance with oxygen. Combustion is another word for **burning.**
Compound	A substance formed by joining atoms of different elements together. The properties of a compound are different from the elements that make it up. The proportions of the different elements in a particular compound are fixed.
Condensation	When a vapour turns to a liquid on cooling. Heat is given out during this change. Condensation is the opposite of evaporation.

Conductor	A conductor will allow electricity to pass through it (electrical conductor) or heat to pass through it (heat conductor). Metals are good conductors of heat and electricity. Carbon, in the form of graphite, is a good electrical conductor but a poor heat conductor.
Corrosion	The wearing away of the surface of a metal by chemical attack. The rusting of iron is an example of corrosion. Rusting requires the presence of oxygen and water.
Cracking	The breaking down of long hydrocarbon molecules with heat and/or a catalyst to produce short hydrocarbon molecules. The short molecules are much easier to sell, especially for making plastics.
Crystal	A piece of a substance that has a definite regular shape. Crystals of the same substance have the same shape. Slow **crystallisation** will produce larger crystals.
Decomposition	A chemical reaction that results in the breaking down of substances into simpler ones. This is often brought about by heating, when it is called **thermal decomposition.**
Dehydration	A reaction where water (or the elements of water – hydrogen and oxygen) are removed. Dehydration of ethanol produces ethene. The substance which brings about this reaction, e.g. concentrated sulphuric acid, is called the **dehydrating agent.**
Deliquescence	Some substances absorb water from the atmosphere and dissolve in the water to form a solution. These substances are said to be **deliquescent.**
Density	The mass of a particular volume of a substance. It is expressed as kg/m^3 or g/cm^3.
Detergent	A detergent is a cleansing agent. There are two main types of detergent – soaps and soapless detergents.
Diatomic	An element whose molecules are composed of two atoms is said to be diatomic. The common gases oxygen, hydrogen, nitrogen and chlorine are all diatomic and are written as O_2, H_2, N_2 and Cl_2.
Diffusion	This is the spreading out of a substance to fill all of the available space. Diffusion takes place quickly with gases and liquids.
Discharge	An ion may be converted to a neutral atom at an electrode during electrolysis by loss or gain of electrons. This is called discharging of ions.
Dissolving	When a substance is added to water it can disappear from view when stirred. This disappearance is called dissolving. The substance is still there and can be recovered by evaporation.
Distillation	A way of purifying a liquid or obtaining the solvent from a solution. The liquid is vaporised and the vapour condensed to reform the liquid. The condensed liquid is called the **distillate.**
Ductile	A metal is said to be ductile as it can be drawn into thin wires.
Effervescence	If a gas is produced during a chemical reaction bubbles of the gas can be seen to escape from the solution. This 'fizzing' is called effervescence and this word is frequently confused with **efflorescence.**

Efflorescence   Some substances containing water of crystallisation, on standing in an open laboratory, lose water to the atmosphere. These substances are said to be **efflorescent.**

Electrode   The conducting rod or plate which carries electricity in and out of an electrolyte during electrolysis. Graphite and platinum are good unreactive or inert electrodes.

Electrolysis   The passing of a direct electric current (d.c.) through an electrolyte, dissolved in water or in the molten state, resulting in the splitting up of the electrolyte at the electrodes. Lead bromide, for example, is split up into lead (formed at the negative electrode) and bromine (formed at the positive electrode).

Electrolyte   A chemical compound which, in aqueous solution or when molten, conducts electricity and is split up by it. Acids, bases, alkalis and salts are all electrolytes.

Element   A single pure substance that cannot be split up into anything simpler.

Endothermic reaction   A reaction which takes in heat.

Environment   The surroundings in which we and other animals and plants live. A person who studies the environment may be called an **environmentalist.**

Enzyme   An enzyme is a protein which acts as a biological catalyst. Certain enzymes only work with certain reactions. The action of an enzyme is best under certain temperature and pH conditions. Enzymes are part of the growing subject of **biotechnology.**

Evaporation   The process by which a liquid changes to its vapour. This happens at a temperature below its boiling point but is fastest when the liquid is boiling.

Excess   In a chemical reaction there is a connection between the quantities of substances reacting. In practice one of the reactants is present in larger quantities than is required for the reaction and is said to be in excess.

Exothermic reaction   A reaction that gives out heat, e.g. the burning of coal. A reaction which takes in heat is called an **endothermic reaction.**

Extraction   The removal of one thing from a group of other things, e.g. separating iron from iron ore.

Fermentation   Enzymes in yeast convert glucose into ethanol and carbon dioxide. This process can be used to dispose of waste sugars in industry.

Filtrate   The liquid that comes through the filter paper during filtration.

Filtration (or filtering)   A method of separating a solid from a liquid. The solid is 'trapped' on the filter paper and the liquid runs through.

Flammable   Describes a substance, e.g. petrol, that catches fire easily.

Fractional distillation   A method of separating a mixture of different liquids that mix together. The process depends upon the different boiling points of the liquids. The liquid with the lowest boiling point boils off first and is condensed. As the temperature is raised, liquids with higher boiling points distil over.

Freezing   When a liquid changes to a solid. It will do this at the **freezing point.** A pure substance will have a definite freezing point.

Fuel   A substance that burns easily to produce heat and light. **Fossil fuel** is present in the earth in only limited amounts and cannot readily be replaced, e.g. coal, petroleum.

Funnel	A piece of glass or plastic apparatus used for filtering. A **Buchner funnel** is a particular type of funnel usually made of china. It produces quicker filtration because the filtrate is sucked through the filter paper.
Giant structure	This is a crystal structure in which all of the particles are strongly linked together by a network of bonds extending through the crystal, e.g. diamond.
Group	A vertical column in the Periodic Table. Elements in the same groups have similar chemical properties.
Halogen	An element in group 7 of the Periodic Table. The word halogen means 'salt producer'. Common halogens are chlorine, bromine and iodine.
Homologous series	The name given to a family of organic compounds, e.g. alkanes.
Hydrated	Contains water.
Hydrocarbon	Compounds made up from the elements hydrogen and carbon only.
Hydrolysis	The splitting up of a compound with water.
Hygroscopic	Substances which, on standing in an open laboratory, absorb water and become damp. They do not dissolve in the water.
Igneous	Describes rocks that have cooled and solidified from molten rock material produced deep in the earth. Granite is an example of an igneous rock. In an igneous rock there are interlocking crystals.
Immiscible	Two liquids that do not mix are said to be immiscible, e.g. oil and water.
Indicator	A chemical that can distinguish between an alkali and an acid by changing colour, e.g. litmus is red in acids and blue in alkalis.
In situ	It is sometimes necessary to prepare a chemical, as it is required, by mixing other chemicals. Ammonium nitrate, which is inclined to be explosive because of impurities, can be prepared by mixing ammonium chloride and sodium nitrate. The ammonium chloride is said to be prepared *in situ*.
Insoluble	Describes a substance that will not dissolve in a particular solvent.
Insulator	A substance which does not conduct electricity, e.g. rubber or plastic. Insulators may be called **non-conductors.**
Ion	A positively or negatively charged particle formed when an atom or group of atoms lose or gain electrons.
Ion exchange	A process in which ions are taken from water and replaced by others. In an ion exchange column used to soften hard water, calcium and magnesium ions are removed from the water and replaced by sodium ions.
Malleable	Metals are said to be very malleable as they can be beaten into thin sheets or different shapes.
Melting	A solid changes to a liquid at the **melting point.**
Metal	An element that is shiny, conducts heat and electricity, can be beaten into thin sheets (**malleable**) or drawn into wires (**ductile**) is probably a metal. Metals usually have high melting points and boiling points and high densities. Metals burn in oxygen to form neutral or alkaline oxides.

Metamorphic   Describes rocks, originally either igneous or sedimentary rocks which were thoroughly altered by heat or pressure within the crust of the Earth, without melting. Marble is an example of a metamorphic rock.

Mineral   A naturally occurring substance of which rocks are made.

Mixture   A substance made by just mixing other substances together. The substances can easily be separated again.

Molecule   The smallest part of an element or compound that can exist on its own. A molecule usually consists of a small number of atoms joined together.

Neutralisation   A reaction where an acid is cancelled out by a base or alkali.

Non-aqueous solution   Solution where the solvent is not water, e.g. iodine dissolved in hexane.

Oxidation   This is a reaction where a substance gains oxygen or loses hydrogen.

Oxides   Compounds of an element with oxygen. A **basic** oxide is an oxide of a metal. It reacts with an acid to give a salt and water only. Some basic oxides dissolve in water to form **alkalis**. A **neutral** oxide such as carbon monoxide CO does not react with acids or alkalis and has a pH of 7. An **acidic** oxide dissolves in alkalis to form a salt and water only. It has a pH of less than 7. An **amphoteric** oxide can act as either an acidic or a basic oxide depending upon conditions. Examples of amphoteric oxides include zinc oxide ZnO and aluminium oxide Al_2O_3.

Oxidising agent   An oxidising agent, e.g. concentrated sulphuric acid, oxidises another substance. It is itself reduced.

Period   A horizontal row in the Periodic Table.

pH   A measure of the acidity or alkalinity of a solution. The scale is from 0 to 14. Numbers less than 7 represent acids; the smaller the number the stronger the acid. Numbers greater than 7 represent alkalis; the larger the number the stronger the alkali. pH 7 is neutral.

Polar solvent   The molecules of some solvents, such as water, contain slight positive and negative charges. A stream of a polar solvent is deflected by a charged rod. A polar solvent dissolves substances containing ionic bonds. Solvents without these charges are called **non-polar solvents.**

Pollution   The presence in the environment of substances which are harmful to living things.

Polymer   A long chain molecule built up of a number of smaller units, called **monomers,** joined together by a process called **polymerisation.** Polymers are often called plastics, e.g. poly(ethene) is a polymer made up from ethene molecules linked together.

Precipitate   An insoluble substance formed in a chemical reaction. This usually causes a cloudiness to appear in the liquid and eventually the solid sinks to the bottom. The precipitate can be removed by filtering or centrifuging.
OR

Precipitate   If a solid which is insoluble in water is produced during a chemical reaction in solution, the particles of solid formed are called a precipitate and the process is called **precipitation.**

Product   A substance formed in a chemical reaction.

Properties	A description of a substance and how it behaves. **Physical properties** include density and melting point. **Chemical properties** describe chemical changes.
Proportional	If a car is driving along at a constant speed the amount of petrol used increases regularly as the distance increases. The amount of petrol used is said to be proportional to the distance travelled.
Pure substance	A single substance that contains nothing apart from the substance itself. Pure substances have definite melting and boiling points.
Qualitative	A qualitative study is one which depends upon changes in appearance only. A **quantitative** study requires a study of quantities, e.g. mass, volume, etc.
Reactant	A chemical substance which takes part in a chemical reaction.
Redox reaction	A reaction where both oxidation and reduction take place.
Reduction	The opposite of oxidation. This is a reaction where oxygen is lost or hydrogen is gained. A **reducing agent,** e.g. carbon monoxide, reduces another substance left on a filter paper during filtration.
Reversible reaction	A reversible reaction is a reaction which can go either forwards or backwards depending upon the conditions. A reversible reaction will include the sign $\rightleftharpoons$ in the equation.
Salt	A substance which is formed as a product of a neutralisation reaction. A salt is the product obtained when hydrogen in an acid is replaced by a metal.
Saturated compound	A compound which contains only single bonds, e.g. methane CH_4.
Saturated solution	A solution in which no more of the solute will dissolve providing the temperature remains unchanged.
Sedimentary	Rocks, e.g. sandstone, composed of compacted fragments of older rocks and other minerals which have accumulated on the floor of an ancient sea or lake, etc.
Semi-conductor	Some substances, e.g. silicon, have a very slight ability to conduct electricity. They are called semi-conductors and are used to make microchips.
Solubility	The number of grams of a solute that will dissolve in 100 g of solvent at a particular temperature.
Solute	The substance that dissolves in a solvent to form a solution.
Solvent	The liquid in which a solute dissolves.
Spectroscopy	The study of the light coming from a substance. Helium was first discovered by examining light from the sun. Helium must be present on the sun.
Sublimation	When a solid changes straight from a gas to a solid **or** solid to a gas, missing out the liquid. The solid collected is called the **sublimate.**
Surface tension	This is a measure of the attraction between molecules at the surface of a liquid. Water has a high surface tension.

Suspension   A mixture of a liquid and an insoluble substance where the insoluble substance does not sink to the bottom but stays evenly divided throughout the liquid.

Synthesis   The formation of a compound from the elements that make it up. This is usually accompanied by a loss of energy.

Titration   A method of investigating the volumes of solution that react together.

Transition metal   A block of metals between the two parts of the main block in the Periodic Table. Transition metals are usually dense metals much less reactive than alkali metals.

Vapour   A vapour is a gas that will condense to a liquid on cooling to room temperature.

Viscous   A viscous liquid is thick and 'treacle-like'. It is difficult to pour.

Volatile   Describes a liquid which is easily turned to a vapour, e.g. petrol.

Water of crystallisation   A definite amount of water bound up in the crystal, e.g. $CuSO_4.5H_2O$.

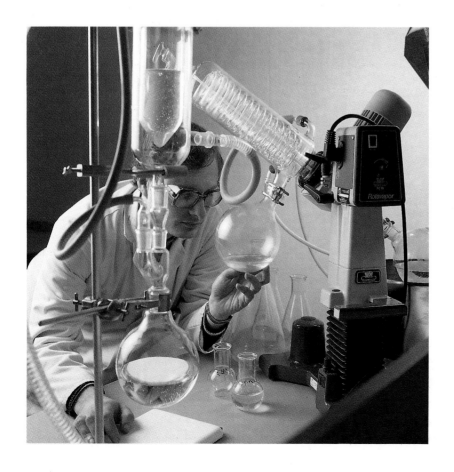

An industrial chemist performing quality control tests on high quality cosmetic and pharmaceutical raw materials.

Careers in Chemistry

The chemical industry

The United Kingdom chemical industry is the fifth largest in the 'free' world – after the USA, Japan, West Germany and France. It is also the fifth largest industry in the UK after food, drink and tobacco, mechanical engineering, electrical engineering and paper, printing and publishing. The industry sold £30 billion (£30 000 000 000) worth of chemicals in 1987, and it employs 5% of the UK workforce.

These figures illustrate just how important Chemistry is to society. It affects our lives in many ways, from the soap we wash with to the tyres on our bicycles. The diagram below shows the main sectors of the chemical industry.

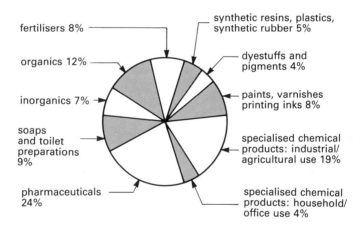

fertilisers 8%

organics 12%

inorganics 7%

soaps and toilet preparations 9%

pharmaceuticals 24%

synthetic resins, plastics, synthetic rubber 5%

dyestuffs and pigments 4%

paints, varnishes printing inks 8%

specialised chemical products: industrial/agricultural use 19%

specialised chemical products: household/office use 4%

The top 10 companies in Western Europe are:

1. Hoechst (West Germany)
2. BASF (West Germany)
3. Bayer (West Germany)
4. ICI (United Kingdom)
5. DSM (Netherlands)
6. Ciba Geigy (Switzerland)
7. Shell (Netherlands/UK)
8. Mondedison (Italy)
9. Rhone-Foulenc (France)
10. Akzo (Netherlands)

If you want to find out more about the chemical industry, you could write to any of these companies and ask for a brochure. You will find their addresses in the reference section of your local library.

Careers in Chemistry

Throughout this book you will find photographs of chemists at work in universities, factories, industrial and research laboratories. These include young people on YTS placements, or studying for a degree, quality control scientists and highly qualified research chemists.

If you are interested in Chemistry as a career then ask your careers advisor about the opportunities available to you. For further information write to The Royal Society of Chemistry, 30 Russell Square, London WC1B 5DT.

If you are studying Balanced Science or Chemistry to GCSE, then you have already taken the first step in a number of worthwhile careers. These include:

Animal technician	Doctor	Laboratory technician	Pharmacy technician
Biochemist	Farm Manager	Materials scientist	Physiotherapist
Chemical engineer	Fish farmer	Medical laboratory	Public analyst
Chemist	Food technologist	scientific officer	Quality control technician
Dental hygienist	Forensic scientist	Metallurgist	Schools science advisor
Dental technician	Fuel technologist	Microbiologist	Teacher
Dentist	Hairdresser	Nurse	Textile technician
Dietician	Home economist	Pharmacist	Veterinary surgeon

For many of these careers you will need to achieve a grade C or above in your GCSE examination. For some you will have to go on to GCE 'A' level and other further education. The table below lists degree course which require 'A' Level Chemistry as an entry requirement.

Agriculture	Chemical education	Geochemistry	Pathology
Agricultural sciences	Chemical engineering	Geology	Petrology
Agricultural biochemistry	Chemical physics	Glass technology	Pharmaceutical chemistry
Agricultural botany	Chemical process	Human biology	Pharmacology
Agricultural chemistry	Chemical technology	Human ecology	Pharmacy
Agricultural zoology	Chemistry	Human sciences	Physical chemistry
Analytical chemistry	Colour chemistry	Inorganic chemistry	Physical sciences
Animal biology	Colour technology	Materials science	Physiology
Animal nutrition	Crystallography	Material technology	Plant sciences
Animal physiology	Dentistry	Marine biology	Polymer chemistry
Animal sciences	Development physiology	Marine botany	Polymer and colour science
Applied biochemistry	Dietetics	Marine zoology	Polymer engineering
Applied biology	Dyeing and dyestuffs	Medical biochemistry	Polymer sciences and
Applied electrochemistry	technology	Medicine	technology
Bacteriology	Forestry	Metallurgy	Science (general)
Biochemical engineering	Earth sciences	Microbiology	Science (history and
Biochemistry	Environmental sciences	Mineral exploitation	philosophy of)
Biological chemistry	Exploration science	Mineral sciences and	Soil science
Biology	Farm animals (physiology	technology	Textile technology
Biology sciences	and biochemistry of)	Minerology	Theoretical chemistry
Biomedical electronics	Fibre science	Molecular sciences	Veterinary science
Biomedical engineering	Food science and	Natural sciences	Virology
Botany	technology	Neurobiology	Wood science
Brewing	Forestry	Nutrition	Zoology
Cell biology	Fuel science	Oil technology	
Ceramics	Genetics	Paper science	

Whatever you decide to do, hopefully the Chemistry you have studied has given you an interest in the subject and its applications in the world around you.

Index